EXILE, WRITER, SOLDIER, SPY

EXILE, WRITER, SOLDIER, SPY

JORGE SEMPRÚN

SOLEDAD FOX MAURA

Arcade Publishing • New York

First North American Edition 2018

Arcade Publishing books may be purchased in bulk at special discounts for sales promotion, corporate gifts, fund-raising, or educational purposes. Special editions can also be created to specifications. For details, contact the Special Sales Department, Arcade Publishing, 307 West 36th Street, 11th Floor, New York, NY 10018 or arcade@skyhorsepublishing.com.

Arcade Publishing® is a registered trademark of Skyhorse Publishing, Inc.®, a Delaware corporation.

Visit our website at www.arcadepub.com.

10 9 8 7 6 5 4 3 2 1

Library of Congress Cataloging-in-Publication Data is available on file.

Cover design by Brian Peterson
Cover photograph courtesy of Magnum Photographs

ISBN: 978-1-62872-917-7
Ebook ISBN: 978-1-62872-918-4

Printed in the United States of America

For my mother

Acknowledgments

I have written about and taught Jorge Semprún's work since 2001. Some of the elements in this biography have been simmering in my mind for the past seventeen years; the bulk of the research and writing have taken five. During this time, many people have helped make this project possible through their support and generosity. These include my colleagues in the Department of Romance Languages at Williams College; Associate Dean John Gerry, and three consecutive Deans of Faculty—Peter Murphy, Denise Buell, and Lee Park.

I am grateful to my editors Miguel Aguilar at Debate, Penguin/Random House in Barcelona, and to Maxime Catroux of Flammarion in Paris for having faith in this project from early stages.

This biography would not have been possible without the help of Dominique Landman and her family—Claude Landman, Mathieu and Cecilia Landman, and Thomas and Anka Landman. I thank them welcoming my project, sharing their photographic archive, giving me the authorization to explore the RGANI archives in Moscow, and for introducing me to Dr. Charles Mehlman.

I must also thank Jorge Semprún's nephews and nieces Georges-Henri Soutou, Danielle de la Gorce, Isabelle Semprún Camenen, Luis Aguirregomezcorta, Ruben de Semprún, Diego de Semprún, and Sylvia Nicolas for sharing their memories and personal materials and photographs.

Many thanks to other family members and friends, who also shared impressions, and unpublished materials: Santiago Valentín-Gamazo, Roger Kase, Yannick Bellon, and Natalia Rodriguez Salmones.

Alfonso Pérez-Maura for giving me access to documents from the Fundación Antonio Maura.

Oscar Fanjul and Plácido Arango for their generosity in connecting me with many of Jorge Semprún's colleagues and friends.

Many thanks to the following people who kindly agreed to speak with me:

Joaquín Almunia, Claudio Aranzadi, Eduardo Arroyo, Josep María Castellet, Leo Barblan, Carmen Claudín, Javier Folch, Constantin Costa-Gavras, Felipe González, Juan Goytisolo, Jordi Gracia, Roger Grenier, Elsa Grobety, Gabriel Jackson, Florence Malraux, Evelyn Mesquida, Beatriz de Moura, Berta Muñoz, Bernard Pivot, Rosa Sala Rose, Rossana Rossanda, Javier Solana, Carlos Solchaga, and Jeannine Verdes-Lerroux.

The historian and Gallimard editor Jean-Louis Panné, who put together the wonderful and extensive chronology to Jorge Semprún: *Le fer rouge de la memoire* (Gallimard).

Alan Riding, for sharing unpublished materials and advice.

Helga Druxes, Peter Starenko, and Betsy Kolbert helped me quickly and expertly with German translations, and Alex Mihailovic translated correspondence from Russian that enabled me to make contact with the Russian Government Archive of Contemporary History (RGANI). Mikhail Iampolski tracked down a potential Russian researcher for me.

Juby Bustamente encouraged me from early on to tackle this subject.

Florence Malraux has been a constant guide. She lived through most of it, and when she told me I was on the right track, I trusted her. Merci, Florence.

Axel Braisz of the International Tracing Service in Bad Arolsen; Daniel Palmieri of the Library and Public Archives Unit, International Committee of the Red Cross, Geneva; the staff at the Bibliothèque Litteraire Jacques Doucet, Paris; Ron Coleman of the Library and Archives

Reference Desk of the United States Holocaust Memorial Museum, Washington; Ilona Denner of the Bundesarchiv, Berlin; Victoria Ramos of the Archivo Histórico del Partido Comunista de España, Madrid; Sylvia Naylor of the National Archives in College Park, Maryland.

The bibliography reflects the valuable contributions made to related subjects by other researchers. The following scholars were very helpful regarding Semprún's references to Yiddish: Ruth Wisse of Harvard University, Matthew Kraus of the University of Cincinnati, and Michael Yashinsky of the Yiddish Book Center, Amherst.

Laura Diez Herrera for her work in Madrid and in Alcalá de Henares at the Archivo Histórico del Ministerio de Asuntos Exteriores, the Archivo Histórico del Partido Comunista Español, and the Archivo General de la Administración; Maria Thomas for her research at the Archivo Histórico del Partido Comunista Español; and Amaury Nauroy, for his help in Paris.

Esther Gómez Parro for deftly handling access to the Russian Government Archive of Contemporary History (RGANI) in Moscow, and for her translation of the materials. Thanks to Juan José Herrera de la Muela for putting me in touch with Esther.

Caroline Delerue, in London, and Antonia Riera Vales, in Madrid, for excellent and speedy interview transcriptions. Thanks to Arantxa Aguirre for the suggestion.

Julia Munemo for her careful copyediting, and for compiling the bibliography. Lorena Bou, Nora Grosse, and the editorial team at Penguin Random House in Barcelona for designing and editing the Spanish-language edition of this book.

John kept my spirits up when I thought I would spend the rest of my life writing this book.

Jeannette Seaver has my deepest gratitude for bringing the US edition of this book to light. I am grateful to her, Beth Canova, and the team at Arcade.

Unless otherwise indicated, all translations from the French and Spanish are my own.

Introduction

Secrets aren't important. They only change things if you're
writing a real biography, but that should only be done
once the subject is dead.[1]
—Jorge Semprún

Homage at the Prado Museum

On a warm Madrid evening in July of 2011, French philosopher Bernard
Henri-Lévy addressed a packed auditorium at the Prado Museum. The
occasion was a memorial service. The audience was interspersed with
politicians, intellectuals, and businessmen who had interrupted their
busy or leisurely lives to spend the evening in remembrance.

To an eavesdropper, it may have seemed that Lévy was honoring the
lives of several different people: a Spanish Republican, a Buchenwald
survivor, a daring undercover agent, a famous writer, an Oscar nom-
inee, and a great European thinker. He also might have added the
following descriptives: Aristocrat, exile, Communist, clandestine
recruiter, Socialist Minister, Catholic, antifascist, Nazi camp survivor,
honorary Jew, anti-Francoist, Germanophile, Spanish, Parisian, anticommunist, grifter, public intellectual, seducer, dissembler, radical,
glamorous, bourgeois, prize-winning novelist, and autobiographer.

All of these were simply the multiple facets of one person: Jorge Semprún, an individual whose life spanned the twentieth century. "Interesting times," as Eric Hobsbawn would say, Semprún rose to every opportunity and challenge presented by his epoch. The outcome was that he was able to live multiple, often contradictory, lives. For those who knew him, his death was more than a personal loss. It meant the disappearance of a key witness to the twentieth century, and of a figure who had become synonymous with Europe's past and present.

Semprún had died a few weeks earlier in Paris, and the main memorial services had been held in France. Yet there was something especially moving about this homage at the Prado Museum, just a few blocks from where Jorge—and his mother before him—had been raised in peace and luxury, blissfully ignorant of the violent century awaiting them. Eighty-seven years later the same trees lined the Paseo del Prado, and the balconies of the former Semprún home looked out on quiet evening streets, impervious.

A Spaniard in Paris

Like Picasso, Semprún was a twentieth-century Spanish icon of creative talent, political engagement, and intense personal magnetism who made France his adopted country. If he had been a painter, Paris might have honored him with a museum in a former *hotel particulier* in the neighbourhood of Saint-Germain-des-Prés. His first years in France were not easy as an adolescent Spanish exile who didn't speak the language. But over the decades, he adapted and conquered the French language. The French came to cherish him, and showered him with opportunities, media coverage, and prizes. He became one of the resident stars of the Parisian intelligentsia, an elegant and aristocratic author, a hero and Nazi camp survivor. He was a dashing public intellectual sought after by French movie stars (Yves Montand) and politicians (Prime Minister Dominique de Villepin).

The French Resistance and the Communist Party

Shortly after the Spanish Civil War erupted in the summer of 1936, Semprún's Republican family fled to France. In exile, the thirteen-year-old Jorge learned French and continued his studies. He was a brilliant philosophy student. By 1939, the Spanish war had ended with Franco's victory and the defeat of the Republic; World War II was destroying Europe. As soon as he could, Semprún joined the French Resistance, hoping that an end to Fascism would liberate Spain as well. He was arrested by the Gestapo in October 1943, and deported to Buchenwald, where he remained a prisoner until the American Army liberated the camp in April 1945.

His experiences as a deportee further cemented his political identity and solidarity with the Communist Party. He became an active militant, and rose to become a leader in the Partido Comunista Español. He spent many years as a brave and loyal clandestine agent, secretly organizing the youth of Franco Spain, but after expressing disappointment with the party's strategy, he was expelled in 1963. Free from the enforced anonymity of his clandestine work, he immediately reinvented himself as a novelist and published his first book, about Buchenwald, *The Long Voyage*. Over a dozen autobiographical works and successful screenplays would follow; most of them fictionalized memoirs that touch on his experiences in Buchenwald, most of them published in France by the prestigious publisher Gallimard and subsequently translated into numerous other languages. Only two of his books were written in his native Spanish.

A European Author and Public Intellectual

Through his writing and the decades of interviews and lectures he gave, Semprún forged an international reputation as a moral authority, as someone who knew both the Fascist and Communist systems inside and out, and who had the education, time, and dedication to reflect on the crises of the twentieth century. He repeatedly contributed to the collective battle against forgetting the Holocaust by mining his own memories, and thanks to his *oeuvre* and political activity he was awarded the Jerusalem Prize, made a member of the Académie Goncourt, and given the German Peace Prize, among other honors. Felipe González, the first socialist President of Spain after Franco's death, made Semprún minister of culture during his first term. Semprún is now widely recognized as one of Europe's leading intellectuals and political figures from the last century and the beginning of this one, an eloquent and prolific witness to the horrors of World War II.

Georges, as he was fondly known in France, was extremely handsome, came from a patrician background, and wrote the Oscar-nominated screenplay for Constantin Costa-Gavras's political thriller *Z*. Yves Montand played Semprún in the latter's autobiographical *La Guerre est finie,* directed by Alain Resnais.

All of these factors came together to make Semprún a tailor-made hero for Post World War II and Cold War Paris: a man of action *and* thought, as much at ease with his false passports and the double-bottomed suitcases of his clandestine work in Franco Spain, as in the cafés of the Parisian boulevards, Les Deux Magots and the Flore, who broke with the Spanish Communist Party, and immediately became an award-winning author. Thanks to literary television shows such as Bernard Pivot's *Apostrophes* and *Bouillon de Culture*, Semprún became a household name in France.

He also became a public spokesperson for deportees and Nazi camp survivors. In Germany he was also revered. He wrote in French and lived in Paris, but he was Spanish and he was not Jewish. His point of view was unique.

Fiction vs. Testimony

Semprún's work is largely autobiographical, yet the fact that it draws inspiration from his experiences should not lead us to assume that it gives us a complete or historical picture of his life. On the contrary, he was outspoken about his right as a novelist to blend fiction and fact, and we can be sure that he freely embroidered, invented, and omitted. To date, there has been no in-depth study that contrasts Semprún's actual experience with his literary work that examines the enigmas and paradoxes that made up his life. We know a great deal about what he said he did, but we know very little about what he really did, or his motivations. It is perhaps only now, since his death, in the absence of his powerful persona, that it is possible to peruse certain sources and reflect on his legacy with some distance. How do his narratives move between historical fact and his brilliant literary self-fashioning? Are there patterns?

Though Semprún rebuilt his life in France as a deracinated exile forced to invent himself from scratch, I suggest that his political and literary ambitions were forged in his childhood in Spain. He liked to say that that the only thing he inherited from his family was his father's copy of Marx's *Das Kapital,* but in fact he shared a profound political vocation with his father, grandfather, maternal uncle, and brother-in-law. The writer Juan Goytisolo has said of Semprún that, "Politics was in his genes."[2] It is important to contextualize his political roots and trace his family background to highlight startling parallels between Semprún's life and that of his famous grandfather Antonio Maura, who started from humble Mallorquín origins but through determination and intelligence became prime minister of Spain for over two decades.

The Price of Power

What was exceptional about Semprún's life is not that it coincided with so many of the historical convulsions that defined his era, but that he involved himself so assiduously in all of them. Like his grandfather, Semprún went a long way in the political sphere, both as a professional revolutionary and as a minister of culture. And, like his grandfather, he preferred to lose everything rather than compromise his ideals. Semprún's highly individual sense of integrity led him to sever ties with political allies, and his convoluted life in exile distanced him from family members. He survived several painful and definitive separations: with the Spanish Communist Party and the Spanish Socialist Party (PSOE); as well as with his father, his once-favourite brother Carlos, and his only son, Jaime. What was the personal price paid for these broken relationships? Was he a political chameleon? Did he consider himself a success or a failure? What was his relationship to power?

Throughout the distinct periods of his life there are themes that define his personality. In every context in which he found himself Semprún looked for a way to stand above those surrounding him. Of his seven siblings, he says it was he who his mother and father designated as the future writer and politician. He was the chosen son. In Paris in the late 1930s he was an exceptional philosophy student; in Buchenwald (1943–1945) his fluency in German and his office job in the camp gave him immense advantages over the other prisoners. Within the Spanish Communist Party (1952–1962), his sophistication and cultural level allowed him to become the legendary Federico Sánchez, the agent in charge of seducing bourgeois university students and turning them into anti-Franco activists. A wanted man, Semprún/Sánchez hid in plain sight in a Madrid crawling with police. For ten years he conducted his "clandestine" work with impunity, wearing elegant clothes and riding around in flashy cars, almost baiting the *guardias civiles* to catch him. These activities were risky, without a doubt, but also afforded him the most glamorous role within the party. He was never caught. While his Spanish Communist colleagues in exile in Paris lived in low-income housing in the city's periphery, Semprún was able to live in comfort and style with his wife, the *parisienne* Colette Leloup, in central Paris. His next act was becoming a world-renowned, prize-winning, Oscar-nominated novelist/autobiographer/screenwriter, from 1963 until his death in 2011. His intense political activity was renewed when he served as Spain's minister of culture from 1988 to 1991.

An Enigmatic Legacy

What Semprún relates in his complex autobiographical *oeuvre* cannot be taken as pure historical fact—nor as pure fiction. His works are a mix of experience dressed in the guise of literature, fiction conflated with memories. Caution must be taken when analyzing them, separating fact from fancy. Semprún was one of the great seducers of the twentieth century, and it is tempting to believe everything he writes. He became an expert at blending in, at knowing how to survive in terrible conditions, calmly changing his identity and name when he knew his life hung in the balance. What were his personal relationships to trauma, memory, and forgetting?

One also has to keep in mind the degree of self-censorship natural to someone at home in a clandestine world. His version of events often gives the impression of being personal and intimate, but time and again they omit key biographical elements. Almost always his narrators speak in the first person singular, with little mention of any sort of family life. Yet Semprún was a brother, a husband, a father, and grandfather. What other aspects of his life might he have left out?

The questions that drive this biography revolve around the enigmas Semprún has left us in the wake of his death. What really inspired him to join the French Resistance? What was his role within the Communist organization at Buchenwald? To what extent are his books based on personal memory vs. received knowledge about Nazi concentration camps? What is his status within Holocaust culture as a non-Jew, and as an author whose testimony was heavily fictionalized? What were the qualities of his work and persona that made him so successful in France? What did he offer the European discourse? What is his legacy?

To answer these questions, this biography moves chronologically and draws on previously unseen archival materials: over fifty interviews with family, friends, politicians, writers, filmmakers, and historians from France, Spain, the United States, and the United Kingdom; the work and lives of other deportees and Communists; close readings of Semprún's own oeuvre: novels, nonfiction, screenplays, and his film *Les deux memoires*; and oral, print, and photographic sources from public and private collections in Spain, France, the United States, and Russia.

I
Origins

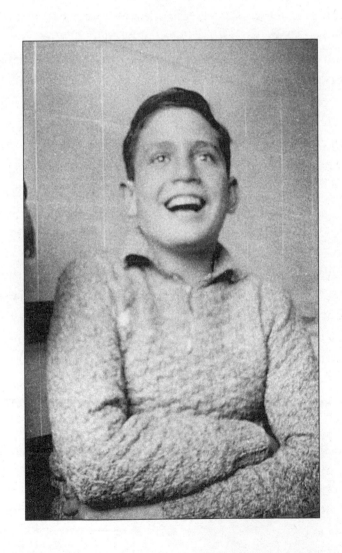

There is not any Spaniard, however poor, but has some
claim to high pedigree.[3]
—Washington Irving

Jorge Semprún is often considered an emblematic French, or
"European," author. Some Spaniards think of him an exiled "foreign" author. Each of these takes on Semprún is accurate; none is
complete. Most accounts of his life begin with his adolescence, in
exile in France, yet his story begins thirteen years earlier in Madrid.
His early life in Spain is simply overlooked, which is not surprising as
Spain is often given short shrift compared to France or Germany, and
has historically been perceived as an isolated, strange appendage to
the European continent. Alexandre Dumas coined the popular French
saying "Africa starts at the Pyrenées," and though these words reflect
their own era, attitudes endure. Spain is still considered by many outsiders as mysterious or irrelevant. Yet Jorge Semprún's blueprint was
formed long before he arrived in Paris, south of the border.

Semprún's childhood was shaped by a cosmopolitan, cultivated,
and politically complex culture. In fact, it was precisely because his
ties to his native country were so deep that he spent twenty years risking his life to try and restore Spanish democracy. His mother's early
death, the Spanish Civil War, exile, and World War II shattered his
family. But before the catastrophes began, Jorge had a cozy, affluent
childhood in Madrid. His was not a typical family, by any means, but
to the extent that it was elite it was part of a particularly Spanish, not
European, elite. To fully appreciate his tragic fall, we must consider
just how high his initial perch was. Unfortunately, his family's status—like a foreign currency—was only valid for Spain.

Jorge Semprún's milieu was steeped in Spanish politics. His first
memory was of visiting his grandfather, Prime Minister Antonio
Maura. The politician's house, on a street near the Museo del Prado
that was later named for him, was both a private home and the Spanish

equivalent of the West Wing. Decades later he recalled this world with Proustian nostalgia:

> For a long time, I thought that my first memory couldn't be real; that I had invented it or at least reconstructed it over time. . . . my first memory was that of a visit to my maternal grandfather, Antonio Maura, in the small palace he had on the Calle de la Lealtad, which has since been renamed after him, just yards from the Prado Museum and from one of the monumental entrances to the Retiro Park. . . . My mother dressed her children for such a solemn visit. She insisted on making us promise that we would be quiet and respectful. . . . When we finally arrived at my Maura grandfather's library-study, on the ground floor of the *palacete*, my grandfather was seated in the dimly lit room. His pointy white beard stood out against his white suit. He had a blanket over his knees.[4]

Young Jorge's first recorded piece of writing was a letter to his grandfather, sent during a summer holiday in 1925:

> Dear Grandfather,
> How are you? I'm sure that you are very annoyed by the strike. I send my regards to everyone. You must answer this shabby letter. My daddy and mummy send their regards to you and your Mrs.
>   A kiss from your grandson Jorge.
>
> Regards from granny.[5]

Perhaps one of his siblings helped him write this simple note, rife with childish mistakes. In any case, both this letter and his first memory establish a fundamental and early connection to his mother's family, to power, and to politics. Antonio Maura had a virtual fiefdom in the most beautiful part of Madrid, and it was in this neighborhood, where his extended family had all clustered around him, like courtiers around a king, that Jorge grew up. To a young boy it must have seemed that his grandfather was omnipotent and that his mansion had always been there, majestic and solid like the *sierra* mountain ranges that towered outside Madrid. But in fact, Maura's power had only recently been acquired. His was an unlikely Spanish success story, that of an island immigrant trying to seek his fortune on the mainland. He was a self-made man. His background sheds light on the family into which Jorge Semprún was born, and also seems to foreshadow his most famous grandson's own story of reinvention in a new city, and his lifelong quest for power.

The family story is reminiscent of Joseph Roth's novel *The Radetzky March*. The opening lines recount the dramatic rise and fall of the Trotta family. The Trottas came from nothing, triumphed magnificently, and returned to nothing, as if they had never existed. The Mauras were, in many ways, a Spanish analogy to the Trottas. Their patriarch, Antonio Maura, was also a provincial, from the then-remote island of Mallorca. It was thanks to Maura's singular rise as five-term prime minister with King Alfonso XIII that he earned the title Duke of Maura. It was thanks to his pride that he rejected the dukedom, replying that "prime minister" was a good enough title for him. His son Gabriel saw things differently, and claimed the title for himself as soon as his father died.

Maura's governments gave way to decades-long cycles of political repression and upheavals: the Dictatorship of Primo de Rivera (1923–1930), and the arrival of the Republic (1931–1936). These dramatic events were, in turn, brutally eclipsed by the Civil War (1936–1939), the Franco regime (1939–1975), and the period known as the Transition to Democracy (1975–1982). Antonio Maura is as distant a memory in Spain today as the Knight of the Trotta family was in Eastern Europe. The wide, patrician street where he lived in Madrid still bears his name, but few people today could tell one just who he was. *Calle* Antonio Maura connects the tree-lined avenues of the Paseo del Prado and the Calle Alfonso XIII, which borders the Retiro Park. It has the Ritz Hotel and the Prado Museum on one side, and Spain's stock market on the other.

The address is a far cry from the Calle Calatrava in Palma de Mallorca, where Maura was born. Calatrava is a narrow, winding street that follows an ancient stone wall that protects the city from the sea. Palma is the provincial capital of the largest of Spain's Balearic Islands, which were relatively obscure until George Sand and Chopin's stay in the Royal Charterhouse of Valldemossa 1838–1839. Sand wrote a well-known book about their experiences called *A Winter in Mallorca* in which she described the island as primitive, and centuries behind the rest of Europe. She said that she had never witnessed people as poor or as sad as the *mallorquines*:

> I have never seen people work the land so patiently and humbly. The most primitive machines are unknown here. The men's arms, which are terribly skinny and weak compared to ours, do all the work—at a snail's pace. Nothing could be sadder or poorer in the world than these peasants who only know how to pray, sing, and work. They never think.[6]

Despite her criticisms of the native islanders, Sand was enthusiastic about the landscape and climate, and her book about the island became a classic. It may be true that there is no such thing as bad publicity, for Sand inspired many travelers—including the painter John Singer Sargent, and writer Jose Luis Borges—to follow in her footsteps and seek out Mallorca's balmy temperatures, turquoise water, and landscapes dotted with palm, juniper, and cypress trees.

Since the 1950s, affordable airline tickets and the proliferation of inexpensive beachfront hotels have made the island a holiday destination for a largely foreign mass tourist industry. Over the decades, international elites have bought up the island's rural *fincas* and replaced farm buildings and fields with multicar garages, swimming pools, and home theaters. Today, German might be the island's most-spoken language, with English coming in second and Castilian Spanish a distant third.

But once upon a time, as Sand's testimony reminds us, Mallorca was a thoroughly Mediterranean, agricultural province, far from the Spanish mainland. It was founded by the Phoenicians in the eighth century BCE, and its traditions, food, and language—*mallorquín*, a variation of Catalan—were utterly distinct from those of any other region of Spain. Because a long sea voyage was necessary to reach other major ports, change was slow to come. Like the Sicilian life depicted in Tomasino Lampedusa's novel *The Leopard*, the Mallorcan rhythms were leisurely, seasonal, and ritualistic. The social hierarchy depended on the landowners. The year was punctuated by harvests and slaughters in the fields, and families and farmers came together for mass, meals, and to recite the rosary. Mallorca was not a destination, but a home to people born on the island where their ancestors had also been born. Nonnative visitors were exceptional, and "a foreigner was a strange sight, to be stared at and whispered about."[7]

This was the Mallorca of Antonio Maura's generation. He was born in Palma on May 2, 1853, to Bartolomé Maura Gelabert and Margarita Montaner y Sampayas. The family business was a leather tannery that occupied the lower part of the house on the Calle Calatrava, which still stands today. Even if the tanning process took place at a distance from where the family slept and ate, it could not have been pleasant to have the traffic of animal hides at home, and in the summer months the heat made the stench of decay and chemicals unbearable.

Antonio was one of ten siblings—five girls and five boys—and when he was thirteen years old he lost his father. His mother struggled on her own to raise and educate her many children, a difficult feat in a completely patriarchal, isolated society. By their culture's standards, Maura and his siblings were orphans, and as such faced an uncertain future and ostracism from not having a male to protect them.

Antonio's older brother, Gabriel, had dreams of becoming a writer in his local *mallorquín*, but he took charge of the tannery so that his fifteen-year-old brother Antonio could be sent to Madrid to study science, the one area in which he had excelled at the local school. The family made personal and financial sacrifices so that Antonio could try his luck on the mainland. An education in Madrid, the capital city of Spain, was an exceptional opportunity that also presented challenges to a young provincial student.

Antonio Maura was unfamiliar with the Castilian language and urban life. Like many young immigrant students he first lived in a boardinghouse in the city center, "La Señoruca," on what was once the Calle del Carbón.[8] Soon after his arrival in September 1868, a revolution broke out, and Queen Isabel II was deposed, launching a long-standing cycle of political chaos and instability. From the window of his rented room, Antonio observed the chaos, street violence, and intense upheavals happening around him. It was more than the adolescent *mallorquín* had bargained for. He knew nobody in the city and had come equipped only with his five years of provincial education. His only "letter of introduction" was not to a duke or a businessman, but to a modest post-office employee.

Madrid was a brutal contrast to Palma. At home he had his family, friends, and the port he loved to explore. Madrid was landlocked, dusty, bustling, and people spoke *castellano* at lightning speed. They were quick to ridicule provincial immigrants trying to communicate in a new language.

The 1868 revolution affected Maura directly. One of the reforms brought about almost immediately was a fast-track three-year law degree. He quickly saw the career potential of law over science and adjusted his plans accordingly. Becoming a lawyer was a rite of passage for those seeking to improve their fortunes, and Maura's widowed mother and siblings had invested everything in him. Lawyers, however, had to know how to speak convincingly and confidently. That would prove to be a great challenge.

The English poet Robert Graves, who lived for decades in Deià, on the northwestern coast of Mallorca, once said that the language of the *mallorquines* "is as old as English; and purer than its closest relatives, Catalan or Provenzal."[9] This admiring view of *mallorquín* was not, unfortunately, shared by the derisive, *madrileño* law students Maura encountered at the university in Madrid, and he felt inferior and ostracized. César Silió, Maura's close friend, political associate, and biographer, wrote the following:

> He distrusted everyone at first. The new setting was confusing to him, and he became shy and isolated. He longed for home, and the streets of Palma, and the port, which he knew like the back of his hand—and where everyone knew him. He had trouble making friends in the university . . . and couldn't fit in. His loneliness was only heightened by his language difficulties. He stammered in Castillian and his accent and syntax were embarrassing. Some of his classmates laughed at him, and he started to live in fear of ridicule.[10]

He was the only nonnative *castellano* speaker in class, a lowly provincial surrounded by young noblemen and gentry. He pored over his grammar books in his room, and spent his nights reading Cervantes, Quevedo, and other classical Spanish authors in his efforts to conquer their unwelcoming language.[11] According to César Silió, it was during this initial period that Maura had defining experiences he would later identify as the moments that drove him to become a statesman and great orator.

One of these life-changing moments came during a language lesson. This should be prefaced by saying that students of the Spanish language are often flummoxed by the abundance of silent "h"s; there are no aural clues to indicate when the letter is necessary or not. Like the dropped "h" in spoken British English, the misuse of the "h" in written Spanish could reveal someone's level of education, and in late nineteenth century Spain, their class.

The professor gave a dictation that included the word *oír* (to hear). Maura hesitated and wondered "h" or no "h"? He finally wrote the word down correctly, "oír." But his insecurities got the better of him, and he looked over his shoulder at the notebook of one of his class-mates, who had written "hoír," and changed his own spelling. The result of his anxious plagiarism was a wrong answer and a poor mark. But the incident, paradoxically, gave him a newfound confidence and sense of self-reliance. Clearly he was better off trusting his instinct and hard work than copying the work of some lazy adolescent aristocrat who didn't need good grades or success and was just going through the motions of becoming a lawyer.

When he spoke in class, he was often silenced by the uproarious laughter of his peers, whose taunts turned into aggressive harassment in the hallways after class.[12] In later years, from his position of power, Maura would remember his difficult beginnings with compassion for the awkward boy he had been:

> At the beginning, everybody looked at me with contempt. Imagine the impression I gave: ridiculous clothes, poor as a church mouse, a mute in a land of orators, fearful, and friendless. . . . I saw how they were preparing to mock and attack me, to bully me brutally. . . . I, who in Mallorca had been treated as little less than a king! The booing filled my ears. I prepared to defend myself with blows, and I cheered myself on in my own dialect. An orange peel whizzed toward my head and knocked my hat off. The crowd laughed uproariously. There were new insults as they closed in on me, threatened me, and I surrendered. But just then, two gentlemen students, well known to all, rescued me from the

> mutiny. At that moment Madrid began to smile at me, and
> I started to feel the city's proverbial seductive hospitality.[13]

The "two gentleman students" he was rescued by were brothers, Honorio and Trifino Gamazo. They were kind to him and urged him to ignore the childish bullies. His relationship with the brothers would change Maura's life. The Gamazos were also provincial, from Valladolid, but they were from a powerful, old family. Their elder brother, Germán Gamazo, had his own law firm in Madrid, and a brilliant political future ahead of him. Germán Gamazo hired Maura as soon as he finished school, and the families united when Maura married Gamazo's sister, Constancia. The marriage produced ten children; the youngest daughter, Susana, would become Jorge Semprún's mother.

As Maura climbed the capital's social and political ladder, he continued to diligently polish his spoken and written Spanish. He would, ironically, after his painfully awkward beginnings, become the most admired and renowned orator of his time, and President of the Royal Academy of Language (Real Academia de la Lengua).

Maura would fend off enemies throughout his career. He was the victim of assassination attempts, and, curiously, of anti–Semitic attacks. This is surprising because Maura and all his family were, apparently, devout Catholics. His brother Miguel was a priest who became the Rector of the Seminary in Palma, and founded an order of nuns, the Hermanas Celadoras del Culto Eucaristico. But Antonio's political opponents claimed that his ancestors were *chuetas*, Mallorcan Jews, and that he was a *converso* or crypto–Jew hiding his true origins. There were even popular postcards for sale with caricatures of Maura that showed him with an exaggeratedly large, hooked nose. Did the family really have any Jewish roots? Nearly a century later, Jorge's brother Carlos explored the accusations his grandfather faced:

It wasn't until I read the *Spanish Labyrinth* by Gerald Brenan
. . . that I discovered I was Jewish: [Brenan] wrote: "Maura
was a man of honor and integrity, who stood out among
the other politicians of Alfonso XII's time despite the fact
that he had Jewish origins. His family was *chueta* from the
Balearic Islands. He was the only Spaniard that the king
addressed formally by 'usted,' vs the familiar 'tú.'" Other
historians, including Hugh Thomas, agree with this statement, and say that the Mauras are Jewish, or *chuetas*, and
even Valle-Inclán, in one of his plays *Luces de Bohemia* . . .
calls my maternal grandfather a reactionary *chueta*. . . . My
mother's mother, on the other hand, was a Gamazo, a perfectly *goy* family. These mixes are common in Spain, and it
is difficult to determine who has "pure blood."[14]

Despite his success in Madrid, Antonio Maura's ties to Mallorca
remained deep. In the summer of 1906, at the height of his political glory, he rented a beautiful house, Can Mossenya, so that his
entire family, including his siblings, could spend the holidays in
Valledemosa. He feared that the island's conditions would not be
up to snuff, and months in advance of their arrival he had the entire
house refurbished to ensure that it was hygienic and comfortable
enough for his wife and children. His wife, Constancia, had a frail
constitution and he wanted to make sure that she could recover in
complete comfort over the summer. His brother Gabriel, the writer
who was in charge of the tannery, was responsible for getting the
house in shape. To satisfy his younger brother's demands, Gabriel
traveled to the house in Valldemossa from Palma forty-nine times.
The following examples clearly show Antonio's concern that everything be impeccable before their arrival. The prime minister's
fanatical attention to the details of domestic matters, from sheets to
plumbing, gives us a glimpse into the immaculate world in which
Jorge Semprún's mother was raised:

We need infinite amounts of linen. . . . We need four sets of horses in the stable and one must always be at the ready . . . and not just any drivers will do. . . . I would like there to be water heaters for baths and lavoratories wherever possible, and as close to the bedrooms as possible. There must be hot water and some chamber pots. . . . All of the pipes running between the house and the water should have traps. Have them installed. Without them we're guaranteed a houseful of typhoid fever. . . . If anything needs to be fixed, cleaned, or whitened, don't spare any expense. The most important thing is that the house be clean.[15]

Another brother, the painter Francisco Maura, lovingly mocked Antonio's complicated and obsessive arrangements. Francisco said that when the ten children, brothers, sisters, and cousins all boarded the train and the ships the porters would think they were a traveling *zarzuela* (the Spanish popular musical genre) troupe that had won the lottery. He referred to the family group as "the tribe." That summer in Valldemosa was the last Maura family reunion on the island. It was a great success, and Antonio was very pleased that his wife's health was much improved because of it. They were tempted to go back the following year, but in the meantime Gabriel died, and without his support it seemed impossible to organize such a fastidious trip again.

Susana Maura y Gamazo, the mother of Jorge Semprún, was born in 1894. She was just a twelve-year-old girl at the time of the summer trip to Valldemossa. Like her four sisters, she attended elite Catholic girls schools in Madrid, and as the youngest daughter of a prime minister, she was positioned to make a great marriage. As Antonio and Constancia's youngest daughter, she was sheltered and spoiled by her parents. She was a society girl and active in charity work, and appeared in the newspapers, opening a tuberculosis clinic for children in Zaragoza[16] and dancing at a fair to raise money for the unemployed. An anonymous gossip columnist described the young ladies at these events as "charming," "lovely," and "beautiful." In contrast, Susana Maura is described as "arrogant." Was she, in fact, arrogant, or was the journalist simply not a fan of her father? Perhaps it was not always easy being the daughter of a powerful man.

When she was twenty-four years old, Susana met José María de Semprún y Gurrea, who was a year her senior. He came from Valladolid, her mother's hometown, and they met at a summer garden party at the Gamazos' home in Boecillo. José María Semprún was a lawyer, and a member of the young supporters of Antonio Maura known as the "Jovenes Mauristas." The engagement and marriage were reported in the society pages. The Semprúns were a noble family with local and national power. José María's uncle was the mayor of Valladolid, and also, for one year in 1927, of Madrid. José María Semprún thus offered, per the *moeurs* of Spanish society, an old family name to the much more powerful, and *nouveau riche,* Mauras. But it was not really an even exchange. Susana was the catch.

The wedding, a surprisingly small affair, took place at the chicest church in Madrid, San Jeronimo el Real. Perhaps her father's health was no longer strong enough for a huge celebration, or the family might not have wanted to draw attention to the fact that she was past the prime marrying age, or that her husband-to-be was not what she might have aspired to. She was given away by her father, who was billed as the "illustrious ex-president Antonio Maura," And her brother, the Count de la Mortera, was one of her witnesses. She was described in the press as a radiant bride in a white satin lace-trimmed dress, holding a bouquet of orange blossoms.[17] The engagement and the small wedding were reported in the society pages of the newspaper *ABC*.[18]

The couple had seven children in rapid succession: Susana (1920), María Isabel (1921), Gonzalo (1922), Jorge (1923), Alvaro (1924), Carlos (1926), and Francisco (1928). They depended on her father for financial support, and on her powerful brother Miguel, a politician like his father, to help José María Semprún professionally. Susana's new husband was not a go-getter. Nor was he averse to asking his powerful father-in-law for help in keeping his youngest daughter and his grandchildren in the style to which she was accustomed. Among the few documentary traces left of their domestic life, there are several handwritten letters José María wrote Don Antonio asking for money. It is difficult to gauge the tone of their relationship. José María addresses the letters to "Papá," and signs off "your son," but also uses the formal second person address "usted." In 1924 he requested 1,750 pesetas to pay for the family's summer holidays, blaming his penury on the "delay, for one reason or another, of various professional payments."[19] He claims to be owed 950 pesetas by an American company, 400 pesetas by some "old and good clients" from La Rioja, and that another "important sum" was on the way as soon as he wrapped up a case for other "old clients." He says there are many other examples he could give—including one in which he is owed thousands of "duros," the old five-peseta coin, but that he doesn't want to be a bore and overexplain.

At one point, José María apologizes for not seeking help from his own father, but explains that would be impossible because the man had already helped him out on "repeated analogous occasions" with much bigger amounts.

In this one, a six-page letter, José María makes a good case for himself, but in doing so he reveals the truth: that he was constantly broke and begging his father, and father-in-law when necessary, to dig him out of a continuous financial rut. He sent another letter the very next day pressing for an urgent reply, with more apologies. In April 1925, he thanked Don Antonio for a one-thousand-peseta payment.

José María Semprún was a lawyer by training, a professor of philosophy of law at the University of Madrid, and an amateur poet. He only practiced law for a few months, as he claimed that he couldn't stomach having to defend people who were guilty.[20] He was fervently Catholic, and his unlikely political career took off during the period of the Republic (1931–1936) when his brother-in-law Miguel Maura had him appointed Civil Governor of Toledo, and later of Santander.

José María also enjoyed composing poems, and self-published a couple of volumes, which he distributed, inscribed to friends and family with authorial dedications. Writing poetry was part of the routine for a certain sort of gentleman *madrileño*. He attended literary gatherings with Federico García Lorca. There were many better and worse amateur poets hanging about and they often fashioned themselves after a well-known master. José María seems to have been a follower of Rubén Darío's style:

> Smiles you laughed,
> tears I cried,
> and the fragrance of the tea rose,
> was so sad
> who knows why![21]

In some of his literary works, Jorge Semprún describes his father as his main political and literary influence. He lovingly remembers his father's library, his political career, and father-son Sunday visits to the Prado Museum as the moments that shaped his destiny. In real life, however, he would soon be looking for other father figures who were more powerful and heroic than his biological father.

Jorge Semprún writes adoringly of his mother, and in his memory she is closely linked to the Republican government and its ideals that she enthusiastically supported. In 1931, when Jorge was eight years old, Spain democratically elected a progressive Republican government. The king was forced to flee into exile, and Spanish Republicans celebrated the dawning of a new, modern era. Susana Maura's brother Miguel was a leading Republican politician, and she was thrilled to raise her children at such an exciting time for Spain. According to Jorge, his mother knew from early on that he would be a writer or a politician: "My future vocation had been decided—with tender irony and amusement—by my mother 'Writer, or President of the Republic!' That's what she used to say. . . . One of the two options was eliminated,[22] and I finally became a writer, though it wasn't easy."[23]

Even before the Republicans came to power, Susana had been a supporter of modern educational values and wanted to be both a mother and a teacher to her children. She turned one of the rooms in their home into a classroom, complete with a blackboard, and taught the older children to read and write. They had their own schedule, and were allowed to spend the rest of their days strolling through the park while the rest of Madrid's children were locked away in schools.[24] Following the fashion of the time, once her children were older Susana continued homeschooling with German governesses. She modeled their education on the ideals of the Institución Libre de Enseñanza, run by Francisco Giner de los Ríos. The approach was strongly influenced by the German philosopher Karl Christian Friedrich Kraus, who believed that education should be free of dogma, and that students should spend as much time as possible outdoors in nature. *El krausismo*, as it was called in Spain, and in Latin America, where it also spread, was considered the height of progress and health. Spaniards thought that the study of German was indispensable to acquiring these ideals, and many affluent and forward-looking Spanish families had live-in German *frauleins* to give their children a bilingual education. These ideas were especially popular from 1931 onward. Though her father had been the king's prime minister for a total of twenty-three years, she was part of a new generation, and she flung open her windows so that the neighborhood could hear the Republican anthem on her record player. She also hung a Republican tricolor flag in all its purple, red, and yellow splendor from the balcony, to the shock of her monarchist neighbors.

In 1929, she came down with an infection she battled for three years. There are different versions of what originated the cause of her death: an infected blister on her foot is one version; a blow to her head from a fall, another. In any case, she seems to have developed septicemia. Her bedroom was gradually transformed into a hospital room and her children lived in a state of anxiety. Jorge was nine years old when she died on January 26, 1932, and he would immortalize her in his memory as his "beautiful, young mother." He later lamented that penicillin, on the brink of becoming available, did not arrive in time to save her life.

The cause of death was not disclosed in her obituary, which simply states "Susana Maura de Semprún died yesterday, in Madrid, after a rapid illness. She was the youngest daughter of the unforgettable statesman D. Antonio Maura. Mrs. Semprún was greatly esteemed by Madrid society, and was married to José Semprún y Gurrea, who has of late, since the onset of the Republic, been Civil Governor of Toledo and Santander."[25] Her funeral mass was held at the Hermanas Eucarísticas de Mallorca (an order founded by her father's brother, the priest Miguel Maura Montaner). The one-year anniversary mass for her death was held at the Church of San Jerónimo, where she had been married just twelve years earlier. She outlived her parents by only a few years: Don Antonio had passed away in 1925, and his wife Constancia a year later.

This was the first, definitive phase of a paradise lost for the Semprún children, and Jorge would cherish the last summer before his mother's death, his last experience of safety, routine, and maternal love.

> The last memories of my mother, before septicemia took her life, are rooted in the landscape of Santander—not only in the house itself, but also the beaches the Piquío rock, the La Magdalena Tennis Club, and further afield, the streets of the old part of the city, the valley of Cabuérniga, all the inland area—it's a place that occupies a privileged position in my memory.[26]

While Susana Maura was alive and in good health, her father's high standards prevailed in the care of her own children. They had a safe and beautiful home, and they could be carefree about their present and future. At the time of Susana's death, the children's *fraulein* was a twenty-five-year-old Swiss woman, Annette Litschi. She was known for her mean streak and quasi-sadistic treatment of the Semprún children. To the children's chagrin, she had José María Semprún wrapped around her finger, and almost immediately after their mother's death he married her. In her new role as stepmother, Annette had full legal rights to treat the children as she pleased. She fired the other servants who had been faithful to their former mistress and who might have buffered her cruelty with the children. Susana's death shifted everything, and launched the seven boys and girls into a Dickensian struggle. With Susana gone, affection, security, and financial stability were all jeopardized. Her death dealt a terrible blow to the Semprún children, who not only had to mourn their mother, but also had to endure a triumphant and tyrannical stepmother worthy of any Gothic fairy tale. After Susana's death, the family also struggled financially. The Mauras were shocked when Jose María remarried so quickly. Semprún defended his choice to wed the young, ambitious governess, saying it was very convenient for his children and that for him it "was better than going to prostitutes."

Jorge referred to Annette as "*la Suiza*" (the Swiss). She had her own means of discipline for the children, and Jorge remembers in particular the punishment of having to write the same line countless times, "*Ich soll gehorchen*" (I must behave). But while the older siblings were better at dodging her cruelty, she had a free hand in torturing the youngest boys, Carlos and Paco. In his memoirs, Carlos does not spare Annette in his descriptions of her beatings and other humiliations. He also tells the story of his father's brother, Iñigo Semprún, being kicked out of their home for insulting Annette by insinuating that their father and Annette were already an item before Susana died:

I don't know much about my father's younger brother, Iñigo, but I later found out that he lived with us for a while in the apartment at 12 Calle Alfonso XI. One day he came in while Annette, the *fraulein* cum girlfriend, was beating us with a broom. I don't remember this, I may have been too little, but I was the world champion when it came to receiving Annette's broom beatings. In any case, I later learned from family conversations that he said to his older brother, "That young lady is monstrous. Not only did she jump into your wife's bed as soon as she died, but she's also torturing your kids." My father kicked him out immediately.[27]

Despite his new domestic arrangements, José María continued to benefit from his relationship with his powerful brother-in-law, Miguel Maura, who was just a few years older. Miguel no doubt wanted to make sure his younger sister's seven children were well provided for.

Miguel had an important, though rocky, political career. Like his father he had started as a monarchist. But in 1923 Spain was taken over by the aristocratic dictator Primo de Rivera, whose alliance with the king tainted the monarchy. Miguel then supported the Spanish Republic because he thought it was the only solution for the future of Spanish politics. When the Republic was elected, his brother-in-law José María was invited to join him and they worked together until the Republic was overthrown in 1936 by the military coup that began the Spanish Civil War. He was used to keeping an eye out for his brother-in-law, and had already helped José María secure posts as Civil Governor of Toledo and Santander.

Historians often paint the Spanish Civil War as a dramatic battle between the extreme right and the extreme left, between Fascism and Communism. This version exists thanks to Francoist propaganda. This imaginary spectrum is very basic: to the right are the military, the Catholic Church, and the aristocracy, and to the left are the working class, peasants, and progressive anti-Catholic intellectuals. These oversimplifications are inaccurate. Miguel Maura and José

María Semprún are examples of Spaniards who defied these categories. They were both politically conservative, moderate, and Catholic
Republicans.

The Republic championed by Susana Maura and her brother was
ill-fated and short-lived. The midsummer outbreak of the Spanish
Civil War caught many political leaders on vacation in remote
mountainous or coastal areas. Miguel Maura was in La Granja, a
summer resort in the mountains in Segovia. He had stood firmly as
a conservative liberal throughout the Republic's unstable five years,
and had made enemies in every camp. After the military coup on the
night of July 17–18, he received death threats and fled the country.
Death threats were serious in 1936 Spain. Miguel was a prominent
target: his own brother, Honorio Maura, a leading pro-monarchist
activist, was arrested and shot by anarchists at the very beginning of
the war. Miguel Maura and his family were flown out of Spain on a
plane specifically arranged for by the Republic's Minister of Defense,
Indalecio Prieto. Many families sympathetic to the Republic were
brutally harassed. The poet Federico García Lorca was assassinated
in Granada by Nationalist far-right militia just a few weeks into the
war.

Though the number of executions of Republicans far surpassed
those suffered by supporters of the military coup, nobody was safe,
and suddenly nobody knew whom they could trust. After three years
under house arrest, García Lorca's family members were among a
small number who were able to flee to New York. The United States
was wary of accepting Spanish Republican refugees, and only a select
few were allowed to enter the country. Franklin Delano Roosevelt's
government had joined twenty-four other countries in signing a
"nonintervention" agreement that they hoped would allow them
to sit out any international conflicts. This policy was disastrous all
around: on the one hand it isolated and dwarfed the Spanish Republic.
Germany and Italy ignored the pact and continued to arm the Franco-
led rebels with weapons and manpower. On the other hand, it did not

prevent the escalation of events into World War II. Mexico, which under the rule of President Lázaro Cardenas was sympathetic to the Spanish Republican plight, was one of the few countries that did not sign the pact. Many Spanish refugees resettled there, but most Republicans, if able to leave Spain at all, could only make it to France. They would remain there for years, in many cases forever. The French put thousands of Spanish refugees in concentration camps, and called the refugees "rouges espagnoles." These exiles struggled to survive in France until the bitter end of the Spanish Civil War, only to learn that Franco had won the war, and they could never go home again. For those who endured the French camps, there was nowhere to turn. When the Nazis occupied France in 1940, things got even worse.

Nobody in the Semprún family was prepared for the summer of 1936. The military coup led by General Francisco Franco and backed by Hitler and Mussolini aimed to topple Spain's Republican government in one fell swoop. Within a month the country was awash in chaos and violence, and friends and relatives were being executed left and right. At the time of the uprising, José María, his young wife, and his children were in a rented summer house near the sea in the Basque fishing village of Leikeitio. He was a much less prominent figure than his brother-in-law Miguel Maura, but he had held offices with the Republic. He got himself and his family out of Spain as soon as possible. They were well connected, enough to avoid living in the abominable French refugee camps, but they left everything behind, and like other exiles, they did not know what would happen next. In a matter of days they fled Spain and became itinerant and impoverished refugees, hoping against hope that it would all be temporary, and that they would soon return to a Republican Spain.[28]

By August 1936, they were all in France. The dates are important, because many Republicans were unwilling or unable to flee Spain so quickly. Jorge Semprún's understated charm and literary flair have often lent a retroactive, dramatic spin to the most basic information about this period. Some sources have his family in Spain, resisting the Francoists until the fall of Madrid in 1939, which is undoubtedly a more romantic version. Journalist Barbara Probst Solomon, who knew Jorge Semprún personally, writes in her obituary of Jorge: "His life had been one of tremendous losses braided with star power and derring-do. His adored mother died while he was still a child: He lost her, her comfortable love, his country, and his language. When Madrid fell, the family moved to Paris."[29] In fact, the family left Spain nearly three years before Madrid fell, wandered around Europe peripatetically, and didn't move to Paris until 1939.

According to Jorge's sister, Susana Semprún Maura, their departure into exile in 1936, when she was sixteen years old, was abrupt and painful. She remembers the anguish during the ship voyage to France, and the sense that her father was fleeing because he was afraid—too afraid to ever return to Spain.[30]

II

Exile

Exile is strangely compelling to think about but terrible
to experience. It is the unhealable rift forced between a
human being and a native place, between the self and its
true home: its essential sadness can never be surmounted.
And while it is true that literature and history contain
heroic, romantic, glorious, even triumphant episodes in
an exile's life, these are no more than efforts meant to
overcome the crippling sorrow of estrangement.[31]
—Edward Said

We were all scattered here and there, blowing on
the winds of exile and chance, which were relatively
benevolent with us. We survived, but, at what price?
What kind of anguish and heartbreak did we endure?
Each one of us, if we're still alive, of course, has his or
her own answer. Maybe they would answer nothing at
all. I, in any case, won't say anything.[32]
—Jorge Semprún

By February 1939 there were half a million Spanish Republican refugees in France. Tens of thousands of them were in makeshift
camps with little food, water, or sanitation. Some of the camps had
been built on the beaches and their residents were forced to stay on
through the bitter winter months. They were treated as prisoners, and
had nowhere to turn. Propagandists sent from Franco Spain made
the rounds and tried to encourage people to return across the border,
making false promises about amnesty for all; but most people knew
that going back to Spain meant imprisonment or execution.

The defeated ones seethed within their barbed-wire enclo-
sures. Many of them could and did slip through the bar-
riers to find extra food or shelter in the homes of friendly

Frenchmen. . . . Civilians and soldiers were now to become preoccupied with the problems of living under virtually prison conditions, of the threat of forced repatriation to Spain, and, later, of deciding whether to remain in France or to seek to emigrate to other countries.[33]

Compared to the vast majority of Spanish exiles, the Semprún family had a relatively more sheltered experience in exile, at least in terms of material needs. They were able to leave Spain in the early days of the war, and had connections to help find lodging and some kind of food at every turn. In terms of their material well-being, their circumstances cannot be compared to those who struggled or died in the French refugee camps. Nonetheless, the family would be driven apart by alienation, fear, and the hardship they suffered. It was a bitter time, and one that Jorge did not really address in his writings until 1998. Sixty years had to go by for him to face his memories of this period.

Between 1936 and 1939 the Semprúns lived in numerous temporary housing arrangements in three countries: France, Switzerland, and Holland. When José María Semprún decided to leave Spain with his family, he was able to cross the border through his connections with the French Catholic journal *Esprit*, in which he had published some articles. *Esprit*, still published today, was the platform for powerful French Catholics. It was progressive, and decidedly antifascist. Its contributors were ready to help Spanish Republicans flee Franco. The family's contact person from the organization was Jean-Marie Soutou, a young *Esprit* affiliate who was sent to Spain in August 1936 on behalf of the organization to help them. He changed their lives, and they would change his. Soutou later remembered his fateful rescue mission:

At the beginning of the Spanish Civil War I met the Spanish correspondent for *Esprit*, José María de Semprún y Gurrea, who was on vacation in the little Basque village of Lequeitio,

. . . I had gone to help them organize their escape into
France . . . I was a good hiker and knew the mountains well.
I used to spend all my holidays in Spain with local shepherds
and mountain dwellers. I knew the area inside out. I also
knew what was going on in Spain. . . . In July 1936 I didn't
waste a minute wondering (like Bernanos or Mounier did)
what side to support. I said to myself, "It's time to back *la
República*, and reject the *coup d'etat*."[34]

The twenty-four-year-old Soutou was from Lestelle Bétharram, a
town in the Pyrénées, and once the Semprúns made it across the border to Bayonne, on a ship called the Galerna, his family took them
into their home. Jorge Semprún recalled the dramatic impact of arriving in Bayonne when he was fourteen years old:

My exile really began at Bayonne, with the landing at
Bayonne Harbor of the Basque trawler Galerna with its
cargo of refugees from Bilbao, fleeing Franco's armies .
. . After Bayonne, if I am to be specific and keep to the
chronological order, there was Lestelle-Bétharram. This
tiny Béarnais village was a place of pilgrimage. There was
a collegiate church, a wayside cross, several religious buildings; school, monastery, etc. . . . We had lost everything
when we arrived in exile, and the Soutou family took us in.
Jean-Marie was the younger son of the Soutou family. He
belonged to the Esprit movement, as did my father. . . . He
was quite a young man, with a singsong, rough accent like
a mountain stream rushing over pebbles toward the Adour
and the Garonne. The accent has gone with the passing of
time, but not the Béarnais ardor of his youth. . . .
    We arrived at Bayonne with nothing, staring rather
vacantly at the spectacle of French peace before us, the band-
stand, the colored flower beds, the bakery windows, the

jeunes filles en fleur—and we called on Jean-Marie Soutou for help. He came at once. He had already taken the situation in hand.

Our stay at Lestelle-Bétharram was quite long. We wandered the highways and byways, my brothers and I, while the lizards warmed themselves in the autumn sun, on the low, dry-stone walls. One day, as we were walking along a sunken road beside the torrent, one of the monks from the monastery at Betharrám called over to us. He recognized us from church . . . (he) presumed we were Nationalists.[35]. . . He congratulated us on being Spanish, on belonging to that valiant people who had risen in defense of the state, in a crusade against the Marxist Infidel. . . . He terrified us. We didn't dare say anything to him. . . . Later we were furious with ourselves. We were ashamed of our childish fear before this pathetic personage.[36]

From the Pyrenées, the Semprún family embarked on the next step in their exile, to Ferney-Voltaire, where the entire family was taken in by the American journalist Gouverneur Paulding and his family. Paulding was another connection through the Catholic network that those affiliated with *Esprit* had access to. Jorge would later recall the lively conversations at lunch—with guests such as George Santayana—and the delicious food that was served at the American family's home.[37] Years later, Paulding recalled, "the Semprúns, a Republican family, left the Spanish Basque country and made their way by sea to France. When they landed at Bayonne, summer people from fashionable Biarritz gawked at them. They were 'Spanish Reds.' As such, they aroused curiosity, embarrassment, and an uneasy feeling that they might be bringing along with them, like a contagious disease, the disaster that had overtaken them in their country."[38]

The next stop was Geneva, where the *Esprit* contacts continued to provide shelter for this rather large family of refugees: Jose María, his

Swiss wife, and the seven children. The girls were sent to a Catholic boarding school there, and the small boys were taken in by Le Foyer, a Catholic charitable home for children run by Mademoiselle Helene Reymond.

Jorge and his brothers were enrolled in the Collège Calvin, where they discovered that Europe's political tensions were apparent even among schoolchildren in 1936. On the playground the Semprún boys were taunted by classmates who disliked the "Spanish Reds." The Swiss boys raised their hands in the Fascist salute and chanted slogans praising the leader of their Swiss canton, Oltramare. Jorge was soon removed from school due to a "heart condition." He later summed up his memories of this period in one word: brutal.[39]

The famous photo of the five brothers with their fists defiantly in the air is from this period. Standing behind them in the photo is a young girl with glasses, Elsa Grobéty. Elsa, known to all as "Pom," was also a foster child at Le Foyer, and she became the Semprún children's best friend in Geneva. Nearly eighty years after that photo was taken, she remembered the entire Semprún family with great affection, especially Jorge, who she says was very kind to her. The boys, and their sister Maribel, especially, were like siblings for her. Elsa used to walk around Geneva hand in hand with Jorge, who she adored. She was four years older than Jorge, and they hit it off immediately. Jorge's brother Alvaro, who suffered from severe depression, was also adopted by Mlle. Reymond and spent most of his life at her home, which she left to him when she died.[40] Alvaro wanted to marry Pom, but she never married anyone, though she stayed by Alvaro's side and helped look after him until his death. Elsa also had a sister, Yvonne, whom Jorge claimed was "his favorite." [41]

To the Semprún children this Swiss interlude in 1936 might have seemed like a temporary adventure,[42] but as Jorge recalled in retrospect: "It was in Geneva that my sleepless night of exile began. A night that has still not come to an end, despite appearances to the contrary, and which will probably never come to an end." [43]

Between 1936 and 1939 José María Semprún was a mid-to-low ranking member of the exiled Republican intelligentsia. He continued to benefit from the protection of his brother-in-law Miguel Maura, a much higher-ranking member of the same group, and he was also looked after by his new friends from *Esprit*.

On November 1, 1936, José María Semprún wrote an article for *Esprit,* which was translated and published on February 3, 1937, by the Spanish embassy in London as a pamphlet in English under the title "A Catholic Looks at Spain." The title alone makes clear that he wanted to prove to the world that Catholics could and should support the Spanish Republic. Since the nonintervention agreement that had been signed in August 1936, Republicans were desperately trying to rally democratic nations to support their side. The United States, Britain, and France had many economic and strategic reasons for not intervening, and to make matters worse, international headlines were tarring the Republicans as violent anti-Catholics. The anti-Catholic image of the Republic spread like wildfire in the United States and England during the Spanish Civil War. Despite energetic diplomatic efforts to counter the charges, by 1938 the *New York Times* quoted Bishop John Mark Gannon of Erie, Pennsylvania, and trumpeted his claims in headlines that read: "16,000 priests slain" and "20,000 churches sacked."[44]

José María Semprún's pamphlet was one of the early attempts to change the Republic's image abroad and attract foreign support for the Spanish government. He clearly thought his point of view, as a devout Catholic and Spanish Republican, might be successful in changing views of the Republic abroad. More importantly, he thought his eloquence and temperance might help rescind Roosevelt's nonintervention policy. He was not successful in this endeavour; nor, of course, was anyone else, yet his efforts leave us with an impression of a concerned, yet ineffectual man, still wholly unaware that his government would lose the war and that he would never set foot in his country again. His text is poignant, but his archaic language, the Spanish of

a deeply Catholic former lecturer of philosophy of law, was useless
in the midst of a wholly modern war with no time for abstractions.
Though his heart was undoubtedly on the side of his government, his
defense of the Republic is awkward:

> In any other European country an attack on a church would
> be a clear sign of religious hatred. In Spain it may be merely a
> brutal manner of expressing a protest or a means of radically
> fortifying oneself against more or less imaginary dangers. I
> have no desire to excuse such acts. I only insist on affirming,
> with a clear conscience of what I say, that they do not corre-
> spond—or they may not correspond—to that state of mind
> which they appear to indicate, and that it would be a serious
> error to measure them by the relationships and judge them
> by the criteria ordinarily valid in other countries.[45]

Written arguments like these were, alas, a feeble counteroffensive
to the violent onslaught on the Spanish republic, including the Nazi
Condor Legion bombing Spanish civilians. José María clearly hoped
to make amends for leaving Spain—in effect abandoning a sinking
ship—by recasting himself as an international spokesperson for Spanish
democracy. He was forty-three years old when the war started, and
was constitutionally more fitted to writing and talking about politics
than engaging in armed resistance. This is important because his son,
Jorge, would strive, successfully, to distance himself from his father's
role as a "gentleman" armchair political activist.

José María Semprún tried to survive the war with his dignity intact,
and was able to get his children out of the makeshift homes in France
and Switzerland. As a former Republican governor, he attended the
Society of Nations meetings in Geneva, and got back in touch with
the Republic's Minister of Foreign Affairs, Julio Alvarez del Vayo. He
requested a diplomatic post, and Alvarez del Vayo was ready to help.
The next stop for the entire Semprún family in late 1936 was The

Hague, where José María was sent as the Business Attachée to the Spanish Republican Embassy. It was a comfortable situation, given the times, and the alternatives. The family was able to live together again in a large house, where receptions and other embassy-related activities took place. Soutou came along as José María's secretary. Soutou must have been quite attractive in his role of valiant savior: both Semprún daughters, Susana and Maribel, fell in love with him. In 1942 Soutou would marry Maribel. Susana, heartbroken by his rejection, made the radical choice of moving back permanently to Franco Spain. She never saw her sister again.[46]

Curiously, the first wife of Chilean poet Pablo Neruda also worked the Spanish Embassy in The Hague. Maria Antonieta Hagenaar was an embassy employee who the Semprúns saw on a daily basis. She had also found a safe haven there for herself and her daughter, Malva Marina, who was stricken with hydrocephalus. With the small salary she earned at the embassy, Hagenaar was just barely able to pay for a foster care home for her daughter, and for a room in a nearby boardinghouse for herself.

Hagenaar, originally from Java, strikingly beautiful, and exceptionally tall, had indeed been caught far from home at the outbreak of World War II. She had been abandoned by Neruda just before their daughter turned two. They had met during one of his consular stints in the Pacific, and despite communication difficulties (he spoke no Dutch, she spoke no Spanish), they were soon married. Unbeknownst to Hagenaar, while she was in The Hague, Neruda had obtained a Mexican divorce from her and remarried Delia del Carril. Hagenaar wrote to Neruda repeatedly, urging him to send her money to look after Malva, and tried to get a visa to go to Chile where they could be closer to him. Neruda, who was also a diplomat with powerful government connections, nixed her visa application, and never saw his daughter, or Maria Antonieta, again. Malva died in 1942.[47]

Though Hagennar had no direct role in Semprún's story, her tragic situation and background presence are illustrative of the characters the family ran into in exile, and she made an impact on the young Jorge. Decades later, in his book *Communism in Spain in the Franco Era: The Autobiography of Frederico Sánchez (Autobiografía de Federico Sánchez)*— written in an unusual second person narration—Jorge Semprún reminisced about his childhood exile in The Hague, Neruda's first wife, and her mysterious presence at the embassy:

> In 1937, at The Hague, where your father was the Business Attaché during the civil war, there was a female employee at the Chancellery of the Spanish Republic's Mission who was a Dutch creole from Java or Sumatra and who had been Pablo Neruda's wife. Only a poet could have married that kind of woman, she was literally so incredibly tall that she looked like a soft sleepy giraffe.[48]

Semprún was one of the few people to ever "memorialize" Hagenaar, who seems to have vanished from history. Her story, and that of her daughter, gives a sinister tint to Neruda's image. The famously antifascist bard, and champion of Europe's beleaguered, made sure his first wife and daughter stayed put in war-torn Europe while he embarked on a new life and marriage in Chile.

The fourteen-year-old Jorge seemed to need a strong father figure, and José María was not cut out for the role. Furthermore, he had betrayed their mother's memory by remarrying the scary governess. Jean-Marie Soutou was the hero who had saved them, and he was the first in a series of influential father figures that Jorge would turn to in his early years. Though Soutou was also a Catholic intellectual, he was closer to Jorge's age, educated, highly literate, and brave. Soutou had important friends in the antifascist underground, and could make things happen. He made sure the Semprún family got to France safely, and he introduced Jorge to French literature. It was in The Hague that the adolescent Jorge heard his future brother-in-law reciting Baudelaire, and borrowed his copy of *Les Fleurs du mal*, which he learned by heart.[49] He seemed to have all of the qualities young Jorge dreamed about, and his admiration would only grow when World War II broke out. Soutou cofounded, along with the Abbot Alexandre Glasberg, a Ukrainian Jew who had converted to Catholicism, the *Amitiés judéo-chrétiennes*. The organization, headquartered in Lyon, was dedicated to saving Jewish children.

In 1998, fifty-two years after they first met, Jorge dedicated his memoir *Adieu, vive clarté* to "Jean Marie Soutou, for his watchful and fraternal lifelong friendship." ("*Jean-Marie Soutou, pour son amitié vigilante et fraternelle de toute une vie.*") In the book Soutou is portrayed affectionately. Curiously, in Soutou's memoirs, Jorge is not mentioned at all, except for in a footnote to the introduction, written by Soutou and Maribel's son, Georges-Henri.[50] Soutou's memoirs are much less personal than Jorge's, but it is nonetheless surprising that he does not once mention his brother-in-law, the famous author and Buchenwald survivor.

In February 1939, Jorge and his elder brother, Gonzalo, were sent to Paris as boarders at the Lycée Henri IV. Jean-Marie Soutou was an alumnus of the elite school and had undoubtedly intervened to secure spots for his brothers-in-law. Franco's victory marked the permanent end of Spain as the Semprúns had known it. The Hague was the last place all seven siblings would ever be together.[51] José María Semprún, his wife, and the remaining children stayed in there until the Spanish Republic officially lost the war on April 1, 1939. At that point its government, including all embassies and consular offices around the world, were shuttered and replaced by Franco Spain's diplomats. For how long, nobody knew.

José María Semprún moved his family to Saint-Prix, an old town surrounded by large estates, north of Paris, high on a hill near the Montmorency forest.[52]

From his new abode, José María Semprún continued to struggle through life in exile. He had a much younger second wife, and seven children to worry about. He was a bon vivant, a gentleman intellectual, and a devout Catholic. There were others like him in Spanish social circles of the 1930s, and they naturally fared much better in their natural habitat than in exile. When José María first married, his powerful father-in-law had provided him with a home and money whenever needed. He had control of his wife's dowry, and his brother-in-law had made him Civil Governor of two important Spanish cities. In France he was adrift, and owed everything to the help of Jean-Marie Soutou, *Esprit*, and Miguel Maura. If it hadn't been for the well-connected and resourceful Catholic group that published the journal *Esprit*, the Semprúns might have ended up on the street, or in another country. The house where José María, Annette, and the younger children eventually settled in Saint-Prix had been secured for them by the organization.

The Semprúns decided to stay in France while many other Spanish Republicans had opted to leave for Mexico. The Mexican Government under President Lázaro Cárdenas had welcomed Spanish Republican refugees more generously than any country in the world. Though it was far away, for most of the Spanish exiles the conditions were infinitely better than anywhere in Europe, and the common language, balmy weather, and Mexico's rich culture made the journey worthwhile. José María's friend, the Catholic philosopher José Bergamín, had resettled his family in Mexico City and urged Jose María to join them. José María's response shows just how despondent his situation had made him:

> If I must set off to join you in order to avoid starving to death, well then I might. But no matter where I am, here or America, or China, I can never be—nor do I want to be— anything but a survivor. I feel like the walking dead, and my only desire is to crawl into my grave."[53]

Though Jorge painted a somewhat romantic image of his father in many of his works, in *Adieu, vive clarté* (1998) a more critical portrait emerges of a rather helpless and deeply self-pitying man. In one instance he recalls his father's behavior at an *Esprit* meeting in 1939 at Jouy-en-Josas:

> He (my father) complained: "How can I be expected to share a room with other people!" The mere idea was unbearable. He muttered something about how impossible and inappropriate it would be to sleep under such promiscuous circumstances. How uncomfortable and humiliating it would be. My father had never known the life of the barracks because he didn't do his military service. Like most young men of bourgeois families he had paid a substitute do the service for him. . . . But this time, in Jouy-en-Josas, I was not sympathetic.[54]

Luckily for José María, he didn't have to share a bedroom with strangers very often. But in his day-to-day routines he was equally inflexible and closed-minded. It sometimes seemed as if he lived in another century and imagined that he was wealthy and had servants and staff to attend to all of his needs. The truth was that he was a penniless refugee stuck in the eye of the storm of World War II, a status that Jorge alternately pitied, and resented:

> He had always been incapable of practical tasks, of doing anything that a servant could do for him. The only exception was that he did like to drive his own cars, which were usually powerful and American. . . . If he had been a sports buff he might have played golf, if he had been a hunter he might have shot clay pigeons. . . . He was a bourgeois intellectual who had bet everything, and lost everything, on defending his liberal ideas of social justice. But getting a letter stamped and putting it in a letter box was beyond him, not to mention dealing with French bureaucracy. . . . Exile and defeat had turned him into

a proletariat, a déclassé of the intelligentsia, and he had been thrown into total despair.[55]

Another painful memory from this period is from early June 1940, when Jorge accompanied his father to the immigration office at the police headquarters in Paris to request French citizenship. The timing could not have been worse, as France was already falling to the Germans. Jorge remembers his father introducing himself and reciting his qualifications and honors—diplomat of the Spanish Republic; Professor of the philosophy of law, University of Madrid; Officer of the Legion of Honor—and asking to share in France's destiny. His request was greeted with laughter by a civil servant who told him that he would make a note of the request, and went through the motions of doing so. José María, seen through his son's eyes and words, seems like a Quixotic figure in this encounter: tall, thin, elegant, and completely out of touch with the world in which he lived.[56]

The humiliating scene of his Spanish refugee father being laughed at by a French official, and denied the chance to apply for French citizenship, helped forge Jorge's sense of his own identity, and nationality. Like his mother's death, the flight from Spain, and his homelessness from that point onward, his father's impotence made Jorge all the more determined to excel in the ways in which his father had ultimately failed: intellectually, politically, and financially. But there would be echoes of his father's character in his own behavior. Jorge would never enjoy menial, practical, domestic tasks any more than José María Semprún had. When Jorge's wife Colette died at age eighty-seven, just a few years before his own death in 2011, he didn't even have a key to his own apartment. Though he strove to distinguish himself from his father's behavior, they shared traits, including little interest in domestic details. It shouldn't be surprising that Jorge needed looking after and while in the Resistance waited for a female comrade to make him coffee in the morning. It was one thing to be an antifascist, but another altogether to rebel against his generation, and his background, which as he himself said was "Catholic, bourgeois, and patriarchal."

Like the little Spanish *pícaro* character Lazarillo de Tormes, Jorge quickly realized he would have to learn to take care of himself, and Lazarillo's awakening to the harsh realities of life befits Jorge's. "I suddenly awoke from my innocent, childish slumber. . . . I realized that I had to be alert and keep my eyes open, because I was alone, and had to figure out how to survive."[57]

It was at the same aforementioned *Esprit* congress in Jouy-en-Josas in 1939 where Jorge met another father figure, a man he identifies only as "Edouard-Auguste F." He usually gives complete names, so the reader wonders: why doesn't he include this man's last name? The fact that only the last initial is provided suggests an ambivalence on Jorge's part toward this older gentleman, and that he may only be giving us a partial portrait of him and their relationship. As it happens the man's last name was Frick, and he was part of the Catholic group Amis de Esprit. He knew Jorge's tutor at Lycée Henri IV, Pierre-Aimé Touchard. He had undoubtedly heard good things about this precociously brilliant sixteen-year-old student and his family's precarious situation in France.

Edouard-Auguste Frick was a wealthy Swiss-born, Russian-bred Catholic, and he was a powerful man. He had been responsible for the creation of the international Nansen passports that enabled World War I refugees to find new homes. Both Jorge and his brother Alvaro, who boarded during the week at the Lycée Henri IV, began to stay at Frick's fancy Parisian house on rue Blaise Desgoffe, in Montparnasse, on weekends.

In his own memoirs, Jorge's brother Carlos claims that Frick was interested in young men, and that he tried, unsuccessfully, to take Carlos to bed[58] while he was living and working at Frick's farm in Bouzon-Gellenave (Gers). The farm produced Armagnac, and was one of many businesses managed by Frick and owned by a wealthy Greek entrepreneur, who is left unnamed.

Thanks to the *Esprit* connections, Frick ended up rooming and boarding, wining and dining three very handsome Semprún boys at both his city and country homes. Thus José María and his wife had three less mouths to feed. In the summer of 1939, just after meeting them, Frick took Jorge and Carlos on a few weekend trips to the beautiful Hotel Roches Noirs in Trouville. Recalling these trips many years later, Carlos said: "I didn't like the dirty old man from Normandy."

Jorge only mentions Frick in his book of memoirs *Adieu, vive clarté*, which centers on his adolescence in Paris. In this book he describes the time he spent living with Frick and makes a point of denying that Frick ever laid a hand on him. During a holiday trip to Biriatou in the Pyrénées, he remembers, they stayed at the home of the Greek arms dealer who employed Frick. The Greek's wife, a beautiful young woman named Hélène, asked Jorge why he was sleeping in a room so far away from Frick's. Jorge immediately realized that she assumed he was Frick's young protegé and lover, and he was enraged. He later set the matter straight, for the record, and ardently defended his heterosexuality:

> Never, during the two and a half months of my stay at rue Blaise-Degoffe, had he made the slightest gesture, nor said an insinuating word that could have been interpreted as untoward. Nothing could have led me to believe that his taste for Greek *paideia* might have been the cause, or the effect, of his latent pederasty.[59]

He says that he flirted with Hélène just to prove her wrong, and he says they continued their flirtation right under everyone's nose, and that she groped him under the table at dinner. This must have been risky right across the table from the undoubtedly watchful eyes of the Greek magnate, and Frick. If Jorge was, as he says, seducing Frick's boss's wife, he was seriously risking his luxury room and board, and school tuition. Jorge also claims, rather defensively, that he was not homophobic, and mentions his father's friendship with Federico García Lorca, as if to prove, if only by association, his open-mindedness on the subject.

Jorge and Carlos had an intertextual debate and memory war about Frick, as they did about so many other subjects over the years. Carlos's memoir came out the same year (1998) as Jorge's description of the Biriatou holiday—sixty years after the events. Their war of words always followed a pattern: Carlos would go public about something shameful from the family's past, and Jorge—without acknowledging Carlos's accusation—would address the subject in a way that discounted, or at least checked, Carlos's sometimes unflattering recollections. If Carlos had not written about Frick, perhaps Jorge would have never brought the matter up at all. Their narrative tandem is a bit like Don Quixote and Sancho Panza: Jorge is the cultivated, idealistic leader, and Carlos is the earthy, funny, and sometimes refreshingly realistic sidekick. He is the younger sibling that questioned and made fun of his older brother the hero, and commented, like a one-man Greek chorus, on Jorge's stories and claims. This competitive brotherly rapport lasted for decades, until their deaths.

If José María Semprún had been a different sort of father, and if Annette Litschi had not been an evil stepmother, the Semprún boys would perhaps never have gone to live with single, wealthy, older Catholic benefactors. The male children lived with a few families, and boarded in different schools along the way, but Frick seems to have made his mark on Jorge. Jorge has enthusiastic praise for the education Frick offered him, and clearly enjoyed the luxurious lifestyle of his patron. His time with Frick, combined with his education at the Lycée Henri IV, gave Jorge the polish he was lacking as a young Spanish refugee. He was beginning to become a writer and thinker. He spent his time reading philosophy and French literature, and made mental notes about Parisian life from his decidedly outsider perspective. Spending the weekends in Parisian splendor with Frick

was incomparably better than traipsing back from school to spend
weekends in gloomy Saint-Prix with his weak father and domineer-
ing stepmother: "My father and stepmother live with my two younger
brothers, Carlos and Francisco (Paco), who suffered their share under
the obtuse and arbitrary rule of "la Suisse."[60] His father barely scraped
by during the Occupation. His only income was from teaching at a
nearby religious school.[61]

In school and out, Jorge was already moving forward, and away
from his family, developing his new French/Spanish hybrid identity,
exploring new relationships, and building his own singular path.

What must have been clear to him by 1939 was that his fortune
would be made in Paris, and in French. In France, and in part thanks
to Frick and the Lycée Henri IV, he quickly outclassed his siblings
and his father. Frick had high expectations for his charge, and he
was pleased with the results. The young Spanish refugee stood above
the norm of most Parisian adolescents in every respect. He was soon
trilingual in Spanish, German, and French, and a prize-winning philosophy student. He had also become irresistibly good looking. His
cheekbones and jaw were chiseled, his dark hair abundant, his eyes
beautiful and intelligent. He was tall for his generation, and had the
strong, lean figure of a long-distance runner. Frick had encouraged
Jorge to become an athlete and he excelled in this area as well. His
natural beauty, combined with his quick wit and his need to survive, made him an expert seducer. He read other people astutely, and
knew how to make himself desirable. This power of seduction was an
extremely valuable talent for a young exile whose family finances had
disintegrated.

To hear those who knew him speak about his magnetism, one
would think they were describing a rock star. Those who knew him
personally always emphasize his good looks and personal charm, along
with his intellectual capacity, cultural breadth, talent, and bravery.

Despite these qualities, Frick made sure Jorge sang for his supper
by doing extra scholarly work:

Edouard Auguste F.'s pedagogical approach was a mixture
of classical paideia and the Montessori Method. It might
have also come from his exposure to the high society of
Calvinists in Geneva, but he had the rigor of an accountant:
everything must be paid for, and nothing in life is free. I had
to earn his generosity. I was housed, fed, and laundered; I
had pocket money, but every week I had to write an essay
on an assigned reading.[62]

If that was indeed all Jorge had to do in exchange for his tuition,
expenses, and housing, it sounds like a good deal. But just before his
final year of high school, the arrangement came to an unexpected
end. For unspecified reasons, and unexpectedly for Jorge, he was sent
back to Saint-Prix. He continued at Lycée Henri IV, but could no
longer call Frick's splendorous apartment his home base.[63] The Sunday
lunches at the most expensive Paris restaurants and the Mediterranean
holidays with Frick's glamorous friends were over. Who would support him while he studied at university?

Jorge did not indulge in self-pity, but being cut off by Frick was
clearly an unpleasant shock. His life had become like that of a picaresque character, going from master to master, and getting the boot, or
fleeing when necessary. He is also reminiscent of Lazarillo of Tormes,
in that he tells his life's story but censors himself in picturesque fashion
as he goes along.

In June 1941, he obtained his baccalauréat degree and was awarded
the second prize of the *concours general* in philosophy. Several factors
would pull him away from his studies and toward an active role in the
war. Losing his benefactor was one of them. Frick's interpretation of
paideia only went so far:

After completing my studies in Philosophy, with my bac-
calaureate degree in hand, and the multiple lessons learned
from Edouard-Auguste F., I was flung out into the world

before my eighteenth birthday. F., whilst a strict adherent of *paideia*,[64] was also absolutely opposed to financial and emotional crutches, including nest eggs. So I was forced to make a living, quite pathetically, by taking on all sorts of odd jobs and private classes. I had to leave the preparatory course that I had started at Henri IV, and that would have allowed me to enroll in the École Normale Supérieure. Surprisingly, I have no recollection at all of that course.[65]

Jorge was an excellent student, but his personal and financial situation limited him. It must have been unbearable to have to drop out of the prestigious ENS, which would very possibly have guaranteed him a brilliant career as a philosopher. But the classes were full-time, and he had to work odd jobs to support himself. Frick's timing could not have been worse.

France was under siege, and while Jorge prepared his *baccalauréat*, on June 14, 1940, the Germans occupied Paris. In November, Jorge took part in demonstrations at the Place de l'Étoile. These were some of the first student-organized Resistance activities that resulted in numerous arrests, injuries, and the closing of the Université de Paris through December 20.[66] By then he had become a Parisian, and was already a regular at the Café Flore and other Saint-Germain-des-Prés haunts. Flore, made famous by its clients Simone de Beauvoir and Jean-Paul Sartre, was also the only well-heated café during the occupation.[67]

Flore was a symbolic spot, and a regular meeting place for Philosophy students from Henri IV and Louis-le-Grand, and for those of us in preparatory classes for *hypokhâgne* and *khâgne*. It was this atmosphere that made me a lifelong fan of the Rive Gauche. When we were seventeen years old, that was where we spent our days, before the Resistance drew most of the people in my entourage into real military and militant action.[68]

Former Spanish Prime Minister Felipe González believes that Jorge's
rebellious spirit had its origins in the milieu at the Henry IV institute
in Paris:

> His sense of moral rebellion began when he went to school
> there. It is a process that is familiar to me because I went
> through something similar. Morally, you seize on one thing
> that becomes absolutely clear to you: to live under a dicta-
> torship is impossible. It is the one thing as an adolescent that
> was very clear to me. And once that is clear to you, then you
> know you must devote yourself to fighting it, and you begin
> to consider options. What is the most effective manner one
> can choose to confront it? He wasn't born a Communist.
> His family were not Communists—far from it—but he had
> that sense of moral rebellion fired up within him, and as a
> young man looking for adventure and influenced by the
> people around him, when he decided to join the Resistance,
> he came to believe that the most effective instrument avail-
> able to him was embodied by the Communist structure.
> And so he joins the Communist Party for the sole reason
> that it is the most committed group willing to fight in the
> Resistance movement against the forces he identified as
> being the enemies of Spain.[69]

Jorge was indeed swept up by his friends and the political events,
and saw a way to put some of his intellectual dreams into action. He
had started reading Emmanuel Lévinas, Husserl, Marx, and Lukács.
He was already a devoted fan of André Malraux, who was one of
those rare literary men of action that Semprún fervently aspired
to be. Malraux had helped the Spanish Republic, and he written
the powerful novel *L'espoir* about the crash of a Republican plane.
Jorge Semprún said very clearly that he knew *L'espoir* by heart, and
that it was in his bag when he was fighting with the *Tabou maquis*,

(underground fighters). He says that if he hadn't read Malraux when he did he would never have become a Communist.[70] The dashing French author was also a pilot, and he had smuggled planes into Spain to arm the Republic against Franco and the Nazi air force. *L'espoir* was considered the most important novel about the Spanish Civil War. Jorge had first read selected extracts when they appeared in serialized form in 1937–1938 in *La Nouvelle Revue Francaise*. His political awakening can be attributed to his own experiences as an exiled Republican, his education, his Parisian milieu, and—though he never says this—his uncertain future.

When he was nineteen, through people Soutou and Maribel knew, he was recruited to join the Resistance group Jean-Marie Action, of the Main d'oeuvre immigrée (MOI). He was assigned a new identity so that if he were arrested he would not be caught with his real identity papers. His alias was Gérard Sorel, and he was supposedly a gardener by profession. His principal mission was to collect arms dropped by parachute during the night. These arms were used to sabotage communications, canals, and railways.[71]

In June 1940, Jorge left his family and began a separate life. His father, in the meantime, fled the onslaught of Nazi troops and left Saint-Prix with his wife, Paco, Carlos, and Susana (who was soon to leave permanently for Spain). Maribel was living with Soutou in Lyon. The family ended up in Saint Jean de Luz, where, in yet another twist and turn of fate, they were taken in by the Chinese embassy to Spain, which continued in exile from Madrid because Chang Kai Chek had refused to recognize Franco's victory. José María knew Ambassador Liu from The Hague, and so the family spent the summer on the Basque coast. They returned to Saint-Prix in the fall.[72] At this point, Annette pulled Carlos out of school, and he was forced from then on to work full time as a farm hand and run errands for her. She turned Carlos and Paco's adolescence into a dismal nightmare. They had gone from being pampered children in Madrid to being Oliver Twists, more or less abandoned in the suburbs north of Paris.

The youngest two brothers hated living in Saint-Prix with their father and stepmother, who Carlos called the bitch, *la chienne*. Carlos and Paco felt the world had abandoned them. As World War II went on they received fewer and fewer visitors. It was just Annette, their father, and the local priest who had dinner at their house once a week enjoying endless conversations with José María. Thanks to Carlos's work on the farm, they all had food, and the father, stepmother, and the two youngest sons scraped by. They lived on rutabagas and Jerusalem artichokes (which were only used for animal feed at the time). Once a month Annette would kill and cook a chicken or rabbit, and Carlos sometimes brought back other vegetables from other farms where he worked.[73]

Poverty, even more than politics, dominated their lives. Carlos and Paco, like their brothers, were good-looking lads who wanted to meet girls, and they were embarrassed to be seen in the same clothes they'd been wearing since 1936. The only shoes available were wooden soled clogs, and Carlos considered himself lucky the day he found an old pair of leather shoes in the rubbish. The soles were full of holes, but he lined them with newspapers to walk through the rain and snow, and says that all the colds he caught were worth it.[74]

Thousands of young men wanted to join the Resistance. Carlos, who always wanted to emulate his big brother Jorge, was jealous when he discovered that Jorge had signed up; he begged Jorge to take him along, but he was too young.[75] Carlos and Paco joined the local Red Cross instead, and got to wear the organization's official armband, but there were no wounded to help in the Saint-Prix area.

Why did Jorge Semprún join the French Resistance? Ideological, political, and moral grounds? Of course he wanted to help defeat the Nazis, Franco's allies, and he certainly hoped that doing so would weaken the dictatorship in Spain. Jean-Marie Soutou, an active antifascist and recruiter for the Resistance, and André Malraux were undoubtedly key role models, and he was eager to pursue a heroic adventure, so why *not* join the Resistance? His family had disintegrated, and his hard-won chance for a glorious higher education at the École Normale

Supérieure had been destroyed by Frick's withdrawal of financial support. He was nineteen and didn't have a penny to his name. Joining the Resistance was a way to become a hero and get regular meals for a time.

Felipe González said the seeds for resistance had been sown in Jorge Semprún's imagination since his time at the Lycée Henri IV, where the atmosphere was left-leaning and decidedly anti-Nazi, though not Communist:

> We talked about things at Henri IV. There was a patriotic, French dissidence . . . the demonstration of November 1940, was organized at Henri IV, we went to the Concorde and toward the Champs Elysées. It was a patriotic demonstration. There were several hundred of us at the end. . . . I was there as an anti-Nazi, not as a French patriot. I was commemorating the Spanish Civil War. But the French police was there, and they started to hold us back, and beat people up. Our march was dispersed, and we didn't make it to Etoile, which was our goal. Armed SS troops were coming up Avenue Georges V, and we split off and with a friend I broke through a line of police officers and we got away on the metro. But some of our friends were arrested. It all started with people saying France is not defeated. France still exists. . . . We passed from a spiritual resistance . . . to actually sabotaging industry and lines of communications, and then widespread fighting in the *maquis*.[76]

His friend Michel Herr also influenced his decision. Michel Herr was the son of Lucien Herr (1864–1926), a Parisian intellectual leader, a librarian, and alumnus of the École Normale Supérieure. Michel Herr had been recruited to join the Resistance by Soutou, and as of May 1943 he started working with the Jean-Marie Action network, which was run by the England's Special Operations Executive (SOE). SOE sent arms from England to France, and Jean-Marie Action, under the command of Henri Frager, a World War I veteran, was responsible for making sure the arms reached Resistance forces in France.

It was Maribel who asked Michel Herr to "get in touch with" Jorge,[77] which seems to mean that she and her husband knew about, and may have supported, his plans. The meeting between Herr and Jorge took place at Lucien Herr's home, 39 boulevard du Port-Royal.[78]

The alternative to joining the Resistance was not attractive to the nineteen-year-old Jorge Semprún. Who wanted to eke out an existence tutoring wealthy children in occupied France? Jorge was young, strong, and had an adventurous spirit. He needed to channel his energy, intelligence, and anger. Life as "Jorge Semprún" had started out well, but had rapidly gone downhill. Perhaps his alias, "Gerard Sorel" the arms distributor, would have more luck.

Semprún's training took place in Yonne, under M. Herr's supervision. The young Jorge was made Herr's second in command, and he was put in charge of organizing anti-Nazi sabotage operations. His unit blew up threshers to make sure the Germans couldn't get their hands on French wheat, and they organized attacks on trains, town halls, and police stations. They stole ration cards, arranged the reception and distribution of arms, and hid the weapons in secret caches. Semprún worked regularly with the *Tabou maquis*, based in Pothières. Luck seemed to be on their side, but not for very long. Two of their men were arrested for blowing up a munitions train in Pontigny. The German police immediately launched a major dragnet operation.[79]

On October 8, 1943, Jorge was hiding out, asleep, at the house of fellow *resistante* Irene Chiot when the Gestapo broke into the home and arrested everyone:

> The house . . . was an old farm, with several buildings built around a grassy courtyard. It was noon, more or less. The night before, we had jumped a Wehrmacht munitions train at Pontigny, and one of the guys from our group [Georges

V.] had vanished. . . . Certain facts made us think he might
have been arrested. Back in Epizy, at dawn, after a sleepless
night, I had dozed for a few hours in my usual room. . . . So
when I finally woke up, it was noon, and I had a pasty, dry
mouth. I walked across the courtyard toward the building
where the kitchen was so that I could tell Irene to prepare me
a coffee. But there they were: the Gestapo. I saw a guy . . .
standing in front of me, wearing a raincoat. . . . I turned
toward him while trying to pull out the revolver I had
slipped under my belt, but the bloody revolver I had that day
wasn't the 11.45 I was used to. It was a Canadian revolver
that we had just received by parachute by the dozens, and
that I had yet to try out. But this bloody revolver had a
wider, rougher barrel than my usual Smith and Wesson.
The barrel got caught on my leather belt, and I couldn't
grab it.[80]

The Gestapo officer gave Jorge a fierce blow to the head with his auto-
matic gun. Irene Chiot was arrested and tortured in a cell at the psy-
chiatric hospital of Auxerre, in front of the prison. She was transferred
from Auxerre to Compiègne, and was later deported to Ravensbruck
where she died.[81] Their leader Henri Frager was arrested, tortured,
and deported to Buchenwald, where he was executed.

Jorge was held at the Auxerre prison for four months. In his posthumously published *Exercices de survie* he described, for the first time,
the interrogation techniques he was exposed to during his detainment at a house the Gestapo had requisitioned near the prison. Only
at the end of his life did he describe the beatings, hanging upside
down and waterboarding. Dr. Hass, chief of the local Gestapo, was
in charge of the questioning. Like a villain in a James Bond movie,
he is described as having a mouth full of gold teeth. His assistant was
a younger fellow, who Jorge remembered as someone who "moved
softly, effeminately. He was the youngest of the torturers and the most

perverse."[82] He also says that after a certain time the Germans realized that they could never break him, and left him alone. What we may never know is whether they gave up on Jorge, or if someone, such as the Spanish Ambassador to Vichy intervened to protect him? As we will see shortly, the Germans knew Jorge had to be given special consideration soon after his arrest, but whether or when they respected these orders is still a mystery.

From Auxerre he was taken to the transit camp at Compiègne, which was a bad sign as it meant the last stop before deportation to a concentration camp by train. If he had entertained any hopes of miraculously escaping his sentence, they were dashed by the time he reached Compiègne. His journey to Buchenwald was the subject of his first autobiographical novel, *The Long Voyage*, which won the international Prix Formentor, just narrowly beating out Mario Vargas Llosa's first book *La ciudad y los perros*. Within the relatively small canon of camp and Holocaust literature published by 1962, his account was innovative in that the entire narrative focuses on the brutal and seemingly endless *trip* to the camp rather than on life in Buchenwald itself. The prisoners—many of them moribund or dead by the time the journey was over—were crammed into cattle cars like upright sardines. The cattle cars had already been described by Elie Wiesel in his 1956 book *Night*, but a full-length narrative on the train voyage itself was an unusual literary approach.

When Jorge arrived at Buchenwald, he was interviewed about his background.

When he told the official in charge of the interview that he was a student, he says he was encouraged to come up with a more useful professional identity:

> The guy explained to me that at Buchenwald it was better
> to have a manual occupation. Didn't I know anything about
> electricity, for example? Surely I at least knew how to hold a
> carpenter's plane. The guy almost sounded angry. I got the

impression that he wanted at all costs to find some ability in this twenty-year-old student who shook his head like an idiot. It then occurred to Gérard[83] that the only manual work he knew anything about was terrorism. Weapons, light arms at least, up to the machine gun of the French army, which I did know about. How to handle them, take them apart, clean them, put them together again. And I knew about plastic. Explosives in general, with their detonators, their Bickford fuses, everything you needed to organize a derailment. . . . But I said nothing about this and the guy, in desperation, put me down a student. So I was no longer a gardener. . . . The day of my arrest, at Epizy, a suburb of Joigny, I was carrying my real Spanish identity papers on me. I was supposed to go to Paris that very evening, to meet "Paul,"[84] the head of my network. And in Paris, my card as gardener from the Yonne would have been suspect. . . . And so, quite by chance, I had been arrested under my real name.[85]

Thus despite all the precautions taken to provide him with a false identity, he was arrested under his own name, and ironically this may have saved his life. Another irony is that it wasn't until his arrest that Jorge Semprún's childhood education in Spain became meaningful. He had spent the first several years of his life under the tutelage of two German nannies, who preceded Annette's arrival, and thanks to these *frauleins* he was completely fluent in German:

I was the only one, among all the Spanish prisoners, who spoke German. Thanks to Fraulein Grabner and Fraulein Kaltenbach, German governesses from my privileged child-hood! So the organization of the Spanish Party had asked the German Communists to have me transferred to the *Arbeitsstatistik*, as its "representative."[86]

In the meantime his family panicked about his detention. How would it affect their status in France? As Carlos recalls, it was Michel Herr who broke the news to his father:

> Michel Herr . . . was an important man in Jorge Semprún's youth. He dragged him into the Anti-Nazi Resistance in occupied France. One day, toward the end of 1943, Michel Herr showed up at our house in Saint-Prix, and announced that Jorge had been arrested by the Germans. . . . He also told us a story that was straight out of a Western movie: that he, alone with a gun, had tried to break Jorge out of the police station, or *Feldkommandantur*, where he was being held. Obviously he was not successful, and he had also been arrested but miraculously managed to escape and to come to Saint-Prix and tell our father about Jorge. The good José María de Semprún y Gurrea turned green when he heard the news. The worst of it was, of course, Jorge's arrest, but the madness of Michel Herr made my father fear . . . that he would lead the entire Gestapo to our door.[87]

It was a good thing that Jorge had been detained under his real name. It made tracking his whereabouts easier for those attempting to help him. From the day of his arrest, Jorge's detainment caused a whirlwind in Spanish-German diplomatic circles. His father, his uncle Miguel, and his brother-in-law Jean-Marie Soutou would all try and rally forces to try and have Jorge released, or at least, perhaps, improve the conditions of his imprisonment. His imprisonment was a liability to the family.

Hitler and Franco had been allies since at least 1936, so the arrest by Germans of a Spaniard from a prominent political family was news. He was, after all, still the grandson of one of the most important political leaders in Spanish history.

A cable was immediately sent from the Vichy police to the authorities in Madrid:

> A few days ago the Spanish citizen JORGE SEMPRÚN Y MAURA was detained by the German authorities. He is 19 years old, and lived with his parents in Saint-Prix (Seine et Oise). He was arrested on October 8th, when said Semprún was en route to a terrorist meeting in the area where his family lives. He was armed with a heavy Colt revolver. It has been established that he has belonged, for some months, to the group of French terrorists arrested in the l'Yonne Department, and that he has been transporting arms and explosives as well as working as a liaison between the l'Yonne group of terrorists and another group in Sein et Oise. He has been moved to the prison of Auxerre (Yonne) where he awaits trial by a competent Military Tribunal.[88]

Franco's diplomats in France, especially his ambassador José Félix de Lequerica, managed to pry some Spanish prisoners out of Nazi hands, including a few Spanish Jews. Surely, he would be able to pull some strings to get Jorge Semprún released.

His brother Carlos remembers weekly visits to Miguel Maura's apartment in Paris. Maura was his mother's brother, and Carlos's godfather. Maura did all he could to improve Jorge's fate.

Miguel was trying to organize the Spanish Republican government in exile. Like many Spaniards, he hoped that once the Allies won the war they would charge right through the Pyrenées, arrest Franco, and restore Spanish democracy.

He and other Republicans in exile were, in fact, making the necessary plans for their return to power in Spain as soon as the Allies won World War II. Miguel Maura, Franco's Ambassadors José Antonio de Sangroniz, José Félix de Lequerica, and his Consul to Paris Alfonso

Fiscovich were all trying to negotiate a peaceful change of government with Franco himself. Maura's message was delivered to Franco: let's make a deal to make a smooth transition from dictatorship back to Republic. But Franco did not accept Miguel Maura's suggestion that he resign. He never replied at all.[89]

While Jorge was still in prison in Auxerre, José María Semprún Gurrea approached Lequerica in an attempt to save his son. Carlos Semprún recalled accompanying his father on this mission to implore the Spanish Ambassador to contact the German authorities on Jorge's behalf. Lequerica was worth asking for help: he had close ties to the Maura family and would not want the death of one of their boys on his conscience. He had started his career in Don Antonio's law firm, and he had become close to his son Miguel Maura. Lequerica and Miguel Maura had apprenticed at the same time in Maura's office, they had been allies and colleagues, and working for Antonio Maura had laid the foundation for Lequerica's success.

José María Semprún wanted to save his son. Perhaps he took Carlos along for company, or he might have hoped that if Lequerica saw Jorge's sixteen-year-old brother he would be moved to act more quickly. As Carlos remembered with his usual tragicomic knack:

> While Jorge was in prison in Auxerre, before his deportation
> to Buchenwald, my father added yet another item to his list
> of useless transactions. He must have thought he had to try
> and do something to get his son out of jail. He took me to
> the Spanish Embassy for a meeting with Félix de Lequerica,
> (Spanish) Ambassador (to Vichy). It was an absurd scene,
> like something out of Ionesco. I can still see Lequerica strid-
> ing through his opulent offices, coming to greet us in the
> waiting room. He had a strange twisted moustache, and he
> threw up his arms and exclaimed "Don José María! What
> a disaster! What a catastrophe! I've heard that your son is
> a terrorist! He blows up trains and kills German soldiers!"

And my father replied, very seriously, "Impossible. It's not
true. It's impossible. A son of mine wouldn't do those things.
It is a mistake."[90]

The ambassador was friendly, and suggested to José María Semprún
that it was not too late for him to change sides and support Franco.
Carlos wondered if this apparent kindness might actually mean that
Lequerica feared that Franco might be deposed after an allied victory
and that he might soon be asking Jose María and other Republicans
for mercy. Nobody was sure yet how the chips would fall.

Carlos concluded from Lequerica's response to his father that
there was nothing to be done about Jorge, but despite his misgiv-
ings, Lequerica did follow up. He brought the matter directly to the
infamous Otto Abetz, Hitler's Ambassador to Vichy. Abetz received
many appeals from family members or friends of people who had been
arrested by the Gestapo in France. The author Irène Nemirovsky,
whose masterpiece *Suite Francaise* was written during the war and
published posthumously in 2004, was arrested in Issey in 1942. Her
husband Michel Epstein also wrote directly to Abetz, "stressing Irène's
'hatred for the Bolshevik regime.'"[91] In Nemirovsky's case, the pleas
were fruitless, and she died a month later in Auschwitz of typhus.
When the poet Max Jacob, a close friend of Picasso's, was arrested,
his powerful friend lobbied for his defense. Gerghard Heller, head
of the Nazi's Propaganda Staffel in Paris, claimed that Jean Cocteau
"lobbied Ambassador Abetz and the German secret service and eventually obtained an order for Jacob's release. But the poet died of bron-
chial pneumonia in Drancy on March 6 before he could be rescued."[92]
Did Abetz help free people from the Gestapo's clutches? Sometimes,
as Alan Riding concludes, "Whether Ambassador Abetz could be
counted on remains debatable, but he spoke French, had a French
wife, and probably helped free some writers from jail."[93]

Lequerica didn't have much to lose by contacting Abetz, for "there
is no doubt about the cordial relations enjoyed by Vichy France and

Franco Spain. Pétain and Franco met at Montpellier on February 13, 1941, to review matters outstanding between the two countries, and from the beginning France had cooperated fully with its southern neighbor."[94] The Spanish ambassador had helpfully prepared a list of eight hundred Spanish so-called "delinquents" (i.e., Franco opponents) in France to be arrested by the Gestapo and Vichy officials,[95] so perhaps he was just hedging his bets when he composed his confidential letter about Jorge Semprún to Otto Abetz. Or perhaps he thought his intervention could at least save the young Jorge from execution? Did it? The Spanish Consul to Vichy, Alfonso Fiscowich, seems to have made the first plea on Jorge's behalf. He attached Lequerica's report and wrote to his colleague Pedro Urraca, Spanish Inspector of Police in Paris:

> Dear Urraca: Vis-à-vis the request I have formulated regarding the arrest of the young Semprún, I am attaching a report in French and German in case The Occupying Authorities can use it to *soften the situation* of said person. With all my affection, Fiscowich.[96]

This long letter, written in Vichy, on December 15, 1943, was received and very carefully read. The letter is underlined by Abetz or one of his staff, in alternating red and blue pencils. Following are the relevant excerpts:

> Permit me to draw your watchful attention to the case of a young Spaniard, Jorge Semprún y Maura, who was arrested on October 8th and has been held at the German section of the Auxerre Detainment Facility since then. He is a young fellow, about twenty years old, and he has no political past. He is an exceptional student, emotional and highly susceptible, and his background is purely intellectual.
>
> So what happened to him? I have no idea, but I dare to bring this matter up to you personally because he is the

grandson of the man who was Spain's most eminent statesman during the first 25 years of this century, Don Antonio
Maura. He was the great champion of the fight against free-
masonry and Judaism. In 1909, Ferrer was executed while
he was Chief of State.[97] This unleashed a truly anti-Spanish
and demagogical crusade against Maura. He was the victim of three assassination attempts, which he miraculously
escaped, and when he died (of natural causes) he was honored as a respected leader.

In 1921, when I was a young member of parliament, I
worked as his under-secretary. It was his last term as prime
minister, and shortly before his death. I remember him
dearly, and that is why I allow myself—just this once—to
bring this to your attention and to that of the authorities
of the Occupation. This young man may have been a victim of threats or of a conspiracy against him by professional
rabble-rousers. I ask you, in the name of the services rendered by his illustrious ancestor, to take a special interest in
this case and to attenuate the situation by any means that
are possible, and compatible with the great responsibilities
incumbent upon the Occupying forces in France.[98]

Lequerica, an experienced diplomat in his early fifties, clearly decided
that the way to get Abetz's attention was to spin Antonio Maura into
an illustrious proto-fascist. It is ironic that Maura's name, once tainted
in the Spanish press as a Jewish *chueta*, was now being used in the name
of anti-Semitism. Lequerica knew how to appeal to the Germans.

Abetz had probably never heard of Maura, but he responded cor-
dially to his Spanish counterpart:

Letter from Otto Abetz to Lequerica. Vichy, January 28, 1944
"I was very touched by your interest in this young man,
Semprún, the grandson of Maura, whom I had responded

to you about and about whom you have provided further details. I myself hope that he wasn't involved in any serious agitations, and that his situation can be sorted out quickly."[99]

But no more news followed after this response, and on January 5, 1944, Lequerica again wrote to Abetz imploring him to do something to help Jorge. This time Lequerica offered to have Jorge returned to Spain:

> I would like to bring your attention again to the case of the young Jorge Semprún y Maura, the grandson of the former prime minister of Spain M. (sic) Maura, about whom I spoke to you in my letter of last December 15, to tell you that I've just received some more favorable impressions about his situation.
>
> The father of the young Semprún y Maura suggests, as a possible solution this difficult business, that his son be transferred back to Spain to free him of the bad influences of certain French milieu. In his own country, he would be able to continue the studies for which he has shown great promise. I find it hard to believe that the grandson of the man who led the great battle against the masonic revolution in Spain, who was wounded numerous times in attempts on his life by anarchists, and who was the victim of the most powerful Judeo-Masonic movement before the war of '14—the one led by Ferrer—could have taken part in any act of violence against the social order. I apologize for bothering you again by taking the liberty of submitting this suggestion to you, and herein express my most sincere gratitude for anything you might be able to do.[100]

This letter is also marked up in pencil. At the top left of the letter "Jorge Semprun y Maura" has been added in by hand, and at the top left someone has written in large letters and underlined the word *eilt* (urgent). The name "Klingenfuss" had also been scribbled in the left margin. Karl Klingenfuss was a member of Hitler's Foreign Ministry.

Further internal correspondence (from February and March 1944) between the Sicherheitspolizei (the Nazi Security Police), and the Sicherheitsdienst (the SD, or German Security Service in charge of tracking down hidden Jews and Resistance fighters in France) and Abetz concluded that Jorge's activities were serious crimes and that the charges could not be dismissed, nor could he be released provisionally:[101] Jorge is erroneously referred to by his second, maternal last name:

[1] German Embassy Paris Paris, Feb. 16, 1944
"Concerning the arrest of the Spanish national. . . .
Because of the above named person, the Spanish ambassador has once again been lodging complaints to us here. With reference to the letter dated January 18 written by the ambassador, he has again asked for the proceedings regarding the facts of the case, the report, and the decisions therein."

[2] March 17, 1944
"To the German Embassy in Paris
Concerning the Arrest of the Spanish national. . . .
File: Missive from January 18, 1944 from Klingenfuss
Because Prisoner Maura's (sic) case concerns the committing of subversive activities; his release from custody is impossible."

[3] March 28, 1944
"The Spanish ambassador has, for some time, turned to Ambassador Abetz and asked for the release of . . . Maura (sic). Based on the reports by the chief of the security police and the SD of the above named subject's subversive activities, he has been taken into custody and will not be, for the time being, released.
Pfeiffer"

Lequerica did everything in his power to have Jorge released. These efforts, which have never been documented before, were probably thanks to his friendship with Miguel Maura, and his lasting affection for the late Antonio Maura. But his urgent communications did not keep Jorge out of a German camp. In January 1944, Jorge was transferred to Buchenwald.

Did the Spanish Ambassador's efforts have any impact at all on Jorge's situation? Miguel Maura would later claim not only that Jorge owed Lequerica his life, but that he himself was saved by the Ambassador. According to Miguel, Lequerica didn't have extreme views, and he wasn't a fanatical Francoist. He was surely ambitious, but not an ideological convert. When Miguel once teased him about having become an extremist *"carlista"* (a nineteenth-century traditionalist movement that supported an alternate line of the Bourbon dynasty, and later supported Franco), Lequerica joked that what he had become was a *"carguista,"* or careerist that he was only interested in his new *cargos* (appointments).[102]

Miguel Maura spent parts of World War II in different parts of the Maritime Alps. He was constantly under surveillance by the Vichy and Spanish authorities, and under suspicion of collaborating to restore the monarchy in Spain. He was thus forced to move from place to place simply to survive. When the Germans expanded their borders to include Nice in their Occupied zone, Miguel Maura was there, and was detained for questioning at the city's new *Kommandatur*:

> Before the interrogation had properly begun, Miguel refused to satisfy the impertinent curiosity of the local boss, and told him that if he wanted to know anything about him he could go straight to Franco's Ambassador to Vichy. That brought the interview to an end.[103]

Miguel Maura later said that he discovered that Lequerica had indeed intervened on his behalf, and on Jorge's, and that his unspecified intervention had, in fact, saved Jorge's life:

> Miguel had already received help from Lequerica once before. As Ambassador, he had successfully intervened to save *somebody close to him*[104] *from a sure death by Nazi hands.* . . . And when he later told Lequerica about the *Kommandatur* arrest, he said, "Oh yes, they asked me about you, and I told them, "Don't lay a finger on my Miguel!"" Miguel always thought that he also owed his life to Lequerica.[105]

From his new post in Berne, Switzerland, as Press Secretary at the French Embassy, Jean-Marie Soutou also worked to help Jorge during his deportation. He specifically tried to pressure Juan Schwartz, the head of the Spanish legation in Berne. If there was anyone in the family who could imagine what Jorge was going through, it was Soutou. He had also been detained in Lyon by the Gestapo and interrogated by the infamous Klaus Barbie, "The Butcher of Lyon." Soutou used his Catholic connections and was eventually let go, thanks to the intervention of Cardinal Gerlier, then Archbishop of Lyon. He and Maribel then escaped to Switzerland where he continued to work for the Resistance and collaborated with the Office of Strategic Services, the intelligence agency of the United States.[106] Soutou's network was international:

> It seems that his collaboration with the American Secret Service was largely based on his activity within the Témoignage Chrétien movement. In the American archives there is a correspondence between Géneral Davet ("René"), the head of the Swiss Resistance Delegation, and "chers amis," which in 1943 includes a money transfer to J.M. Soutou and Témoignage Chrétien.[107] Other documents

show that Soutou had organized a courier service between Lyon and Turin, nicknamed "Chris Service."[108]

The fact that he was known as an important member of the Esprit family helped open doors in Switzerland, where Emmanuel Mounier was greatly admired in enlightened Swiss intellectuals milieus, as well as by intellectuals and political men who had taken refuge in the Confederation. From 1943 onward, he became the attaché de presse of the MUR (Mouvements unis de la Résistance) delegation in Switzerland, under the pseudonym "Béraud." He was in charge of editing the MUR news bulletin in Switzerland, which was delivered to the Swiss press agency, Reuters, and United Press. Its mission was twofold: to inform the Resistance members inside France about what was going on internationally, and to present a reliable image of France to the outside world. He asked Jean Laloy, who he met at Esprit, to help him in his mission. He translated the federalist documents of Ventotene in Milan and distributed them in France. His pseudonym in OSS code was "Pierre." In 1945, Soutou was made secrétaire adjoint of the French Embassy in Belgrade, and later went on to become secrétaire général of the Quai d'Orsay.[109]

In January 1945, Soutou and Maribel made inquiries about Jorge to Juan Schwartz. They apparently had a cordial relationship with the Spanish diplomat, and Schwartz wrote to Soutou on January 30 to say that "after speaking to my Minister, urgent action is underway in the attempt to satisfy you entirely."[110] The "Minister" being referred to was none other than Lequerica, who by this time had been promoted from being the Spanish Ambassador to Vichy's Ministry of Foreign Affairs (replacing Franco's own brother-in-law, Ramón Serrano Suñer). The only letter from Schwartz, dated from May 22, 1945, after Buchenwald had been liberated by the US army, makes clear what the "urgent action" was, and apologizes for not being able to achieve his promise:

> You can imagine what pleasure it gives me to receive your letter of May 18th, and the joy I felt at knowing that your brother-in-law has finally been able to return to Paris. I am only sorry that it was not possible to *shorten his stay in Germany*, which the minister [Lequerica] and I both desired. Now, thanks to the new regulations of the Spanish government, your brother-in-law will easily be able to return to Spain. *There, thank God, peace and prosperity are complete.* If you are interested, I would be delighted to send you a copy of these regulations.[111]

Like Lequerica, Schwartz was gracious and had also lobbied to get Jorge out of Buchenwald. But he was also impotent vis-à-vis the Nazis and unable to wield his influence. His smooth words, after the fact, were no solution for the recently released Jorge. Why would he, a Nazi camp survivor, have wanted to go back to Franco Spain?

Given that all of these efforts have never been put together, it is worth reviewing the ensemble: between October 1943 and January 1945 Miguel Maura, José María Semprún, Soutou, Lequerica, Fiscowich, and Schwartz had all lobbied on Jorge's behalf. They had appealed to high-ranking figures within the Vichy context: Pedro Urraca and Otto Abetz. Given the circumstances—the arrest of a young student with family connections—these efforts make perfect sense. Who would not want to help free their son, brother-in-law, or nephew from a German prison or concentration camp? What is most interesting about the substantial lobbying done on Jorge's part is that he does not mention it explicitly in his many autobiographical works about the camps. Did his family never say to him, "We are doing, or we did, all we can to help you"? Is it possible he didn't know about the copious correspondence exchanged, and meetings held on his behalf? Was he embarrassed?

Lequerica is only mentioned in one of Semprun's many auto-biographical novels. In *Le mort qu'il faut*, the narrator is a Spanish Communist prisoner at Buchenwald named Jorge Semprún. His comrades worry when they learn that a message has arrived at the *Politische Abteilung* office requesting information about Jorge. This type of communication usually preceded deportation to a death camp. Because it happens on the eve of a weekend, they agree to wait until Monday to find out more. In the meantime they find *"le mort qu'il faut,"* a necessary victim: they locate a young prisoner who is on his deathbed, and have everything in order to swap his identity with Jorge Semprún's if their suspicions are confirmed. But on Monday, they discover that the message was nothing more than a friendly inquiry about Jorge's well being from the Spanish Ambassador to Vichy. It is implied that this ambassador is asking as a favor on behalf of the prisoner's family, whom he has known since before the war. Because of this preferential treatment, Jorge is immediately suspected by his fellow comrades of consorting with the enemy, and has to explain that he has had nothing to do with this. He admits only that the Ambassador was an old family acquaintance. This is an embarrassing situation for the character in the novel. The episode also highlights the practice of his Communist colleagues in the *Arbeitsstatistik*, of protecting their own at all costs. Moribund prisoners were deported to save the lives of comrades. It was as simple as erasing a name on a list and replacing it with another.

Le mort qu'il faut is the one book in which Jorge raises these two thorny issues: his job in Buchenwald at the *Arbeitsstatistik*, and—obliquely—the efforts made to get him released from the camp and/or to "soften his situation." This novel, his fifteenth published work, came out in 2001. It is interesting that he finally chose to bring up up these subjects that he had been avoiding for so long. And the reason may have been another case of *cherchez le frère*. In 1998 Carlos had published his own memoirs, *El exilio fue una fiesta*. These were brought out by Planeta, a major Spanish publisher with wide-reaching distribution. It was in this book that Carlos talked about going to see

Lequerica with his father to try and help Jorge, and where he reveals Frick's attempts to molest him. Was *Le mort qu'il faut* a counteroffensive move to check Carlos's leak about subjects that had been taboo for Jorge? Was it his way of saying, "Lequerica achieved nothing. Nobody did me any favors. For the record." It is possible that Carlos was once again in his Greek chorus role, egging on his big brother to bring his skeletons out of the closet. Jorge responded by writing novels in which the subjects were addressed in ways that he could control. If, thanks to Carlos, he could not keep his secrets, he could at least spin them.

III

Buchenwald

KL.: BUCHENWALD

Häftl.-Nr.: 44904 8

Häftlings-Personal-Karte

Fam.-Name: Semprun   Oberstellt   Personen-Beschreibung:

Vorname: Georges   Grösse: cm

Geb. am: 10.12.23 in: Madrid   am: an KL.   Gestalt:

Stand: led.   Kinder: —   Gesicht:

Wohnort: Saint Prix / Seine-Oise   am: an KL.   Augen:

Strasse: 47 rue Auguste Rey   Nase:

Religion: r.-kath. Staatsang: Spanien am: an KL.   Mund:

Wohnort d. Angehörigen: Vater: Ohren:

José Maria S., Saint Prix,   am: an KL.   Zähne:

w. o.   Haare:

Eingewiesen am: 29.1.44   am: an KL.   Sprache:

durch: B.D.S. Paris

in KL.: Buchenwald   Bes. Kennzeichen:

Grund: Polit. Spanier

Vorstrafen: Entlassung: Charakt.-Eigenschaften:

                                    am: durch KL.:

                                    mit Verfügung v.:   Sicherheit b. Einsatz:

Strafen im Lager:

Grund: Art: Bemerkung: Körperliche Verfassung:

KL. 3/8.44 - 500 000

Individual experience is the only truth. There are no values,
just lives, and what makes sense for one person is useless to
another. That seems to be the lesson of Lázaro's story.[112]
—Francisco Rico

Images of Nazi camps have come to us over the decades in the form of
documentary footage, photographs, feature films, testimonies, and literature. Whatever "Nazi camp" signifies to each one of us has been
shaped by these sources. Our own varied interpretations are fed back
into the general cultural narrative when we write or talk about the subject. As a survivor, witness, and author, Jorge Semprún had a singularly
significant role in the historiography of German camps in World War II.

Semprún wrote so much, and so often, about his experience in
Buchenwald that it really became his identity badge. There is no doubt
that being imprisoned from the ages of nineteen to twenty-one years
old was the defining experience of his life, and that he meant it when
he claimed—as he often did—that he was neither Spanish nor French,
but "*un deporté de Buchenwald*."

His versions of his deportation and camp experience have not been
fully examined in light of available documentary information, nor
within the larger framework of Holocaust culture. Contextualizing
certain aspects of his oeuvre in a historical background provides
the framework for a more nuanced understanding of his novels, and
enables readers to further appreciate his artistic flourishes and separate
them from some of his actual experiences.

Semprún based his literary career on the crafty intermingling of
fact with fiction, but when it comes to the Nazi camps—the very
existence of which some people still deny—it is worth considering
certain biographical facts in their own right, separate from his literary
flair. Understanding how Semprún recast his camp experiences in his
work helps pinpoint themes and issues that run through his life and
how he forged his public persona as a writer.

From his very first book, *The Long Voyage*, we see him echoing his literary idols (Malraux, Hemingway), and we catch a glimpse of the burgeoning screenwriter. His dialogues are taut and tough, à la Humphrey Bogart in *Casablanca*; his scenes are blatantly literary and cinematic. He proudly flaunts his novelistic imagination and his international literary and philosophical references.

Semprún has been misclassified as a testimonial author, when what he in fact writes is a sophisticated autobiographical fiction most akin to the picaresque. As a *pícaro*, Semprún as protagonist/narrator/author inscribed himself in a deeply Spanish genre of grifters and storytellers. Like his literary ancestor, Lazarillo de Tormes, he recounts his life selectively and artfully. And like the classic *pícaro*, he is always several steps ahead of us. He learned much too early how to fend for himself without love or shelter in a brutal world where the only rule is "every man for himself." Picaresque heroes are orphaned at a young age, and forced to seek protection from a succession of cruel masters, often venerated clerical figures who introduce them to the sordid and secret underbelly of society. *Pícaros'* lives are episodic and random, and devoid of any of the coherent structure of the grand epic until they have the opportunity to tell their own story and rebrand their lives as meaningful and respectable. The most important lesson the picaresque hero learns from his hypocritical masters is the art of self-defense through concealment. Through clever self-fashioning and retelling his own suffering and travails, he acquires the social status that has always eluded him. The *pícaro* is the quintessential self-made man, made not through work in the capitalist sense, but through literary invention. The *pícaro* develops an angle.

Semprún acknowledged and defended his use of fictional devices: "Ever since *Le grand voyage*, I've always used fiction, sometimes as a shortcut, sometimes to take things up a notch, and other times because there was simply no alternative."[113]

In fact, he thought that fiction was more powerful than history as a medium to communicate atrocities. As Lilah Azem Zanganeh writes: "Semprún allows that testimony is vital to historians, but he notes that testimony, too, is not always precisely reliable, and that historians, alas, are never quite as effective as novelists at conveying the essence of experience. 'Horror is so repetitive,' he says, 'and without literary elaboration, one simply cannot be heard or understood.' Hence, he argues, 'The only way to make horror palpable is to construct a fictional body of work.'"[114]

Semprún himself elaborated on this potentially thorny issue, and staked his claim that fiction was not the best but the *only* way to represent the Nazi camps:

> I will always defend the legitimacy of literary fiction in expounding historical truth. In the case of deportation, both Jewish and non-Jewish, it is simply not possible to tell, or write, the truth. The truth we experienced is not credible, and this is a fact the Nazis relied upon in terms of their own legacy, for future generations. If we tell the raw, naked truth, no one will believe us. . . . It needed to acquire a human shape, an actual form. This is where literature begins: narration, artifice, art—what Primo Levi calls a "filtered truth." And I believe ardently that real memory, not historical and documentary memory but living memory, will be perpetuated only through literature. Because literature alone is capable of reinventing and regenerating truth.[115]

We could say that the studies of his work and life, including this one, are doing exactly what he hoped: using his own literature as a springboard to perpetuate the memory of the Nazi camps, and more generally of twentieth-century Europe's violent crises. In doing so, we will also keep in mind broader questions about his approach to a "filtered truth." How do readers respond to lies told for the sake of "truth?" Why do most readers conflate his fictional heroes with Jorge Semprún the author? Are his narrators reliable? They seem completely sincere in what they say, yet we also know they are holding things back.

Though Semprún passionately defended his work as fiction, excerpts from his books are frequently cited and regarded as historical fact. Semprún established himself as a respected and even authoritative voice on the concentration camp experience. Even if he made things up, his status as a witness transformed everything he said into history.

The converse is also true: even if he was a witness, he made things up. Shouldn't we have some respect for his claims about the power of invention? After all, it isn't easy to tell a good story. Shouldn't the reader be wary of a seductive author who spent many years of his adult life operating under false identities, a master dissembler? How do his narratives relate to information about his life found in historical documents? What scraps of secrets underlie Semprún's masterly autobiographical discourse? Wasn't his experience as a prisoner quite unique, as he repeatedly points out, because of his distinctive background: a Spanish exile from an upper bourgeois family with an elite education, a philosophical-literary vocation, who was fluent in German? And how did this background affect the experience and memory of his Buchenwald imprisonment?

Class and camaraderie are themes that run through his narratives. During World War II, in the European political arena, class, politics, race and religion intersected in a myriad of complex ways. Within the camp, particularly in Semprún's case, the stigmas and privileges of class continued to resonate, though he says he forged fraternal bonds that defied class differences, and that his commitment to the Spanish Communist cause was cemented by his experiences with his comrades in the camp.

Semprún wrote at length about his time in Buchenwald in three of his major books about the camp—*The Long Voyage*, *What a Beautiful Sunday!*, and *Literature or Life*. These books have been translated into Spanish, English, German, and many other languages, and he gave dozens of interviews on the subject. They present certain issues and recurring themes that can be seen from a broader context than the author's exclusive point of view.

The overarching issues in this respect are what made Jorge Semprún's time in Buchenwald unique, and how did it shape his future? These questions will be answered drawing from his own accounts, but also from historical documents and the testimonies of other Buchenwald prisoners. By sifting through contrasting and complementary evidence, our sense of his life as a prisoner, and more importantly his own perspective, will come into focus.

Semprún was arrested by the Gestapo on October 8, 1943, and held at the Maison d'Arret in Auxerre. His crime was being a member of the French Resistance *maquis* "Tabou." He was nineteen years old on the day of his arrest, and turned twenty on December 10, 1943, in prison in France. Before being deported to Buchenwald, he describes that he endured months of torture. He only fully recounted the torture he underwent in the posthumous *Exercises de Survie*;[116] it took him nearly seventy years to do so.

But in his first book, the 1963 *The Long Voyage*, he doesn't tell that story. His only comments about his imprisonment in France are the following: "I've told myself I would write the story of the Auxerre Prison. A very simple story: the exercise period, that long conversation, in short snatches, each one of us on our own side of the bars. . . . And now I have a chance to write that story, and I can't. The time isn't right, my subject is this voyage."[117] In this first novel, he focuses, as the title suggests, primarily on the harrowing trip to Buchenwald from France in a cattle car.

On January 29, 1944, he was registered as prisoner 44904 at Buchenwald. Numbers were crucial to the Germans, and all the more so in the camps as space was in short supply. The camp was built to hold a mere fraction of the 250,000 prisoners held there during the war.

Thanks to the Germans' recordkeeping, we know details of Semprún's arrival at Buchenwald that seem both irrelevant and chilling in their minutiae. Among the personal effects he was forced to hand over to the authorities when he registered were one coat, two pullovers, and one set of underwear.

Semprún was brave and young, strong and fit. He never discusses fear in any of his books. What was he thinking? How much worse could the camp be than the Gestapo prison in France? Could it outdo the actual train journey to Buchenwald, the endless days and nights crammed into a windowless, airless space with people screaming and dying around him? How long would he be trapped in this nightmare? When and how would the war end?

His only consolation, as his character says in *The Long Voyage*, was that it had been his decision to join the French Resistance. As a prize-winning philosophy student, he prided himself on his ability to reason. Thanks to his will and his lucidity, he had chosen his path. He was not a victim, but a fighter. He had done the right thing. He had tried to battle the Nazis in France and hoped that would help to undermine Franco's regime in Spain. He had fought for justice, following the anti-Francoist slogan often repeated during the Spanish Civil War: Better to die standing than to live on your knees.

> I've been free to go where I had to go, and I had to get on this train, since I had to do the things which led me to this train. I was free, completely free, to get on this train, and I put that freedom to good use.[118]

He had chosen freely, but he was headed to a Nazi *lager*, surrounded by barbed-wire fences, dirty snow, disease, humiliation, and death. Was he going to die on his knees, after all? Had he made a monumental mistake?

For anybody who has read his books, it is a bit shocking to see the archival documents of his registration at the camp. Sometimes historical documents *are* more powerful than fiction. His *oeuvre* creates such a compelling alternate universe, and we know his fictional heroes so well—from *The Long Voyage*, *Le Mort qu'il faut*, *Literature or*

Life, or *What a Beautiful Sunday!*—that it is uncanny to see the records pertaining to the *real* arrest of the *real* Semprún. We are reminded that he was, in fact, just a person before he turned himself into a legend, or into literature. It seems improbable that anyone whose circumstances involved their own Nazi camp registration card could have survived. The thick, yellowed paper, with its sinister Gothic lettering, has a definitive air of death about it.

The card lists his father's home address in Saint-Prix, his religion as Roman Catholic, his father's name, and his classification: Spanish political prisoner. His name was replaced by his identification number: 44904. His identity had already changed multiple times in the first twenty years of his life: Semprún Maura in Madrid, *Georges* Semprún in exile, Gérard Sorel the gardener/Resistance fighter, and now to Prisoner #44904. On two very official-looking preprinted cards, his profession is listed as "student," but on another entirely handmade card, only his name and profession are listed, and here it says *stutakeur,* or stucco worker, instead of student. This mystery card adds yet another identity. It is stamped "Paris BDG" (Befehlsaber des Gendarmerie, Commander of the local police) January 29, 1944. Where and when was this card filled out, and by whom?

According to Semprún:

> Printed in advance, 44904 was the number that was destined to me. I mean to say: destined to the deportee, whomever he might be, who arrived at that exact moment to sit in front of the man in charge of filling out the card. By chance, it was me. Truly by chance. The mere fact that I had been inscribed as a "stucco worker" probably saved me from being sent in one of the massive transports to Dora. . . . I didn't know that until later, of course. . . . The anonymous communist who tried to make me understand the situation was right. To survive in Buchenwald it was better to be a skilled laborer, *Facharbeiter.*[119]

When Semprún saw this card fifty years later, upon his return to Buchenwald with his step-grandsons Mathieu and Thomas Landman, he concluded that this card had "possibly" saved his life.[120] A student would have been considered useless in the camp, and might have been sent to Dora. But a stucco worker could be useful, and therefore his life had a higher chance of being spared. Semprún commented that this anonymous camp bureaucrat who rewrote his fate—by changing one word—was a "fraternal" and experienced German Communist. He says he was lucky not to have stumbled upon an immature party upstart who would have been annoyed by the "intellectual arrogance" of the young, handsome, bourgeois detainee. Many of the Communists in the Buchenwald administration had been there for years, and were, according to Semprún, "sordid and heroic, bloody and generous, deadly and moralistic."[121]

David Wingeate Pike, an expert in German camps, succinctly recaps what Semprún saw as his advantages:

> Semprún, a survivor of Buchenwald, defines the secret of
> his survival in terms of three factors: sufficient knowledge
> of spoken German, skill in a trade (or the pretense of having
> it), and pure luck.[122]

He was not as unlucky as his predecessor on the registration card whose information was on the flip side. As everything was scarce in wartime, the prisoner registration cards were recycled, and Semprún's card had first been used for a Boris Matwejew, political prisoner #29664. Matwejew's arrival had been registered on October 18, 1941. His information was typed on the card, and a diagonal red pencil line had been added at some point along with the stamp "*Verstorben*." Deceased. The date of his death, or at least the death on his card, was stamped in the bottom right-hand corner: July 4, 1942. Matwejew's profession was car mechanic ("*autoschlosser*"), a trade that would surely have been useful to the Germans, if usefulness indeed counted for anything. But he didn't even live nine months, or perhaps it is exceptional that he lived almost nine months. Semprún says he was only shown a (one-sided) photocopy of his registration card, so he may never have known whose card he inherited, or that he was the B side to Boris Matwejew's fate. Why was Semprún luckier than Boris Matwejew? Was it luck that destined him to Buchenwald instead of another camp? After 1940–1941, there were three types of Nazi camps: "Category I (work camps) represented the mildest form. Category II meant harsher living and working conditions. In category III were the "death camps." Buchenwald was at first Category II, then Category I."[123]

Thousands of the prisoners died due to the brutal conditions and inhumane forced labor in quarries. Had Semprún been sent to Mauthausen, however, like many of his Spanish compatriots, the odds for his survival would have been even lower. That said, Buchenwald was not much of an improvement: over fifty thousand of Buchenwald's prisoners died, and all of those who survived knew that it was by the skin of their teeth. In addition to disease and hard physical labor, each day at the camp presented many other random opportunities to lose one's life. Just looking at someone the wrong way or walking too slowly in a line could result in death. Buchenwald also had a fair share of Spaniards. Ten thousand Spanish prisoners died in the camp.

How did Buchenwald fit into Jorge Semprun's fate? In addition to his literary ambitions, Semprún had always envisioned a grand destiny for himself. *The Long Voyage*, in all its Hemingway-esque coolness, is a brilliant play at refashioning himself as a reluctant hero, the man of action and words he had always wanted to be, and about whom Malraux had written so beautifully. Semprún strove to stand out amid the deportees; he did not want to be a young *goy* who had been caught in the wrong place at the wrong time waving guns around and getting himself arrested by the Gestapo. His own family, especially his fearful father and harsh Swiss-German stepmother, must have cursed him for his brazen recklessness. What kind of son would commit such folly?

Two dominant, and perhaps opposing, images come to mind after reading Semprún's books on Buchenwald. One is that of a beautiful oak tree known as "Goethe's tree," and at the other end of the spectrum, the stinking, disease-ridden latrines that the prisoners were forced to use.

> *Gärtnerei*, or "gardening," was the euphemism for the worst job of all. It consisted of two men, quickened by relentless blows, carrying heavy wooden pails . . . overflowing with natural manure. This assignment was most commonly called "shit work."[124]

Within the Semprún family history, the mass latrines are a distinct counterpoint to the impeccably modern and hygienic plumbing Antonio Maura had demanded for his family. Maura had been almost hysterically protective of his family's health, and germophobic. He was fortunate not to have lived to see that germs were the last things his descendants would have to worry about. One of his sons, Honorio, had been executed in 1936, and another—and countless grandchildren—had fled into exile only to land in Nazi occupied France. In one generation, the family evolved from omnipotent and Spanish to powerless and homeless, its mortal enemies had gone from bacteria and viruses to the Gestapo. The German language the Semprún children had learned years ago in Madrid, the language of progress, logic, and enlightenment, was, ironically, useful to Jorge for primitive survival in Buchenwald. Summer holidays, private toilets, and the most basic human rights were long-lost luxuries. In the camp machine, prisoners' excrement became the manure that made the Nazis vegetable gardens thrive.

A forest of beech trees was razed to build Buchenwald in 1937. The one tree left standing within the gates of the camp was an oak tree, rescued because it had supposedly been Goethe's favorite tree in the area. He had, legend says, written parts of *Faust* and the poem "Wanderer's Nightsong" while sitting under the shade of this tree. Though it may have been "Goethe's tree," it also may have just been randomly identified as such to give the camp a touch of sentimentality, High Culture, and German essence. What was truly German, after all, the eternal Goethe or this temporary camp? It is debatable whether "Goethe's tree" was real, or an apocryphal legend created by the Nazi propaganda machine. Apparently, Goethe had many favorite trees in Germany. In any case, Goethe had spent summers in the area of the camp, and Jorge Semprún cherished the imagined connection to the German author.

> At Buchenwald, twenty-five years earlier, I sometimes dreamed that Goethe, immortal and Olympian, Goethean, in other words—was still walking on the Ettesberg, accompanied by that distinguished fool Eckermann. . . . What would Goethe have said if he had noticed, as he walked along the Avenue of Eagles, one December Sunday, for instance, the wrought-iron inscription on the monumental camp gate?[125]

The gate at Buchenwald is mentioned repeatedly in *The Long Voyage*, and there is in fact a crescendo of references until the camp's liberation when the inscription is finally revealed and emblazoned on the page in capital letters:

> I show my pass to the American sentinel and glance up at the inscription, in large, wrought iron letters, set above the bars. ARBEIT MACHT FREI. Freedom Through Work. It's a fine paternalistic maxim, it's for our own good that we've been imprisoned here, it's through forced labor that they have taught us the meaning of freedom.[126]

The gate was of paramount importance to Jorge Semprún's camp narrative, but the strange thing is that *Arbeit Macht Frei* was not the inscription over the gates of Buchenwald. It was the inscription placed over the gates of Auschwitz. The gates of Buchenwald were inscribed with the words: *Jedem das Seine*, roughly translated as "to each his own" or "everyone gets what they deserve."

It is hard to imagine that Semprún would have fumbled something as historically significant as the inscription on the gate of Buchenwald, so we must look to other factors for this fictional inscription, or borrowing of an inscription from the gate of another, more famous camp.

By the time Semprún started writing about his camp experiences in 1960–1962, Primo Levi and Elie Wiesel had already made the Auschwitz gates unforgettable in their respective novels *Se questo è un uomo* (Italian edition published in 1947, English translation, *Survival In Auschwitz* in 1959, German and French editions in 1961); and *Night* (first published in French as *La Nuit* in 1958 before being translated to English in 1960).

The inscription above the Auschwitz gates is mentioned three times in *The Truce* and *If This Is a Man*. In "On the Bottom," the second chapter of the latter, the camp is in the first chaotic stage of liberation. The inscription suddenly seemed to be miraculously declawed:

> For the last time there filed before my eyes the huts where I had suffered and matured, the roll-call square where the gallows and the gigantic Christmas tree still towered side by side, and the gate to slavery, on which one could still read the three, now hollow, words of derision: *"Arbeit Macht Frei,"* "Work Gives Freedom."[127]

The words are also prominently featured in Elie Wiesel's *Night:*

> But no sooner had we taken a few steps than we saw the barbed wire of another camp. This one had an iron gate

with the overhead inscription: ARBEIT MACHT FREI.
Work makes you free. Auschwitz.[128]

Alain Resnais's 1955 short film *Nuit et Brouillard* (*Night and Fog*) was
the first movie to use footage and archival materials from concentration camps. Resnais received numerous accolades for the project,
and Francois Truffaut called it the best movie ever made. In the film,
which was broadcast on French television and watched in homes
throughout the country just ten years after the end of the occupation
and the war, one of the most unforgettable images is of prisoners
entering through the gates of Auschwitz, under the sinister words
"Arbeit Macht Frei."

It is difficult to believe that Semprún, who was fluent in
German and a crafty writer, would misremember the inscription at
Buchenwald. There seem to be only two alternatives: either he never
saw the inscription, or he deliberately chose the "Arbeit Macht Frei"
because it already had a resonance in the discourse of Holocaust culture, thanks to Levi, Wiesel, and to the filmmaker Alain Resnais.

It makes sense that Semprún, launching his career as a writer
rather late in life—he was forty when *The Long Voyage* was published—would co-opt the most well-known representations of the
Holocaust that had come out to date. He wanted a place at the table
of Holocaust authors; he didn't want to lurk around in the literary
margins. He wasn't even French. Semprún didn't want to "just" be
an obscure Spanish *ecrivain concentrationnaire*. Writers such as Robert
Anthelme were highly respected in France, but not internationally
recognized like Holocaust authors Wiesel and Levi. Like a budding
musician sampling the most famous notes played by his masters,
Semprún inscribed himself into the canon of Holocaust literature, not
deportation literature, by associating himself with the most famous
Nazi camp gate inscription, not the inscription of his own camp. And
he called Buchenwald a *death camp*. Though thousands of prisoners
died in Buchenwald, it was not a death camp like Auschwitz. It is

perhaps in these distinctions that his conflation of literature, life, and memory become most fraught.

Sixteen years after *The Long Voyage*, Semprún published *What a Beautiful Sunday!* (1980), his second major novel/memoir about Buchenwald. In this book, the inscription of the gates appears again, but stands corrected. However, there is no reference to the misquoted inscription so prominently cited in *The Long Voyage*.

In *What a Beautiful Sunday!* the narrator imagines Goethe walking along the Avenue of Eagles in Buchenwald, and seeing the camp's inscription:

> What would Goethe have said if he had noticed . . . the wrought iron inscription on the monumental camp gates, *Jedem das Seine*, TO EACH HIS DUE? . . . In 1944, as I stood there imagining what Goethe would have to say about this inscription over the Buchenwald gate, TO EACH HIS DUE—a cynically egalitarian notion.[129]

The narrator in *What a Beautiful Sunday!* makes a big deal about the inscription, and claims that the legend of this infamous camp inscription had even traveled to the USSR, where Russian author and Soviet concentration camp prisoner Varlam Shalamov immortalized it by writing, "It is said that over the German concentration camps there appeared a quotation from Nietzsche: Everyone for himself."[130]

The narrator of *What a Beautiful Sunday!* chides the Russians responsible for deforming the legendary inscription through mistranslation, and chides Shalamov himself for relating the words to Nietzsche:

> *Jedem das Seine* ended up as *Jeder für sich*: TO EACH HIS DUE had become EVERYONE FOR HIMSELF. Which, of course, is not at all the same thing. In fact, the only rather surprising thing in this whole business is that Shalamov

should have attributed this banal expression . . . to Nietzsche. Why Nietzsche? I still haven't found the answer.[131]

It is puzzling that Semprún should ruminate obsessively on pinpointing the exact words and meaning of an inscription that he did not correctly cite until 1980. In fact, Shalamov's *Kolyma Tales* (written over many years) were only finally published in 1978. Was it Shalamov's work that finally tipped Semprún off to what it really said above the Buchenwald gates? Though his narrator split hairs over Shalamov's take on the inscription in *What a Beautiful Sunday!*, Semprún himself was an enthusiastic admirer of the Russian's work. In an interview given in 2010, a year before his death, Semprún praised Shalamov:

> In any case, the most spectacular book on the memory of deportation is the Russian book, *Kolyma Tales*, by Varlam Shalamov. People often bring up the books written by old deportees of the Nazi camps such as Primo Levi's wonderful book, but no one ever talks about Shalamov, because his story is not part of our European collective memory.[132]

The question of the inscription over the gate at Buchenwald is just a specific example of the issues related to memory, poetic license, and intertextuality surrounding the often-contradictory *oeuvre* of Semprún. If our narrator/author comes full circle swapping one inscription—so physical, and unmistakable in its wrought iron existence—for another, how are we to trust him on other matters? Perhaps he is simply catching up with himself and history, reflecting other works of camp literature that he read and assimilated as the genre developed over the decades.

The Nazi camp gates and their inscriptions have retained their symbolic power over the decades. The one at Dachau, which had the same inscription as Auschwitz, *Arbeit Macht Frei*, was stolen in November 2014. Buchenwald's gate slogan, *Jedem das Seine,* would go on to be as famous as *Arbeit Macht Frei*: in 2009 German Esso Petrol Stations sparked a controversy by advertising the coffee product Tchibo Espresso at seven hundred stations with the slogan "Jedem das Seine." The posters were all removed by legal order.[133]

It seems that Jorge's fluent German was key in landing him an office job within what is referred to as the "Communist underground" network that ran the camp. "Underground" is an ambiguous term: the members of the organization were Nazi prisoners, but their captors also trusted them to run most of the camp's operations. The prisoners were divided into work squads, *Kommandos*, and each section had a Kapo, or boss, who was charged with keeping things going to the Gestapo's satisfaction. On the one hand, these prisoners were working for and with the Nazis, but on the other, they had no choice and some of them managed to use their power to secretly sabotage Nazi plans.

The fact that Semprún had an office job among the high-ranking Communist prisoners at Buchenwald may have been *the* crucial factor in increasing his odds for survival. The differences between working inside or outdoors in a brutal wintery climate were enormous. But why was he, a strong, healthy, twenty-year-old athlete assigned to an office job? What did a Spanish-Parisian philosophy student know about the work that went on in an office of labor statistics in a Nazi concentration camp? Why did he survive when the head of his Jean-Marie Action group Henri Frager was killed at Buchenwald, and Irene Chiot, who owned the house where he had been arrested, was sent to the death camps Bergen Belsen and Ravensbruck? Was it just the luck of the draw? Or did he have a priority rank thanks to the combined efforts made on his behalf by his uncle, Miguel Maura, Spain's ambassador to Vichy, Lequerica, Nazi ambassador to Vichy Otto Abetz, or his brother-in-law Soutou?

As he tells it, he was selected for this plum position because he was Spanish and spoke German. It is nonetheless interesting that he was so quickly vetted by the hard-core Communist underground within Buchenwald. He was young and quite inexperienced, and his Communist credentials were virtually nil: after all, the Resistance network he had joined, Jean-Marie Action, was not really French or Communist. It reported directly to London.

Shortly before his death, Jorge Semprún grappled with pointed questions about some vague issues related to his work within the Resistance and in Buchenwald. Had he joined as a Communist, or not? Did it matter? When the writer Jean Lacoutoure pressed him as to why he joined the Resistance through a British unit, he replied:

> I am really the perfect candidate for a Stalinist trial. I had, in fact, joined the British network thanks to the encouragement—or orders—of the French Communist Party. Communist or not, it was important to get the arms to those who were doing the actual fighting. But there is no written proof of this (what I am saying). If France had trials like those of the Eastern Bloc, I would have been accused of working for the British Intelligence Service. How can it be proved that the French Communist Party asked me to work with the English?[134]

It still remains mysterious that he was immediately chosen to be a top member of the underground in the camp. He says that, in addition to his knowledge of German, it was in part thanks to a member (unnamed) of the Resistance group FTP (*franc-tireurs et partisans*) who he had met in Yonne. This person tipped off the Spanish members of the Communist organization within Buchenwald. So, apparently it was the Spanish prisoners who were expecting his arrival and ready to whisk him off and protect him.[135] Because of this tip-off, soon after his arrival, a Communist higher-up interviewed Semprún and determined that his "references were credible" and he was registered as a stucco worker. After that conversation, and thanks to the Spanish clandestine Communists, he immediately became a camp VIP. Thanks to his knowledge of German he was chosen to represent the Spanish Communists in the *Arbeitsstatistik* and become a part of the camp's *nomenklatura*.[136] The paradoxical facets of his situation were multiple, and he would spend the rest of his life unraveling them: a Spanish haute bourgeois in a Nazi camp that was in fact run by Russian communists.

The obscurely and bureaucratically named "office of labor statistics" where he worked was a serious business. Most of their tasks involved organizing prisoners to be shipped off in work squads (*kommandos*) of three thousand or more to destinations of hard labor and sure death, such as Dora.

In his history of Buchenwald, André Sellier describes the office where Semprún, and approximately twenty-five other men, worked:

> The other organization was the *Arbeitsstatistik*, based within the camp, and was, at Buchenwald at any rate, truly managed by the prisoners. Its role was the allotment of work to everyone. Some were assigned a quiet administrative role. Other Kommandos, like those working in the quarries, were especially hard. Skilled laborers who found work in factories dependent on the camp were better off than those who did heavy manual tasks. Thus the *Arbeitsstatistik* had significant power; it became significant when it was time to draw up the "transport" lists for the outside Kommandos. This was the case, for example, when it was necessary to supply the SS with the five hundred prisoners they demanded one particular day for Dora, Langenstein, or Ohrdruf. . . . Even in subordinate positions, camp bureaucrats were privileged. After joining the *Arbeitsstatistik*, Birin slept in a block divided into separate rooms, with eight individual beds in each. The food, moreover, was not as bad. We were given our rations in the office itself, and there were often extras which we were able to share with many of our comrades.[137]

The French war hero Pierre Julitte was also deported to Buchenwald, and in his 1965 autobiographical novel *L'arbre de Goethe*, he describes the superior living conditions of the few prisoners who had the privilege of working indoors:

> It was also true that, in some of the *kommandos* of the camp itself, the work was light and done indoors. This was the case with the *kommando* assigned to making and repairing socks and the one assigned to tailoring. The work of these deportees consisted solely of darning, sewing, and mending. They spent their days sitting indoors, sheltered from the harshness of the weather. It was even claimed that they were served a supplementary ration of soup at noon and that they were counted for the evening roll call in their shops instead of being forced to stand for hours in the cold. But the total complement of these indoor *kommando* groups was very small. It was clear to everyone that these groups were reserved for certain privileged individuals who benefited from protection in high places. The fact that a deputy to the French National Assembly was employed in the *kommando* for socks was cited as proof of this. But one of his fellow deputies worked in the quarry, although they had belonged to the same political party and had arrived at the camp at the same time.[138]

Julitte, a dashing Resistance hero, thirteen years older than Semprún, and also an alumnus of the elite Lycée Henri IV, is an interesting counterpoint to Semprún. Moreover, he was an engineer, and thus had skills that would have been valuable to the Germans. But Julitte, and the French resistant fighters with whom he was arrested, were all assigned to labor Kommandos in harsh outdoor conditions. Julitte did not speak German. Was that the main difference between their fates? Julitte, despite withstanding the daily torture of hard labor, became a hero in Buchenwald. He bravely continued his Resistance work from within the camp, and when he discovered the Mibau, a German rocket-building factory within Buchenwald's grounds, he managed to communicate the information to the Allies. The Germans were building the V-2 rocket with which they hoped to win the war, and thanks to Julitte, the Allies bombed the Mibau and destroyed their plans. In the process, they also destroyed Goethe's tree, which was blown up and burned through the night.

Julitte's narrative also gives us vivid details on the inner workings of the *Arbeitsstatistik* office, where Semprún spent his days:

> When a convoy for Dora had to be made up, it was in the quarry *kommandos* that the *Arbeitsstatistik* found the necessary men. The appearance of the recruiting team spread terror among the deported, and they scattered in every direction. But the S.S. troops gathered them together again with bludgeons and, if necessary, with guns. They herded them into a corner of the quarry and noted down the numbers of the healthiest among them. The next day, these men were sent away and nothing more was ever heard of them.[139]

Charlie, a character from *L'arbre de Goethe* who is a close friend of the narrator's, was a healthy young fellow who was a prime candidate for one of the convoys to Dora. In order to discourage the S.S. from taking him, he cut his leg with a piece of stone, and walked around bleeding and limping. He couldn't have guessed that far from sympathy, his wound would only cause laughter and titillate those around him.[140]

Charlie, who was fluent in German, hoped to get himself a job as an interpreter, or at least an assignment to a *kommando* that didn't work in the quarry. A *Kapo* in charge of a small *kommando* told Charlie that in order to get a "good" assignment he would have to hand over the chocolate and cigarettes he got in his care packages. Charlie, like many prisoners, didn't know if the *Kapo* would keep his end of the bargain.

What Julitte makes clear in his book is that nobody was assigned to one of the choice indoor *kommandos*—especially not the almighty *Arbeitsstatistik*—unless one had friends in very high places or a special skill. Did Semprún have these? Was he treated exceptionally because of the FTP fellow from Yonne who vouched for him, or did his family's entreaties to Lequerica and Otto Abetz have long-term benefits? Did a German official say to Lequerica: "We can't release him, but we will make sure he is protected"? If this happened, and if Semprún knew about any such arrangements, he does not mention them.

In an interview, I asked his nephew Georges-Henri Soutou if he thought that Jorge was aware of all the efforts that had been made on his behalf to help him, and if he had ever spoken about them. He replied:

> I am unable to answer that question. I have to think he was intelligent and well informed enough to consider it, but it is a complicated issue for various reasons. First of all it was not at all like him to speak about such things. He was very reserved. We never spoke about his camp experiences. I only brought it up once, when *The Long Voyage* came out. You also have to keep in mind that the family atmosphere was not easy, there was a lot of tension there. When I asked him about the camp that one time we were with his brother Paco. Jorge began to say "Well the camp was designed to hold ten thousand people and we were fifty thousand." At which point Paco interrupted him and said, "Those poor Germans, they must have been overwhelmed!" And with that the conversation came to a screeching halt, neither Jorge or I said another word.[141]

Jorge did admit that his day-to-day life was better than that of most prisoners. Willi Seifert was the Kapo of the *Arbeitsstatistik*, and Semprún clearly had a fraternal relationship with him.

Willi Seifert offered me one of his cigarettes when we met in
his *Arbeitsstatistik* office for a one-on-one meeting. *Machorka*,
the Russian herb rolled into cigarettes with newspaper bits,
was not for them. It was for the masses of Buchenwald. It
was sunny out . . . when I took a drag of this privileged cigarette. But for the most part I was one of the masses, when it
came to tobacco and food, at least . . . I survived exclusively
on the camp rations.[142]

A typical day, described in terms of the paltry food rations, proceeded
thus:

Wake up was at 4:30 in the morning (if that can be called
morning), and the prisoners were brought a cup of foul liq-
uid passed off as coffee, a slice of bread and a pat of mar-
garine. Sometimes they got a slice of sausage like cold cut.
After work, they went back to their barracks and had watery
soup, except for Sundays when a more filling, and much
awaited, noodle soup was served.[143]

One of his main tasks of his job was to read the German newspapers, make a summary of the Nazi press coverage, and translate it
into Spanish for the heads of the Spanish Communist Party.[144] Many
of his comrades in the *Arbeitsstatistik* were older and had much more
political experience than Semprún, so his experience in the office was
something like a crash course in Communist leadership. Some of his
colleagues had been in German camps for years. Willi Seifert was a
born-and-bred Communist; he had been politically active since he
was twelve years old and after the war went on to become minister
of the interior of the German Democratic Republic. Semprún clearly
picked up a few tricks from these veteran comrades. Working with
these men may not have given Semprún access to extra rations, but
he admits that the office exuded prestige and power. These were the

people in charge of determining the fate of the vast majority of prisoners. An assignment to the Dora *kommando* meant a one-way ticket to death. The *Arbeitsstatitsik* staff decided who was sent to Dora, and who was assigned a warm, safe job in the camp's laundry, the infirmary, or the general store.

Working within the *Arbeit*, as it was known, gave Semprún prestige within the camp hierarchy, as he himself describes it:

> I can address the heads of the blocks and the *Kapos* as equals. They know I am *Arbeit*, and they've seen me with Seifert, or with his deputy, Weidlich. They listen to my requests, whatever they might be. They don't take my number, which indicates I'm a new arrival, into account. It doesn't matter to them that I've only been here a year. They're not surprised to see the S for Spanish printed in black above the red triangle on my shirt, just over my heart. The ones in charge are mostly Germans or Czechs from the protectorate of Bohemia-Moravia . . . but . . . though I am only twenty years old . . . they listen to me. With me they are attentive, servile, even polite, within the limits of their crudeness. This is in part because I speak to them in German, and because they know I am a member of the *Arbeitsstatistik*. I am a bureaucrat and an authority figure.[145]

Eugene Kogon, a historian, politician, and Buchenwald survivor, describes the importance of the Arbesitsstatistik and supports Semprún's description of its power:

> The relations between the leader of labor service and labor deployment and the prisoners were taken care of by the so-called *Arbeitsstatistik*. It registered the workforce of the camp in professional card indexes and accounted the hours worked. Its significance grew immensely in the course of

time, when the leader of labor deployment himself was
no longer capable of compiling the transports for sub-
commandos. Here again prisoners had an immense, partly
beneficial, but partly also fatal influence due to a powerful
key position in the camp. Hundreds of valuable people could
only be saved thanks to the help of the *Arbeitsstatistik*, partly
by being secretly deleted from death transport lists, partly by
being smuggled to sub-commandos when their lives were
threatened in the main camp. Owing to dark activities and
intrigues, however, many camp mates were also brought to
places inside and outside the camps where they were either
seriously hurt or perished. The task to be accomplished by
the *Arbeitsstatistik*—it could happen that they had to provide
thousands of prisoners within only two hours—was difficult and unrewarding. Some of the mates who worked there
have rendered extraordinary services.[146]

Kogon raises the morally ambiguous role placed by those in the
underground in charge of assigning fellow prisoners' fates. Critics of
Semprún's have argued that his work—and that of his comrades—in
the *Arbeitsstatistik* compromised them morally. How was it decided
who was to be saved? How did it feel to have the power to take someone's name off a transport list, by the simple act of erasing it, and
pencil in another's name? How many non-Communists were sent to
a sure death in order to save the lives of more "valuable" party members? In the many decades after the liberation, how did Semprún's
view of his role in the camp evolve?

Semprún often tried to shirk difficult questions about his work,
especially when people, including his own brother Carlos, publicly
accused him of working as a boss, or Kapo[147] at Buchenwald and sending thousands of people to their deaths. Semprún vehemently denied
that he was a Kapo, making clear that he got none of their special privileges or food. The Kapo of the *Arbeitsstatistik* was in fact Willi Seifert,

a seasoned German Communist twice Semprún's age. In his defense, Semprún had neither the experience nor the status to be a Kapo in the German-run organization of Buchenwald. And yet, this does not mean that his experience in the camp was without moral challenges. The Communists justified their administrative collaboration in the Nazi camp by saying that it allowed them to save and protect useful men, to sabotage Nazi plans, and that if they hadn't been in control someone else—someone worse—would have replaced them. To this standard party response, Semprún later added a defensive stance culled from an intermingling, perhaps, of his Catholic background and training in philosophy, or perhaps poached from *Esprit* thinker Jacques Maritain:

> In a concentration camp, or other very unusual circum-stances—such as clandestine resistance to occupying forces—many matters that would be considered deceitful, criminal or evil in civilized life can no longer be defined as such. They take on a different moral nature, and thus become objectively justified, and ethical.[148]

This is a disconcerting rationalization of the concentration camp as a space that imposes circumstances that redefine morality and ethics. It seems to strive to give the survivor, especially the privileged survivor, a retroactive *carte blanche*. Twenty years later, after reading Alexander Solzhenitsyn and learning about the Gulag camps, Semprún seemed to absolve himself:

> Was there blood in my memory? . . . No, there was no blood in my memory. . . . There was nothing to be particularly proud of, either. Maybe it was a question of age. Maybe I was five or ten years too young to have blood on my hands.[149]

Semprún had a superior rank in the camp, and it was this power—not that the *Arbeitsstatistik* offices had electric burners to reheat coffee throughout the day, though that may have helped—that enabled his survival. Like any prison, Buchenwald's detainees were split up into rival factions. The SS weren't the only fearsome presence; prisoners grouped themselves into the equivalent of neighborhood gangs. Semprún was protected from all of these dangers by the Communists in charge of running the camp, and in particular by Willi Seifert. He may as well have worn a sign above his "S" for *Spanier* saying "Hands Off."

Though "camp memoirs" are often grouped loosely in one category, the camp experience of a political prisoner and member of the Communist underground resistance was surely a very different experience from that of other inmates, and particularly of Jewish prisoners who were segregated in the "Small Camp" of Buchenwald. Elie Wiesel, who as a boy survived this Small Camp, where his father died, found the distinction worth highlighting in one of his memoirs:

> Many years later Jorge Semprún and I were exchanging memories of Buchenwald. He had been in the main camp. Working the Shreistube, the office, he did not endure the hunger and cold. He knew the small camp at a distance. The fate of the Jews was unlike that of the non-Jews. We were in the same place, and yet.[150]

Semprún also received special care packages. Such packages were a form of life insurance, and contained extremely valuable goods that the prisoner could use to fortify himself or to barter for favors. They are not mentioned in any of his books. This is curious, as the packages show that his family was thinking of him and possibly putting themselves at risk to send him vital supplies, that he had—at least from time to time—more to live on than the average prisoner, and that the Red Cross was doing good work in the worst of times by trying to prolong and save the lives of Nazi prisoners:

The Red Cross also attempted to help those in concentration camps. Here, they met with mixed results. Attempts
to get the names of those in the camps met with failure. In
1943 the Nazis did agree that Red Cross parcels could be
sent to named non-Germans in the concentration camps.
Somehow, the Red Cross got hold of a few names and sent
food parcels to these names. Receipts for these parcels were
returned to Geneva—sometimes with as many as a dozen
names on each receipt. This method allowed the Red Cross
to collect more and more names. By the time the war ended,
the Red Cross had a list of 105,000 names of people being
held in concentration camps and over 1 million parcels were
sent out—even to the death camps in Poland. As the war
came to its end, to observe what went on in the concentration camps, a Red Cross delegate stayed in each camp.[151]

According to International Red Cross records Semprún received several packages:

> Semprún received 6 times a package from the ICRC and
> one time a double package. Generally, they were standard
> parcels (indicated by the number 3, last column on the right)
> containing foodstuffs, but Semprún received also a parcel
> containing vitamins (indicated by the number 7).[152]

It is true that many prisoners never received their care packages
because they were stolen at some point along the way, but the archives
of the International Committee of the Red Cross in Geneva has seven
receipts that were signed by Semprún. Chocolate and cigarettes, food
and vitamins weren't treats in the camp, but the currency of survival.

The receipts show that the packages were sent from a "D.
Semprún" and a "G. Semprún" at 17 rue de Candolle in Geneva. "G."
might have been Gonzalo, but there is no "D." Semprún. His sister

Maribel and Jean-Marie Soutou lived at that address[153] so it seems that Maribel was looking out for her brother and sending him the packages. Did she disguise her name, or was the complete surname "De Semprún" simply transformed into an initial D. somewhere in the bureaucratic process? Maribel may have wanted to be discreet about having a brother in a German camp in the middle of World War II.

He also mentions that he did not have to hobble around in the standard camp wooden clogs, because he acquired a pair of boots at the camp's *Effektenkammer* (storage building). These boots appear in his narratives a few times, and were clearly an important point of pride, and comfort, for a young male prisoner in a bitterly cold climate. When the camp was liberated by the Americans, Semprún was ashamed of the rags he was wearing, but proud that he was armed and wearing boots, a key detail that he mentions repeatedly:

> What was I wearing? It must have been a curious outfit: mismatched rags, however, on my feet I wore soft leather Russian boots; and slung across my chest was a German machine gun, a clear sign of authority in those times.[154]

His camp narratives, in general, avoid any kind of self-portrayal as a victim. On the contrary, he retains an unusually healthy sense of vanity, humor, irony, and a kind of literary showmanship that other survivors have found disquieting. His incorporation of the better known Auschwitz gate inscription might be an example of appropriation for the sake of narrative punch, and his salacious descriptions of Ilsa Koch, the infamously lascivious and sadistic wife of the camp's commandant Karl-Otto Koch—and her sexual preferences for strong young prisoners with tattoos—have been offensive to some, including the Hungarian Holocaust survivor and Nobel Prize winning author Imré Kertész.

Ilsa Koch was tried and imprisoned, and became known as the legendary Witch (or Bitch, depending on the source) of Buchenwald. She also became the subject of exploitation films and gruesome lore.

In the following quotes, Kertész writes about her role in Semprún's first book. He first reproduces the offending passage in question, then he analyzes it:

> At the time I was reading a novel published under the title *The Long Voyage*, and in it came across Sigrid, the beautiful blond fashion model who, I read, was "there only in order to make us forget the body and face of Ilse Koch, that straight, stocky body planted solidly on her straight sturdy legs, that harsh, sharp, incontestably German face, those fair eyes . . . Ilse Koch's eyes fixed on the naked torso, on the bare arms of the deportee she had chosen as her lover a few hours before, her gaze already cutting out that white, sickly skin along the dotted lines of the tattoo which had caught her attention, her gaze already picturing the handsome effect of those bluish lines, those flowers or sailing ships, those snakes, that sea-weed, that long female hair. Those pinks of the wind, those sea waves and those sailing vessels deployed like screaming gulls, their handsome effect on the parchment-like skin— having, by some chemical process acquired an ivory tint— of the lampshades covering every lamp in her living room where, at dusk, she had smiled as the deportee brought in first as the chosen instrument of pleasure, a twofold plea-sure, first in the act of pleasure itself and then for the much more durable pleasure of his parchment-like skin . . . criss-crossed by bluish lines of the tattoo which gave the lamp-shade its inimitable stamp, there reclining on a couch, she assembled the officers of the Waffen-SS about her husband, the Commandant of the camp, to listen to one of them play some romantic melody on the piano, or something serious from the piano repertory, a Beethoven concerto perhaps."[155]

I stopped reading. There it was, blood, lust, and the demon encapsulated in a single figure, indeed, a single

sentence. Even as I read, it offered definitive forms: I can fit
them with no trouble at all into the ready-made tool box of
my historical imagination. A Lucrezia Borgia of Buchenwald;
a great sinner, worthy of Dostoyevsky's pen, settling up
with God; a female example of Nietzsche's horde of splendid blond beasts, prowling about in search of spoils and victory, who "go *back* to the innocent conscience of the beast of
prey." Yes, indeed yes, our thoughts are still held captive by
the delusions of dove-conscience intellectuals, a more bal-
anced era's simple-minded visions of the daring grandeur of
depravity, although they never pay the required attention to
the details. There is some kind of unbridgeable discrepancy
here: on the one hand, drunken paeans to the first blush of
dawn, a revaluation of all values, and a sublime immorality,
and on the other, a trainload of human cargo which has to
be disposed of as rapidly—and most likely as smoothly—as
possible in gas chambers that never have enough capacity.[156]

For Kertész, Semprún exploits a kitsch image of the evil Nazi, with
Ilsa Koch. He doesn't explore who she really was, her mundanity and
her gray role in a death machine in which she is just a speck. Kertész's
seemed upset by what he saw as Semprún's literary opportunism:

> As I was working on *Fatelessness*, Semprún's *The Long
> Voyage* was published in Budapest. The book was much cel-
> ebrated—yet Semprún had chosen the wrong technique,
> narrating only the most spectacular of events and mangling
> temporality in the process. It's a spectacular method, but it's
> just not true. Whereas if you tell the story of a child, you
> have to conceive of a temporality that is appropriate, for a
> child has no agency in his own life and is forced to endure
> all. So as Semprún's book was reaping so much praise, it
> became clear to me that if I were to be true to the story

I had to tell, I would have to describe, from beginning to end, a situation—any situation—in which my protagonist finds himself, rather than opting merely for the spectacular moments. Take, for example, the famous twenty minutes it took to unload the trains at Auschwitz. That's just how long it took, and a lot happened in these twenty minutes.[157]

Semprún's singling out and demonization of Ilsa Koch as the face of evil of the Nazis is intriguing, given that he came into contact with so few women in his camp experience, and yet there were so many men! Male solidarity is a theme throughout his work, and women are generally relegated to marginal roles, as almost cartoonish characters. Their portrayal is often idealized, and sometimes vilified (e.g., Koch) but it is consistently superficial.

In *Le mort qu'il faut* (2001) Semprún retold his Buchenwald experience yet again and imbues his portrait of Ilsa Koch with what seems like a firsthand immediacy. He says she liked handsome prisoners, and he undoubtedly would have qualified. The impersonal French third person pronoun "*on*" permits a Semprúnian ambiguity, but what is clear is that the author relished the grotesque story of the perverse Nazi woman: "Ilsa, we might recall, was fond of handsome inmates; she would undress them in her bed, to take her pleasure, and then admire their tattoos, if they had any."[158]

The truth is that he never crossed paths with Ilsa Koch or her husband. Karl Koch and his wife Ilsa were transferred to Majdanek concentration camp in occupied Poland in 1941—two years before Semprún joined the Resistance—so he never laid eyes on them. The moral of this story is that there are revealing patterns in Semprún's narratives, and that he knows an attention-grabbing character and detail when he finds one, but we must also take everything he says with a grain of salt. The novelist outweighs the witness, which is fine as long as the reader knows it. Art has its own rules, and Picasso did not have to see the Condor Legion's bombing of Guernica with his own eyes in order to create the most iconic work of art of the Spanish Civil War. Picasso's *Guernica* is an artistic creation, like much of Semprun's work.

Kertész is also troubled by Semprún's literary idealization of the strong, masculine bonds forged between men in Buchenwald. This special kind of friendship featured by Semprún, inspired, perhaps, by Malraux's statement that fraternity and absolute evil are opposites,[159] is first described in *The Long Voyage*:

> In the camps, man becomes that animal capable of stealing a mate's bread, of propelling him toward death. But in the camps man also becomes that invincible being capable of sharing his last cigarette butt, his last piece of bread, his last breath, to sustain his fellow man.[160]

Semprún returns to this type of image repeatedly, and the emphasis on these warm relations are clearly meant to humanize the camp experience, and to make us understand his deepening attachment to Communism.

This idealized vision of masculine friendship seemed to go in tandem with an often hostile and immature take on women. Florence Malraux recalls that she and Colette were often taken aback with Jorge's descriptions of women: "Female characters in particular were never his strong point. At the end of *The Long Voyage* he had included an additional chapter concerning women that was riddled with one stereotype after another. It destroyed the whole manuscript. And so I told him and Colette did as well, that he simply could not end his otherwise wonderful book with such a banal final chapter." According to Florence Malraux, Jorge always took Colette's observations very seriously.[161]

In *The Long Voyage*, after Buchenwald's liberation, a group of women from the French Mission come to see the camp on April 13, 1945, and he repeatedly describes them as "dolls." The narrator, whose tone is macho throughout the novel, is especially brutal in his

description of these young women. The language reads like a rip-off
of gangster-speak from an old Hollywood B movie. The narrator is
the prisoner who guides them around the camp:

> They had hair, lipstick, silk stockings. . . . The girls were
> simpering, they were chattering, they deserved a couple of
> good slaps. . . . I took these living dolls toward the camp
> entrance.[162]

The vision of the camp that Semprún creates with its touches of *kitsch*
disconcerted Kertész. That said, it stems from his style and sense of
artistic freedom. Literary scholar Jordi Gracia spoke to me about
Kertész's comments and Jorge's tendency for invention:

> I understand what bothers Kertész in his book *Fatelessness*.
> Though he doesn't mention Semprún by name he does
> allude to *The Long Voyage* when he questions the practice
> of eschewing direct testimony by dressing it up with liter-
> ary flourishes, but I have to say that Semprún's argument is
> also valid; that literature is the vehicle of reconstruction in
> which one's liberty is absolute. I am on Semprún's side on
> this issue. It is another thing however to evaluate to what
> extent his literary version persuades the reader, and I would
> dare to say that in this respect, for me as a reader, it is unsat-
> isfying and a disappointment. These texts of his that are arti-
> ficially fictionalized are not convincing. This is something I
> have not said very often and it should be said, because there
> is something disquieting about it as a reading experience. It
> doesn't happen to me with *The Long Voyage* but it does in
> the rest of his novels, perhaps because *The Long Voyage* con-
> tains the sort of spontaneity often found with a first-time
> novelist, something that, paradoxically, makes it the best of
> his novels about the camp experience. It was written before

he went about constructing the myth of the survivor, the
victim of Buchenwald. There is still a freshness there and a
lack of literary artifice that works.[163]

For Semprún, Buchenwald was a multilingual experience: German,
French, and Spanish. He said repeatedly that knowing German saved
him, and French was the language of his adolescent home and his work
in the Resistance. German was the language and culture of his own
education. He had, after all, been "homeschooled" in German and
one of the family's Swiss-German governesses had even married his
father. German was his stepmother tongue. Spanish was maternal, loving and secure. German was demanding, stimulating but somewhat
threatening; it was the language of survival, and of betrayal. German
was most definitely the language of an all-powerful stepmother, not
just for Semprún, but for occupied France. He was very proud of how
rapidly he had learned to speak French fluently. In *The Long Voyage*,
the protagonist Manuel makes a point of describing his flawless French,
after a French prisoner says, "You talk exactly like us."[164]

I don't feel like explaining to him why I talk exactly as
they do, why I talk like the Colonel, without any accent,
that is, with a real French accent. This is the surest way of
preserving my status as a foreigner, which I cherish above
all. If I had an accent, my "foreignness" would be constantly
apparent. It would become something banal, exteriorized. . . .
That's why I don't have an accent.[165]

In the first film Semprún wrote, the autobiographical main character
Diego receives the same compliment about his uncanny native fluency in French. The screenplay states explicitly in the opening scene
that the protagonist "has no accent."[166]

His obsession with speaking French fluently echoes his grandfather, Antonio Maura, who had been determined to shed his native

Mallorquín and speak Spanish without an accent. The theme of the ambitious immigrant who knows that the appearance of assimilation is fundamental to success is classic, but among Spaniards these stories are rare. From the Inquisition onward, Spaniards tended to stay where they started unless they emigrated to one of Spain's colonies. They minded their place, class, regional identity, and language, and knew that any attempt to change or improve their lot would be akin to folly. Antonio Maura and his grandson both reinvented themselves in record time.

Semprún's linguistic versatility was not just limited to the world of high culture. It was crucial to all aspects of his survival—in the French schools, in the Resistance, in the camp, and later in the Spanish Communist Party—situations where he needed to be able to speak like a tough guy. So while he admired poets and philosophers in all three (and other) languages, he needed to speak like a *mec,* or a bit of a hoodlum, to adapt to the dangerous and lawless situations posed by adolescence in exile, combat, concentration camp, and political intrigue. He was proud of his chameleon-like qualities, and there is no doubt that he used them to blend in when his life depended on it, or whenever it suited him. Semprún may have been prolific on the page, but the many literary alter egos he created are not chatty types. Manolo, Diego, and other Semprúnian protagonists don't waste their words, and in dialogues they always have the last one. He was always trying to blend in with "them:" the French, the other prisoners at Buchenwald, the Spanish Communists, and later on, the Spaniards in Franco Spain during his clandestine trips in the 1950s and '60s. Yet he never wanted to *become* a part of any group. This tension followed him through his life. In the camp he tried to act like a "regular guy" prisoner, but says other prisoners teased him about his upscale upbringing and the fancy cars his father had before the Civil War. Yet nobody in the camp could have known what kind of cars his father had unless he himself had told them, and we readers wouldn't know if he hadn't written about them. The general response he elicited from those around him was astonishment. The Germans, the Spaniards, the French, none of them could believe that he spoke each of their languages fluently along with two others.

The narrator in *Le mort qu'il faut* relishes telling how the Spanish prisoners in Buchenwald would get together and sing, rather than recite, García Lorca ballads, so close in rhythm to Spanish *coplas*. He also remembers his bunkmate, Spaniard Sebastian Manglano, reciting "Córdoba/Lejana y sola." Elsewhere Semprún criticized the folklore of Lorca's *Romancero Gitano* (*Gypsy Ballads*), and he makes it clear that Manglano is working class, but in the world of this novel, poems are celebrated as a unifying cultural force that boost the prisoners' morale. The singing temporarily erases class lines, and is reminiscent of scenes from other fictional visions of war. In Jean Renoir's great film *La Grande Illusion* (1936), French and British soldiers are held prisoners by the Germans, and at two crucial moments in the story the prisoners sing, respectively, "La Marseillaise" and "It's a Long Way to Tipperary." Though Renoir's story is set during World War I, it was a prescient film and has many themes and attitudes that resurface in Semprún's work. Many of his alter-ego narrators can be seen as a cross between the two pilots in the film: the lanky aristocrat played by Pierre Fresnay, and a handsome working-class fellow played by Jean Gabin. Both are noble, ironic, unemotional, and brave in an offhanded way.

Kafka, García Lorca, Primo Levi, Solzhenitsyn, Borges, René Char, Wittgenstein, Aragón, Dostoyevsky, Louis Armstrong, Victor Hugo, Rimbaud, Lamartine, Mallarmé, Apollinaire, Breton, Heidegger, Husserl, Levinas, Hegel, Nietzsche, Schelling, Malraux, Melrau-Ponty, Hemingway, Bakunin, Marx, Velázquez, Goya, Ribera, Picasso . . . This is just a smattering of the names of writers and thinkers that Semprún drops throughout his work. A complete list would take up too much space. In his books we can find three names to a page, and even three in one paragraph. In *Literature or Life* the cultural name-dropping starts in the chapter titles. The abundance of names makes it apparent that he is eager to prove that culture is his niche. Semprún was an extremely prolific, multilingual reader, but he was also a writer of fiction. Some of his cultural references are thus also fictional constructs. For example, he claimed never to have read Proust until quite late in life. Yet in *The Long Voyage*, the young narrator claims a long-standing connection to Proust's work:

> I spent the first night of the voyage reconstructing *Swann's Way* in my mind, and it was an excellent exercise in abstraction. . . . I too used to go to bed early. . . . And that hawthorn hedge, Lord, that hawthorn hedge was my childhood too. I spent the first night of this voyage reconstructing *Swann's Way* in my mind and recalling my childhood. I asked myself whether there wasn't something in my childhood comparable to the phrase of the Vinteuil sonata. Unfortunately, there was nothing.[167]

If it is true that he very deliberately put off reading Proust for decades,[168] then his twenty-year-old alter ego narrator cannot have been reminiscing about events from Proust's masterpiece—Swann coming to dinner, the Vinteuil sonata—during the trip to Buchenwald. Semprún is constantly merging two strategies, cultural references and fiction, to ennoble this work that, to the naked eye of the average reader, is based strictly on firsthand experiences and memory. Embellished testimony is the key to the Semprúnian flair: an apparently spontaneous candor is in fact artful mise-en-scene. His narrator might have been trapped on a cattle car for days and nights headed to a Nazi camp, but he is chatting wittily about wine with another prisoner, and when he's quiet, he's reconstructing Proust. Whether Semprún had read Proust or not, he wanted his character to come off not only as a Proust reader, but as a modern day Marcel: refined, critical, sensitive, ironic. In *The Long Voyage*, the protagonist's single Parisian Jewish classmate is named Bloch, just like the younger of the two male Jewish characters in *A la recherché*.[169] This is surely not a coincidence. Semprún's Bloch is forced to wear a yellow star on his uniform, and the narrator repeatedly refers to the boy's "sad pride."

His characters, we are constantly reminded, are part of a cultural elite even in the worst of circumstances. Their deep identities are not political but artistic and intellectual, and their artistic destinies and genealogies are interrupted by history, wars, and their consequences. The one time Semprún heard his number called over the camp loudspeaker system it was because he had overdue library books. Even as a prisoner he found time to be a faithful borrower from the camp's library. In Buchenwald he read Faulkner and organized cultural events and poetry recitals with his Spanish comrades. His culturally rich, often convivial narratives of his camp experiences thus diverge dramatically from both those of Jewish survivors (Kertész, Levi, Wiesel, Amery) and those of non-Jewish political prisoners (Antelme, and Julitte, among others).

Semprún's characters have the power to overcome political circumstances, and high culture is akin to a religious faith that saves them and brings hope to their most desperate moments. When his fellow prisoner and former professor, the philosopher and sociologist Maurice Halbwachs, is dying, Semprún holds him in his arms and recites Baudelaire as if it were a prayer. Here poetry takes on a religious role, and Semprún becomes a son to the gentle, wise, paternal elderly man:

> I had also taken Maurice Halbwachs in my arms, that last Sunday. I slid my arms under his shoulders, and bent down over his face to talk to him up close, as softly as possible. I had just recited Baudelaire's poem to him, as if I had been reciting a prayer for the dying.[170]

If we flash forward to the camp's liberation, we also see Semprún with the one surviving prisoner from the Small Camp. He finds this nameless "Jewish survivor," half-dead, half-alive, muttering the Kaddish (in Yiddish, surprisingly), and also takes him in his arms as he is dying.

> I have knelt down next to the Jewish survivor. I don't know
> what to do to keep him alive, my Christ of the *kaddish*. I
> speak to him quietly. I end up holding him in my arms, as
> gently as possible, afraid that he might break between my
> fingers.[171]

Luckily, thanks to our narrator, the survivor is given medical attention and, last we hear, it seems that there's hope for him. At the same
time, Semprún manages to convey his sympathy for the Jewish plight
by imagining the survivor's story and the tragic circumstances that
brought him to the Small Camp, all the while giving himself the significant role of lifesaver.

　　This chapter is titled "Kaddish," and Semprún says:

> But that is a story I have already told. Not the one about
> the Jewish survivor that Albert and I met, because he was
> singing the prayer for the dead in Yiddish. This is a story
> I am telling for the first time. It is part of the stories that I
> haven't told yet. I would need several lives to be able to talk
> about so much death.[172]

In 1945, would Semprún have recognized the Kaddish? Or Yiddish?
It is possible, but it is not likely that someone would have recited
the prayer in Yiddish, as he says. The Kaddish is in Aramaic, though
it is written in Hebrew letters. This strange scene, of a moribund
Jew singing the Kaddish in Yiddish, is another example of Semprún's
poetic license. If he had truly recognized the Kaddish, and heard it
in Yiddish, his character may have said "It was incredible. The dying
man sang the Kaddish in Yiddish, of all things." Is this a display of
creative fireworks—a made-up Kaddish in Yiddish—or simply a lack
of knowledge about Jewish prayers? In any case, the noteworthy cultural reference is disconcerting in a chapter charged with death and
emotions, and designed to be an homage to Jews.

Though Semprún's life had its own particular tragic elements of loss, abandonment, and exile that were shared with the fate of the Jews of the 1930s, as a non-Jew he was careful with the subject of Jewish Holocaust victims. He makes clear that he is fully aware of the differences between their destinies and his own. Yet, as he distinguishes, he is fully aware of the narrative power gained by featuring Jewish characters. In *The Long Voyage* he turns his best friend in the Resistance into a Jew, though he was actually a French Christian from Burgundy.[173]

American bombs arrived at Buchenwald long before the troops, but the air raids were a good sign for the prisoners. As previously mentioned, one of the casualties of an attack in August 1944 was the oak known as Goethe's Tree, and its destruction seemed to symbolize the end of Germany's brutal endurance:

> On the esplanade, between the kitchens and the Effektenkammer, the S.S. had saved the oak tree in whose shade, so the story goes, Goethe used to come and sit. I think of this beech tree, between the kitchens and the Effektenhammer. I'm thinking that now they couldn't come here, the tree is all charred and burned inside, now it's nothing but an empty, rotting carcass, an American incendiary bomb liquidated Goethe's beech tree.[174]

The arrival of American soldiers at Buchenwald is a crucial narrative focal point in Semprún's oeuvre. Coming face-to-face with the Allied liberation sets up the opening of his much praised *L'écriture où la vie* (1993). This work was translated into English as *Literature or Life* in 1997, and Semprún won the Jerusalem Prize the same year.

He describes the chaotic, exhausting period before the liberators appeared. By the time the Americans arrived at the camp, the prisoners had been unsupervised for several days. The last roll call had been on April 3, and the prisoners within the camp's underground

Resistance used rifles they had been collecting and hoarding since 1942 to shoot the remaining Nazi guards. It must have been a very long week waiting for the Americans.

On April 3, the camp's Resistance leaders sent a Morse-code message in several languages to the allies:

> To the Allies. To the army of General Patton. This is the Buchenwald concentration camp. SOS. We request help. They want to evacuate us. The SS wants to destroy us.

A few minutes later, they received a response: "KZ Bu. Hold out. Rushing to your aid. Staff of Third Army."[175]

Semprún, as an elite member of the camp's Resistance organization, was not evacuated, and was waiting at Buchenwald when the Allied soldiers arrived. In his version, he received three British soldiers in rags, but wearing his soft Russian leather boots, and armed with a German machine gun.[176] The camp Resistance network only had one machine gun, and ninety-one rifles,[177] so Semprún must indeed have been highly ranked. While one might imagine surviving prisoners welcoming the Americans with glee and relief, Semprún greets them with skepticism. These soldiers are inexplicably puzzled by everything they see. He must patiently explain everything to them: the stench is from the crematorium, there are no birds because of the stench of burning human flesh. He enjoys telling these soldiers what's what, and leading the way. He is impatient with them, and accusatory: they have arrived, but they are too late.

Eventually, he warms to the foreign soldiers, and his trademark masculine fraternal relationships take on a new, international, liberated charm: an American soldier from New Mexico chats with him in his "singsong" Spanish and gives him a Camel cigarette, and he eventually befriends Lieutenant Albert Rosenfeld, his slightly fictionalized version of Lieutenant Albert G. Rosenberg, part of a special unit sent by General Dwight Eisenhower to collect evidence at Buchenwald.

Rosenfeld is the ideal friend: though a naturalized American, he's German-born and fluent in German, he is Jewish, he is well versed in German literature and philosophy, he went to Spain to fight for the Republic during the Civil War. He is especially interested in Heidegger, is quick to catch a reference to Kant, and he has a jeep. Semprún is summoned to share information about the workings of the *Arbeitsstatistik*, and the two young men discover they are kindred spirits. They go together to see Goethe's summerhouse, recite poetry, and lose track of time talking about everything from Léon Blum to the nature of evil. The visit to Weimar is a sort of gift Rosenfeld has come up with to celebrate Jorge's name day. Rosenfeld remembers that April 23 was Saint George day. With such a man, Semprún can finally express his deepest thoughts about the Nazi camps:

> "What's essential," I tell Lieutenant Rosenfeld, "is the experience of Evil. Of course, you can experience that anywhere. . . . You don't need concentration camps to know Evil. But here, this experience will turn out to have been crucial, and massive, invading everywhere, devouring everything. . . . It's the experience of radical Evil." Startled, he looks at me sharply. *Das radikal Böse!* Obviously, he has caught the reference to Kant. Is Lieutenant Rosenfeld a philosophy student, too?[178]

Rosenfeld is a visibly idealized creation, and a kind of doppelgänger for Semprún's narrator. He is like a good father, who remembers his son's name day, a brother, a peer, and a savior. Through his role we see the author's flair for colorful characterization, his ability to weave all his greatest passions—German philosophy, heroism, Spanish Civil War, Nazi camps, liberation—into one scene. At the same time, he reveals a romantic imagination that is almost childlike, and that can produce an imaginary friend that is part André Malraux, part Hollywood. It was precisely this creative talent that ensured Semprún's literary and

cinematic success in later years, and eventually led him to be a nominated for an Oscar for best screenplay in 1968. He knew how to put
a cinematic spin on the least probable subjects—Buchenwald, or clandestine Communism—and his own life.

Nearly fifty years would go by between the liberation and the
writing and publication of *Literature or Life*, which was the culmina-
tion of his literary success. When he left Buchenwald, his first book,
The Long Voyage, was still eighteen years off.

After his release from the camp in April 1945, many surprises and
challenges awaited. The first major blow was that the end of Nazi
Germany was not the end of the Franco regime in Spain. Hitler and
Franco had been great allies, and the exiled Spaniards thought it was
just a matter of time before Franco was deposed. How could the allies
liberate the rest of Europe, but not Spain? Semprún captured this poi-
gnantly in *The Long Voyage:*

> The end of the camps is the end of Nazism, which means the
> end of Franco, obviously, beyond all shadow of a doubt.[179]

When he was released from Buchenwald, Jorge couldn't imagine that
thirty years later Franco would still be in power in Spain.

IV

Return To France: Postwar

"You see," she says, "it's a matter of the repatriation bonus.
Only French citizens are entitled to it."
"I'm not a French citizen," I explain to her. "In fact I'm
not a citizen, period."[180]

If Jorge Semprún had hoped for a hero's welcome after his release from Buchenwald, he was very much disappointed. Apparently, being a foreign member of the French Resistance didn't get one very far in the immediate postwar period. In *The Long Voyage*, he describes his return to France after Buchenwald in 1945 with a group of French soldiers. The issue of nationality immediately arose and separated him from the other Resistance fighters. The French prisoners were excited, crossing into France to finally see French trees. For Semprún, the trees had no personal meaning and the crossing of the border into France only brought back memories of crossing the French border into exile from Spain with his family nine years earlier:

> I'm lying in the truck, looking up at the trees. It was at
> Bayonne, on the docks next to the main square of Bayonne,
> that I learned I was a Spanish Red. The next day I got my
> second surprise, when we read in a newspaper that there
> were Reds and "Nationalists." Why they were Nationalists
> when they fought the war using Moroccan troops, the
> Foreign Legion, German planes, and the Littorio divisions,
> was more than I could fathom. That was one of the ini-
> tial mysteries of the French language I had to decipher. But
> at Bayonne, on the docks of Bayonne, I became a Spanish
> Red. There were big beds of flowers, and lots of summer
> vacationers behind the *gendarmes* who had come to see the
> Spanish Reds disembark. We were vaccinated, and they
> let us disembark. The summer vacationers looked at the
> Spanish Reds and we looked at the shop windows of the

bakeries. We looked at the white bread, the golden *croissants*, all these things from out of the past. We were like fish out of water in this world from out of the past. Since then I've never stopped being a Spanish Red. It's a way of life that was valid everywhere. Thus, in the camp I was a *Rotspanier*. I looked at the trees and I was happy to be a Spanish Red.[181]

Semprún's indifference to their countryside baffled his companions—who had even forgotten that he was foreign because his French at this point was absolutely fluent. He had to explain: "I'm not home. I'm not French."[182] Ironically, we soon learn that this declaration is supported by the French authorities. It is a fact, and upon arrival at the repatriation camp where all the liberated prisoners are given a physical examination and the repatriation "bonus" of one thousand francs and a supply of cigarettes, the official handling the paperwork says that she cannot give him the bonus because despite fighting for France and surviving Buchenwald, he is not a French citizen and only French citizens are entitled to reparation. His French companions protest, outraged that someone who fought "for France" and who speaks fluent French could be formally excluded. But Semprún does not protest against this absurd bureaucratic injustice, and says that he prefers to preserve his identity as a Spanish Red.

He eventually—and one can only surmise that it was through his well-connected brother-in-law, French diplomat Jean-Marie Soutou—got his papers in order, and was able to go "home." Home was the dreary house in Saint-Prix, where his exiled father, stepmother, and two younger brothers continued their penurious existence.

Since 1939, the family's diasporic situation had deteriorated. Jorge's eldest brother Gonzalo was studying architecture in Switzerland, and his sister Susana had returned to Spain at the end of the Spanish Civil War after being heartbroken by Jean-Marie Soutou. She was taken in by Semprún family relatives in Madrid. Things must have been difficult for her at first in Spain as the daughter of an exile. Eventually she met her future husband, José Antonio Aguirregomezcorta Soria, and they married and moved to Cádiz, where she remained until her death.

Meanwhile, the atmosphere in the house in Saint-Prix was grim and violent. Alvaro, who had a lifelong battle with psychological problems, had come back to live with the family for a while. In his memoirs, Carlos remembered this difficult time period. Alvaro and his father, José María Semprún, eventually came to physical blows, and Alvaro left for good. His father and stepmother had little contact with him from then on.

> I'm in bed with the flu and I hear a violent argument in the dining room. I even hear noises that sound like blows. That is what they are. Alvaro, who has come to live with us in Saint-Prix and work as a gardener, like us, because he is afraid of starving to death elsewhere. . . . He didn't work for long, because people found him "strange." We lived under the weight of terror and hunger. We lived, thanks to the bitch and her husband, in an abnormal and morbid atmosphere. And the war and its shortages, which were all too real, gave them an excuse to turn us into slaves. . . . I don't know how it started, but for some reason José María slapped Alvaro, and Alvaro slapped him back. . . . A few weeks later, Alvaro . . . returned to Spain, wrote a letter to his father asking for for-giveness, and soon afterward he was interned, for the first time, in a mental institution.[183]

Alvaro never saw his father again. He first went to Spain, where he stayed on and off in a boardinghouse run by his father's sister, Mercedes de Semprún, where his sister had stayed. He obtained a scholarship to study medicine, with room and board at the university. He also did his military service, which was obligatory under Franco. So between 1953 and 1955 when Jorge was "Federico Sánchez," voluntarily working for the Communist Party in Madrid, Alvaro was a reluctant sublieutenant in the same city, serving the other side. He was discharged from the military for health reasons in 1955, and didn't complete his medical degree. He returned to Presinge, Switzerland, where he lived for the next two decades under the care of the family's old friends, Elsa Grobéty and Hélène Reymond.

The tense family atmosphere that Jorge returned to after his liberation was not smoothed over by the joy of his return, which might have presented a glimmer of hope. World War II was over, France had been liberated, and perhaps that meant a better future for everyone.

At Saint-Prix, Carlos awaited Jorge impatiently, looking out the window expectantly. The return of his big brother, the Resistance fighter: the hero. Carlos was only three years younger than Jorge and they had been close, though it was always a challenge to keep up with Jorge's magnetism and superior education and attitude. Carlos's only description of his brother's homecoming was written decades later, and tinged perhaps with some envy and fraternal tension:

> We, the family, gave my brother Jorge an unequivocal hero's welcome, me especially. The heroic vision of the Resistance fighter, the deportee, the "professional revolutionary" endured for years, but as I began to uncover his lies—along with the greater lie of communism—the image of "positive hero" started to crumble. It was replaced by indignation and contempt. I can admit today that no matter how great my admiration had once been, my disappointment was even greater. Even more so because he was my brother.
>
> During the few days he spent in Saint-Prix with the family he made our apartment on rue Auguste Rey his legal residence. To do so he had to take care of some paperwork at the town hall, and I accompanied him. Predictably, the modest municipal employees were thrilled to meet a deportee just arrived from Germany, and they all said the same thing: "It must have been terrible!" And Jorge, with a

humble smile, answered, "It wasn't exactly pleasant . . . !" It was the same with friends and acquaintances of my father's. My father would proudly introduce Jorge as a recently liberated deportee, and everyone would exclaim, "How he must have suffered!" And Jorge would smile the same smile, and give his evasive line, "It wasn't exactly pleasant!"

At the beginning I was baffled by his modesty, and I told him, "To hear you talk about it, one would think that being a deportee was no worse than being a prisoner of war." Later I convinced myself that his pride and false modesty were trademarks of the revolutionary hero, of the man of iron, who doesn't stoop to sentimentalisms or complaining. That was until I understood that he had been a *kapo* and that's why he wasn't a walking corpse, and in fact was so healthy. It was true that he was thinner, and his hair was cut very short. Buzzcuts weren't in vogue then, but they protected one from lice. But Paco, our younger brother, who had spent the whole war in Saint-Prix, was much thinner.[184]

Carlos's accusation that Jorge was a *kapo* in Buchenwald must be contextualized. By the time Carlos wrote his memoirs of Jorge's return, they were no longer on speaking terms and he was eager to question his older brother's credibility. He did not keep in mind that Jorge turned twenty years old just before arriving in the camp, and was a relatively inexperienced political activist, surely not savvy enough to be made a leader. On the other hand, it is possible that Carlos suspected from his brother's appearance and health that Jorge's time in the camp was not that of a run-of-the-mill prisoner, which it wasn't. The office job, the care packages, his knowledge of German, and possibly the influence of Spanish Ambassador Lequerica had all contributed to a deportation that was a far cry from that of Robert Anthelme, for example. But it is one thing to suggest that Jorge somehow became a protégé of a Kapo, and another one altogether to accuse him of being one himself.

After spending much of the war in Geneva, Jean-Marie Soutou, Maribel's husband, had been posted at the French embassy in Berne in 1945, and Maribel had rented a house in Locarno for herself and their young son, Georges-Henri. Gonzalo was studying in Switzerland at the time, and kept Maribel company, and Jorge spent several months there after sorting out his papers in Saint-Prix. When and why did Jorge go to Switzerland to be with his sister, Gonzalo, and his small nephew Georges-Henri? Did Jean-Marie help Jorge with passports and other official documents so that he could travel legally?

Jorge was a recently liberated deportee, but he was also an urbane twenty-two-year-old Parisian, itching to resume his life. He was not much of a family man, and lakeside Switzerland with his older sister, her toddler, and visits from his brothers may have made him restless. It was beautiful, and he could rest, but it was also another dislocation.

Yet again, he really had nowhere else to go. Saint-Prix clearly didn't have much to offer him except for family feuds and hunger. Even the fragile semblance of a family home wouldn't last for long. His father and stepmother moved to Rome soon after the end of the war, and left Carlos and the youngest brother Paco to eke out their existence as best they could. José María Semprún had been offered the post of Ministro Sin Cartera (Minister without Portfolio) representing the Spanish Republican Government in Exile to the Vatican State. Working as a Minister without Portfolio for an exiled government without a country may sound disheartening, but as a devout Catholic the Vatican was an ideal post for him. Before leaving Saint-Prix, he paid the rent for a few years, but the boys had no money for day to day life. They had to scrimp or go without water and heat, and they had no formal education between the two of them. They lived like scamps.

Jorge surely had no interest in spending any more time than necessary with his younger, teenage, impoverished brothers in a northern suburb of Paris; but who was going to support his yearning for the Saint-Germain-des-Prés lifestyle?

Was there any political reason why it might be better for Jorge to ride out the first few months after his liberation in neutral Switzerland, as opposed to Paris? Georges-Henri Soutou, Maribel and Jean-Marie's son, has pointed out that food was certainly more abundant. The rations in France were minimal in the postwar years. Georges-Henri traced, as closely as he could, the dates of Jorge's stay in Switzerland. Jorge's correspondence with his sister was spotty, but the basic time line is there, as are glimpses into Jorge's, or "George's," personality as seen by his sister, Maribel:

> My mother's journal shows that Georges (sic) arrived in Berne on October 5, 1945. My father left to start his position as French Ambassador to Belgrade on October 11. My mother stayed behind with Georges and Gonzalo. On November 1 they left Berne to go to a rented house in Locarno-Solduno. On January 10, 1946, my mother had appendicitis followed by peritonitis. . . . Following that, she wrote that Georges had left for Paris, but she doesn't give a date. Judging from the context, it must have been in February or March 1946. There's very little personal information. . . . in December '45 she wrote "Georges is working on the 1940s (a manuscript, presumably); Gonzalo is really kind, certainly more so than that rascal Georges. . . . Georges went back to Paris, in his usual Torquemada mood. Such a pity. He had many plans. He wrote me two letters in a row, and then silence. Spring, his writing, a girlfriend, or his party. Perhaps all of the above or perhaps just his negligence.[185]

From these entries, we can conclude that Jorge was in Switzerland from October 5, 1945, through early 1946.[186] He was a "rascal," moody, and elusive. From Maribel's photographs it is clear that he wrote, and that he spent time with a childhood friend from the first phase of the Semprún children's exile in 1936, Elsa Grobéty.

Nearly eighty years after she first met him, Elsa Grobéty still remembers Jorge with great affection. She kept a wonderful charcoal portrait of a very handsome Jorge that she drew during this period. Seeing the remarkable likeness she created seventy years before was all the more moving because by the time we talked she had been blind for some time. She recalled that the Semprún children had a huge role in her life. She remembered Paco as the funniest, and says that when she learned of Jorge's "disappearance"—when he was arrested and sent to Buchenwald—she spent many "*nuits blanches,*" sleepless nights. She had fond memories of walking hand in hand with Jorge around Geneva. She acknowledged that her relationship with him was rather unique. They had a playful, affectionate dynamic, but she admitted that with other people he was often more tense. He was not, she recalled, a relaxed, loving person. But she cared deeply for him.

There seems to have been a woman with whom Jorge had a romantic elationship with in Locarno. In *Literature or Life* she appears as "Lorena," and Jorge appears as "Manuel." Her real name is not mentioned, but she was a recent divorcée, and her family owned a big pharmaceutical company. Semprún's writing about women is never his finest, but of all the women who walk through his pages, Lorena is written about with the most tenderness. She seems to have been his first love after Buchenwald, but it is not clear whether they continued to see each other after his return to Paris in early 1946.

Carlos claimed that he read the first version of *The Long Voyage* sometime in 1946–1947, which means that Jorge wrote a draft quite soon after his liberation from Buchenwald. "It turns out I had read the first incarnation of *The Long Voyage*. The thing was that he couldn't get it published then, back around 1947–1948."[187]

Jorge's story about the genesis of his first book, told in several print versions and many interviews, is very different. He said that he couldn't write about his camp experience for many years, because he was convinced that reliving it would have led him to suicide. He said he only wrote this first book about Buchenwald in 1963, during a ten-day period hiding out at a fellow communist's house in Madrid. His reason for finally writing, he explained, was that his host had also survived a German camp but was a terrible storyteller. He was forced to write *The Long Voyage* so that the world would actually have a decent account of what it was like to be a deportee. Subsequently, he says, he took advantage of this dull period to plow through writing his first draft.

Carlos's claim that Jorge wrote *The Long Voyage* much earlier was thus an open and challenging contradiction to Jorge's own description on how and when the book first came to be. Evidence from Maribel, Jorge's older sister, supports Carlos's memory of this first draft. She kept a photograph of Jorge, taken some time in the fall of 1945, that shows him in Switzerland, writing in a notebook. On the back of the photo she wrote "*Le Grand Voyage*, first version, Locarno-Solduno."[188]

In this and other photographs—and Elsa Grobéty's pencil portrait—
from this period, Jorge is decked out in a head-to-toe *zazou* look. The
zazous were a French youth subculture during World War II, and they
wore their hair long and styled as high up as possible, defying gravity;
big shoes, and high-waist trousers with flared, cuffed legs. Their inspiration was taken from the "zoot suits" of American jazz musicians. Jorge
never wrote about his fashion choices after the liberation, but the photos
show that he was a hipster before, and after, the war.

> For a period of about twelve years following the liberation
> of France in 1944, a generation of French intellectuals, writ-
> ers, and artists was swept into the vortex of communism.[189]

After Geneva, Jorge found work in Paris as a translator at UNESCO,
and he met the actress Loleh Bellon. Loleh was the daughter of the
famous photographer Denise Bellon, and the sister of filmmaker
Yannick Bellon. She was two years younger than Jorge, a young, beautiful, Parisian bohemian. Simone de Beauvoir immortalized Loleh in
La force des choses:

> Soon after V Day, we had a lovely evening with Camus,
> Chauffard, Loleh, and Michel Vittold. We were at a bar
> in Montparnasse, and when it closed we headed to the
> Louisiana Hotel. Loleh was walking barefoot on the asphalt,
> and she said "It's my birthday today. I'm twenty years old!"[190]

Loleh seduced audiences, writers, and Jorge Semprún. On July 26,
1947, their son Jaime Semprún was born in Paris. Jorge was twenty-four; Loleh was twenty-two. They lived together for close to three
years, a period that Jorge describes as "relatively conjugal,"[191] but in
1949 they split up.

While he lived with Loleh, and worked at UNESCO, Jorge
attended meetings of the Spanish Communist Party in Exile and of

the French Communist Party. Once the couple split up, Jorge set about to become a true Communist militant, and to earn the respect of the Spanish Communist Party (PCE) leader Santiago Carrillo, who selected people for clandestine work in Spain.

He also became a member of the most glamorous cell of the French Communist Party: *cellule* 722. Its members included the major writers and intellectuals of the day who hung out at the iconic Café Flore and Deux Magots, a couple of blocks from the writer Marguerite Duras's flat at 5 rue Saint-Benoît, the home base of the Parisian intelligentsia. The group included: Dionys Mascolo, Claude Roy, Edgar Morin, Raymond Queneau, Michel Leiris, Georges Bataille, Clara Malraux, Romain Gary, and even Lacan, from time to time. Duras, seductively charming, an already well-known author, and former Resistance member, was the queen bee.[192]

Everyone on the scene was a Communist or a fellow traveler, and spent their time talking about literature and politics. There were other larger stars in the constellation, orbiting around the inner circle, among them the philosopher Jean-Paul Sartre, the singer Juliette Greco, and the actress Simone Signoret. The lives of these people unfolded within two Parisian blocks, and it was in the postwar era that the popular, Hollywood-ized image of Saint-Germain-des-Prés was forged: slim intellectuals sitting at smoke-filled cafés and underground jazz bars, wearing black turtlenecks, discussing Marxism and the experimental novel, and dancing. This is the world that seduces Audrey Hepburn's character in the musical film *Funny Face*, and it was Jorge Semprún's first adult milieu: cash poor, antibourgeois, *mais très chic*.

Jorge had political credibility because he was a Buchenwald survivor, and because as a Spaniard he was the only member of 722 whose country was under a Fascist dictatorship. He was also in his early twenties, conversant in philosophy and literature, and extremely well suited to wearing black turtlenecks. He was a star of the *cellule* 722.

There was another Buchenwald survivor in the cell, Marguerite Duras's husband Roger Antelme. He and Jorge shared many interests, and were close in age. Antelme was six years older than Semprún, but unlike Jorge he had subsequently been deported to the death camp at Dachau and barely made it back alive. Immediately after the liberation of Dachau, Antelme was on his deathbed with typhus and held in quarantine. Lucky for him, his friend and Resistance coworker François Mitterrand was sent by de Gaulle as the official French representative of the liberation at Dachau. He helped Antelme escape the quarantine and took him back to France for treatment. Antelme wrote about his experiences in the Nazi camps in his 1947 book *L'espèce humaine*, and joined the French Communist Party in 1946.

Semprún, under the pseudonym "Georges Falco," had been the first to write about Antelme's book on July 4, 1947, in *Action*, an illustrated magazine that supported the Communist Party.[193] The two survivors had been friendly for some time, but Semprún, according to Antelme, turned on him and subsequently denounced him to the party superiors.

Why would Semprún turn on his friend? According to Antelme, the tensions began in 1946. Antelme had started a publishing house, Cité Universelle, and bought the rights to the German novel *Stalingrad* by Theodor Plievier. Jorge was out of work at the time, and Antelme offered him the job of translating the novel, paying him in advance. Jorge, according to Antelme, spent a year and a half working on the book, but only translated a few fragments. In the end, Cité Universelle lost the rights to *Stalingrad*, and soon afterward the publisher went under. Antelme says that Jorge was clearly uncomfortable about his failure to keep up his end of the deal, and that at the same time he became palpably hostile toward everyone associated with the publisher: Antelme, Duras, and Mascolo. This hostility annoyed Antelme, who had been eager to publish a great antiwar novel in French.[194]

There had been some heated discussions among cell members in May and June 1949.[195] These arguments occurred in friendly contexts, where people spoke freely thinking they were simply hanging out. Amid talk about new trends in literary criticism, which inevitably led to the thorny issue of the role culture played in the party, Jorge and Duras showed each other pictures of their children,[196] and others spoke about their upcoming summer plans.

Semprún later reported the tenor of these conversations to party higher-ups, and it led to formal denunciations. Jacques Martinet, the cell's secretary. Jorge Semprún allegedly accused Antelme and Duras of decadent bourgeois behavior, among other things. Duras was formally accused of "dubious morals" and "probable nymphomania."[197] She was expelled from the French Communist Party in February 1950.

She mused on how quickly she had fallen out of favor with her comrades and how appreciated she had been early on, and she blamed the change on Semprún:

> At that particular time, however, the criticisms leveled against me were very different from the present ones. "You're doing too much, you're going to make yourself ill," people kept telling me. Now those same comrades, whom I have not seen since I transferred to 722, send reports into the branch where they accuse me of being a "whore." Perhaps they accuse me of being a whore because they can find no other insult. It's easy to accuse a woman of being a whore, it's vague and facile. Is it because I'm divorced? Because I live with a man I'm not married to? I find that difficult to believe since my accusers, Semprún and Martinet, are themselves divorced and the majority of comrades from the cell cohabit like us.[198]

Duras was right. There was a good deal of partner swapping in their milieu. In fact, soon afterward, Martinet's wife, the film editor Colette Leloup, split up from Martinet and Jorge moved in. Colette became Jorge's second, and last, wife.

Antelme, and Duras's lover Dionys Mascolo, were both expelled as well. Semprún always denied that he had anything to do with this expulsion, and it was one of the few subjects that never ceased to infuriate him.[199]

Antelme was accused of serious treachery, and the ideas attributed to him included typical anti-party lines such as criticizing the Molotov-Ribbentrop pact and speaking in favor of the United States' Marshall Plan. Most notable, however, was Antelme's "attack" on the Communist Party's role within Buchenwald, a sensitive subject for Jorge, who had played an integral part in the camp's underground.

Both men had been in Buchenwald, but Jorge worked in the office that assigned men to work transports. Antelme had been the victim of such a transport, to Dachau, a camp that few people survived. Massive numbers died in Dachau toward the end of the war, from the same typhus epidemic to which Antelme had fallen prey when Mitterrand rescued him.

According to Antelme, he had appealed to Jorge once, as a fellow Buchenwald deportee. He had expressed his view that having been assigned to a transport to Dachau was a sacrifice he knew he had made for the greater good of the cause. He followed up saying that many had died so that the best militants could live: "Each comrade should know which path was the real, or the theoretical, road to revolution. Many men died so that they, those Communist comrades, the best militants of the revolution, could live."[200]

He insisted that the right way to be a Communist was to see it as a responsibility that entailed sacrifices, not as a superior privilege, and he claims that Jorge took this general observation as an attack on his own role in the camp.[201] As revenge, Antelme said, Jorge reported all of Antelme's comments back to party superiors to make sure he was expelled.

To his last days, Jorge denied any involvement in the accusations or expulsion of his comrades. In 1998, in *Le Monde*, he published a response to the accusations that he was a *mouchard*, or informant who had ratted out his comrades:

> I do not accept I had a hand in their expulsion. It's mostly
> myth, a kind of family fiction. It's as though they needed

to hound me, metaphorically, because I was closer to them than the others. I discussed it with Robert Anthelme at the time. . . . In fact, when the wheels were in motion to expel them from the party, I had already moved out of the area to Monmartre, because I didn't want to get involved. And I took advantage of the situation not to renew my membership. I belonged to the Spanish Communist Party, and that was enough![202]

But Antelme's second wife Monique, to whom he was married for forty-two years, also maintained until the end that Semprún had informed on Antelme, and that her husband had never understood or fully recovered from this betrayal:

I was the wife of Robert Antelme for 42 years, and I confirm that Jorge Semprún was present, contrary to what your *Débats* page has just published, at the Communist Party meeting of March 7; the meeting where we were kicked out: Robert Antelme, Bernard Guillochon, and myself. I confirm that Perlican, secretary of the CP's 6th arrondissement section, read out loud a defamatory report directed primarily against Robert Anthelme. It was said to have been written by Jorge Semprún. I would rather not intervene at all in this sordid affair that made Robert Antelme suffer terribly, but Jorge Semprún's remarks, published in June 26 in *Le Monde*, leave me no choice. By denouncing what he abusively calls "the group of la rue Saint-Benoît," Semprún betrayed Robert, and he betrayed friendship. . . .

Now they are all dead. Robert. Marguerite Duras, Bernard Guillochon, Dionys Mascolo, Eugène Mannoni. I am the only witness, and that may not be enough, but I am not making anything up. I would like to add that, after our expulsion, Robert Antelme twice asked Jorge Semprún to meet and explain himself. They saw each other twice. He never explained himself. The second time they said good-bye without shaking hands. Robert always asked himself: why? I could only find one reason, and I won't mention it here because it was only a supposition on his part.[203]

Jorge's brother Carlos also claimed that Jorge had snitched on Antelme, Duras, and Mascolo, and that he denied his involvement to avoid prob-lems. Jorge, according to Carlos, said as much to him and to fellow Spanish Communist Fernando Claudín: "Of course I lied! How could I do otherwise? They wanted to tar and feather me, and I couldn't let that happen."[204]

But Carlos never forgave him, and accused Jorge of lying and cov-ering up his behavior to protect himself:

Forty-eight years later he thinks he can lie about it. Now that almost all the players in that masquerade are dead, he thinks he can deny that he wrote the report, and deny that he was at the expulsion ceremony. He writes that Robert Antelme, after being expelled, asked to meet with him twice . . . and one of the things that he wanted to know was why Semprún, who was (at the meeting) "present, at the back of the room," never spoke up. Forty-eight years later Jorge Semprún responds to Antelme that, according to him, "I never spoke up because I wasn't there, I remained silent because I was absent." And he concluded his article in Le Monde saying: "A few months before, I had switched from the PCF of the 6th District to that of the 18th, and I took advantage of the change to not renew my party ID. I was already a member of the Spanish CP, and that was enough for me. That is why I did not attend the expulsion meeting, and no report was read in my name. All of that is nonsense and family romance."[205]

In any case, Antelme was expelled from the party in 1950 after accusations signed by Semprún and Martinet. That was the end of Semprún's friendship with Antelme. Martinet's wife, film editor Colette Leloup, would become Semprún's second wife after Loleh Bellon. Coincidentally, Semprún's two wives had been classmates when they were little. Jorge was still in exile, but he had finally found a new home through the tight-knit world of Saint-Germain-des-Prés. By the time he left the French party, he was already working his way up the rungs of the Spanish Communist organization.

Why would someone with bourgeois roots who had survived a Nazi camp adhere to a severe party ideology? Why would the young, talented, handsome Jorge want to bury himself deep in the sordid infighting and ambitions of the French or Spanish parties?

To understand his motivation, it is important to keep in mind both his personal circumstances and the larger political context. He had no money, home, or family of his own to rely on. His father and stepmother, never much help, lived quite independently in Rome. His siblings were scattered about. His first marriage had fallen apart and he had a small son, Jaime, to worry about. He had already met Colette Leloup, and they were building a life together. He also had political ambitions, and the Spanish Communist Party seemed like an organization where he could have a role. He was eager to join the anti-Franco struggle. He yearned to be assigned the clandestine trips to Spain. These missions were dangerous and glamorous. Using various pseudonyms he would be able to show up to dazzle Spain's young intelligentsia, and lead them around like the Pied Piper until they saw the light of the PCE. He was also put on party salary after 1952, once he had left his job at UNESCO in September of the same year.[206]

Until September 7, 1950, when its activities were made illegal by the French Socialist Secretary of State Jules Moch, the PCE operated freely in France. As Franco Spain became a prominent North American ally during the Cold War, France couldn't afford to be seen as harboring

Antonio Maura and his family. *Blanco y Negro* magazine, from the collection of Danielle de la Gorce.

Antonio Maura with King Alfonso XIII, from the collection of Roger Kase.

The wedding of José María Semprún Gurrea and Susana Maura Gamazo, 1919.

José María Semprún (center, second row), Annette Litschi Semprún (center, first row), children and guests. Embassy of Spain in The Hague, 1937, from the collection of Dominique Landman.

Carlos and Francisco Semprún, 1931, from the collection of Sylvia Nicolas

Miguel Maura with his children, from the collection of Manuel Maura

José María Semprún, Annette Litschi, Carlos Semprún, and Paco Semprún, from the collection of Sylvia Nicolas

Jorge Semprún, from the collection of
Dominique Landman.

Jorge Semprún in profile, from the collection
of Dominique Landman.

Jorge Semprún's identification papers from
Buchenwald, courtesy of the International Tracing
Service Archives.

Gonzalo Semprún, top, and Jorge
Semprún, center, with his nephew
Georges-Henri Soutou (son of Maribel
Semprún and Jean-Marie Soutou). Lugano,
winter 1945–1946, from the collection of
Sylvia Nicolas.

Elsa Grobéty with Maribel and Gonzalo
Semprún. Lugano, winter 1945–1946, from
the collection of Sylvia Nicolas.

Jorge Semprún. Portrait by Elsa Grobéty.
Lugano, winter 1945–1946. Courtesy of
Elsa Grobéty

Carlos Semprún, 1952, from the collection of
Sylvia Nicolas.

Wedding of Carlos Semprún, seated at the left, and Sylvia Nicolas,
standing, right, 1952. Seated from left to right: Jorge Semprún,
Maribel Semprún, unknown, and Paco Semprún. From the collection
of Sylvia Nicolas.

Congress of the Spanish Communist Party, 1954. Kneeling, left to right: Gergorio López Raimundo, Fernando Claudín, Tomas García Ramón Mendezma and Santiago Alvarez. Standing, left to right: Ignacio Galician, Jorge Semprún, Enrique Lister, Dolores Ibárruri, Santiago Carrillo, Antonio Mije, Francisco Romero Marín, José Moix, Antonio Delgado. Courtesy of the Spanish Communist Party Archive.

Semprún and Carrillo families on vacation in the USSR. Courtesy of the Spanish Communist Party Archive.

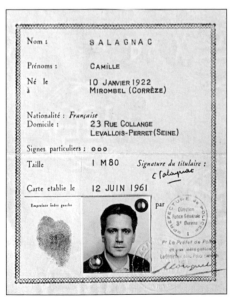

Jorge Semprún's fake identification card under the name "Camille Salagnac," from the collection of Dominique Landman.

Jorge Semprún and
Bernard Pivot.

Jorge Semprún
and Bernard Pivot,
from the collection
of Dominique
Landman.

Jorge Semprún and
Colette Leloup dancing,
from the collection of
Dominique Landman.

anti-Franco fighters, so after 1950 it was forced to go underground. But in 1947, when the party leadership could still meet openly, Jorge met many of its members, including the legendary Dolores Ibárrurri, aka Pasionaria, at the PCE's Parisian headquarters on Avenue Kleber. In addition to the impressive Pasionaria, he met many people who inspired him, and he longed to be a part of the inner circle. They were from all walks of life, but all, like Jorge, were Spanish exiles in Paris, and Communists.

> That word "Kleber" had an aura of mystery to it. People would say "I've heard it said at Kleber," or "That will have to be discussed at Kleber," or "We'll see what Kleber decides." . . . and Kleber took on a symbolic meaning of indisputable patriarchal or religious power, one that was both distant and close to us.[207]

A person who specifically influenced him at this point was Benigno Rodriguez, who had been Republican Prime Minister Juan Negrín's secretary during the war:

> Benigno Rodriguez was an autodidact, and fabulous character in the Spanish political scene. He was the son of a horse and buggy driver, an ex-anarcho-syndicalist, and had been assigned by the Communist Party to be the secretary of Juan Negrín during the Civil War and part of his exile, in London. There was nothing he hadn't seen.[208]

There was an adventurousness to the political world that Jorge was drawn to. It also provided a connection to Spain, and he relished meeting with the other exiles at one of their homes and sharing a hearty meal of Spanish home cooking:

> I ran into Enrique Líster a few times; some of them, sitting around a plate of Asturian *fabada*, or a Galician *potaje*,

a Valencian *paella*, or a *cocido madrileño* (it is a well-known fact that we exiles loved the typical dishes of our lost and beloved homeland; eating them in the company of friends was like a communion with our national essence).[209]

There was a daredevil aura to this work that appealed to Jorge. The Communist world was repressive but familiar, oppressive but secure: "Today it's difficult to understand why, being anti-authoritarian, they were so keen to remain in the party. But party membership was a way of life, a way of hope, of building a future—whether glorious or not—and of being part of a 'family.' Party membership meant you were never alone."[210]

Though Antelme never forgave Jorge, his ex-wife Marguerite Duras rolled with the punches, and didn't hold a grudge. On the contrary, she always had a weak spot for Jorge, and was eager to turn him into a screen idol. In 1960, director Peter Brooks made a film version of her best-selling novel *Moderato cantabile*, which starred Jean-Paul Belmondo and Jeanne Moreau. The great Belmondo was, in fact, her second choice for the male lead. Duras had her heart set on Jorge, who had never acted in his life. She pursued him, but he refused the opportunity to become a movie star.

In 1960 his commitment to his clandestine life in Spain was still his top priority. His long-standing involvement with the Spanish party had to do with many factors, and among them his relationship with party leader Santiago Carrillo must be given special consideration. Jorge depended on organizations and VIPs throughout his life to survive: his brother-in-law Soutou, his adolescent benefactor Frick, the *Arbeitsstatistik* in Buchenwald, and the intelligentsia of cell 722. He now he was ready to move on to PCE leaders Santiago Carrillo and Dolores Ibarruri and deepen his political and personal connection with his Spanish roots. Jorge and Carrillo had an unusual relationship that cut across deep class lines, and would prove to be mutually beneficial. Santiago Carrillo would be Jorge's new father figure, for a long time, but not, of course, forever. He would also be the last paternal leader Jorge would follow.

As Jorge ascended through the PCE ranks, his personal allegiances underwent a permanent shift. He would see less and less of his son Jaime, and when they did see each other, their relationship was increasingly tense. He was rebuilding his life with Colette Leloup, and came to think of her and her daughter, Dominique Martinet, as his only family. His estrangement from his own son would become radical and definitive. It still haunts Jorge's biography as a sad and murky rupture, not unlike his own break from his father, and some of his own siblings.

V
Alias: The Spanish Communist Years

> I am the son of a vanquished class, of a world in ruins.
> And in the sound and fury of the struggle that is life, of
> what prospers or dies, from me there has spurted the blood
> of this wound.[211]
> —Jorge Semprún

> It snowed all over Spain yesterday. . . . Yet the atmosphere
> is warm and welcoming. More than ever. All my friends
> are showering me with invitations, and I'm going
> non-stop. I am very pleased about this, and plan on having
> a wonderful time this season.
> —Caja 92, Carpeta 64[212]

Jorge's clandestine return to Spain would inaugurate what was, perhaps, the happiest period of his life. He had just turned thirty years old, and he was offered the chance to create a meaningful role for himself in the country his family had been forced to flee seventeen years earlier.

Because of the secretive nature of his life and his work, it is challenging to form a clear idea of his true motivations and impressions. He split his time between Paris and Madrid, between French and Spanish, and this duality only reinforced his ability to reinvent himself and to compartmentalize his identities. He had years of practice dealing with new and destabilizing situations: his mother's illness and death; his father's remarriage; the outbreak of the Spanish Civil War; exile in France, Switzerland, Holland, and France; the French Resistance; and Buchenwald.

Returning to Spain secretly to influence students was a game compared to what he had been through. It was a game he was good at. Most people in Madrid could not imagine what his life in France was like, nor vice versa. France and Spain were geographical neighbors, but they may as well have been on different planets. He was singularly equipped to navigate the particular milieus of each country, and each time he crossed the border he became completely independent of those he had left behind. The Spanish communist leaders Santiago Carrillo and Dolores Ibárruri could not return to Spain, and Semprún became their inside man. His wife Colette never seems to have had a great interest in Spain, nor did she speak any Spanish. His life in Madrid had nothing to do with her, and his upper-middle-class Parisian life was far superior to that of his Spanish comrades. His individuality was thus insulated from everyone, and he even managed to keep a low profile vis-à-vis the French and Spanish authorities without sacrificing his personal flair. Far from cultivating a mole-like image, he remained loyal to his acquired cosmopolitan style.

The fact that Jorge was an elegant clandestine agent reveals his self-confidence—some might call it arrogance—and astuteness. He could have tried to blend in with the dowdy crowds of early 1950s Spain, but he chose not to. Vanity aside, he knew that having a chic air might, in fact, put him above the law. Spanish authorities were not looking for posh Communist agents. Class and politics were indivisible under Franco's very basic system: "Reds" were shabby, poor, and detestable, while upstanding loyal citizens were neat and starched. The small percentage of wealthy individuals with style were an elite that intimidated the police, and they were thus untouchable. Jorge was wise in choosing a third option: fighting for his Marxist ideology while dressing with panache. His two successors in the clandestine position in Spain did not have Jorge's style or sophistication. It wasn't long before they were arrested. Jorge was never detained. Nobody would know he was a Communist. Nobody could guess he had fought in the French Resistance and survived a Nazi camp. Legend has it that he sat front and center in the best seats at the bullfights in Madrid, and that once he calmly enjoyed the spectacle a few seats away from Franco himself. Clearly Jorge had a *torero* streak and enjoyed tempting fate.

The writer Juan Goytisolo remembers how Jorge's unique style and attitude stood out when he met him in the late 1950s in Madrid:

"A meeting was arranged, and I saw Jorge at a café on the Castellana. He was very elegantly dressed, and completely at ease. Nobody could have guessed that he was a wanted party leader; he always held his meetings in upscale places."[213]

So what was he actually meant to be doing in Spain? There is extensive documentation about his clandestine years. Much of it is official party correspondence or Jorge's dissident memoirs in which he selectively discloses, retells but also reneges on his Communist past. Through these sources, combined with testimonies from his Spanish and French friends and colleagues, we can cobble together a portrait of his life during these clandestine years, with a focus on the evolving nature of his mission, and the close and conflictive relationship with his new boss. Santiago Carrillo and Jorge Semprún were an odd couple. Carrillo was eight years older, from Asturias, and had started working as an adolescent. His father was a well-known Spanish Socialist Party leader, Wenceslao Carrillo, and Santiago was active in the Socialist youth organization until he became a Communist when the Spanish Civil War broke out in 1936.[214] Carillo had also broken off relations with his father.

They met in Paris shortly after World War II, and Carrillo was immediately impressed by Jorge's enthusiastic and sincere militancy. He also saw the value of Jorge's unusual life story: the grandson of Antonio Maura, son of a Republican politician who got involved with the French Resistance and ended up in Buchenwald. All of these factors combined to make Jorge an attractive young recruit. The old Komintern rules about only accepting workers as party members had become obsolete, so Carrillo saw no obstacles in bringing this young bourgeois, educated, charismatic exile into the fold.[215] All the leaders of the PCE valued Jorge and considered him a diehard Stalinist. As Carrillo said, "He shared the behaviour and reactions of the prototypical communist militant from the time, and he was as Stalinist as anyone."[216] Carrillo became more than a professional father figure; he was also a friend and ally. In 1956 Jorge was unanimously elected, at Carrillo's suggestion, to the Central Committee of the PCE. The party leaders had a month's paid summer holiday every other year, and Jorge and Colette and her daughter Dominique spent two summers in Sochi and Crimea, respectively, with Carrillo and his family.

Carrillo and Semprún worked together to infiltrate a small, burgeoning Spanish anti-Franco intellectual sector. Their center of operations in exile was the flat where Jorge lived with Colette on the boulevard Saint-Germain. Colette was, according to Carrillo, "kind and discreet"[217] and let them use the apartment for years. It was especially important to have such a space at their disposal since the PCE had been outlawed in France since 1950. Many Spanish intellectuals and writers passed through her home, and it was there that the next steps for the "interior" were mapped out. For the PCE, Spain was always referred to as "the interior," and France and the rest of the world as "the exterior."

As usual, Jorge's day-to-day life was paradoxical. His militancy did not require renouncing a certain element of glamour that was never far from him. Even as a secret agent in Madrid staying at "safe houses" and cheap *pensiones,* Jorge's life was not all gray, dull, anonymous austerity. He would get to know a range of people from all walks of life, from the writer Ernest Hemingway to Luis Miguel Dominguín, the famous bull-fighter, and long-time lover of actress Ava Gardner, who also lived in Spain in the 1950s.

For most outsiders, and even Spaniards, the role of the PCE is unfamiliar territory. The larger questions worth asking are: what did the party leaders hope to achieve? A real revolution, or an opening for a pacific future change in power? Were their goals realistic? Were their methods effective? How did the former and the latter evolve as the years, and decades, went by? There is an extensive bibliography of books, almost entirely in Spanish, on the subject, and the non-specialist can easily be put off by the endless lists of unfamiliar names, acronyms, infighting, and bureaucracy. Yet the Partido Comunista Espanol's (PCE's) history during Jorge's years is fascinating. What was

Jorge Semprún's specific role within this big picture? What did he venture as a PCE agent, and what did he gain or lose? What price did he and others pay for backing the PCE?

Part of his job was to be the PCE's eyes and ears on Spanish soil, and to type up regular reports sent back secretly to the party leaders in Paris. These reports are intriguing documents that reveal his first impressions of the brutal transformations Spain had gone through since the Civil War, thirteen years of postwar poverty and economic stagnation.

Two things are immediately clear from Jorge's accounts. He was thrilled to be back home, no matter what the conditions, and he was deeply committed to the anti-Franco fight. His descriptions and analysis show the mind of a lucid observer and the passion of a fledgling, but talented, writer. This writing in these reports is a far cry from the overtly propagandistic writing he started out with. The classified interoffice party memos he was required to submit from Spain put Jorge into the habit of writing regularly. Once he started he would never stop. His clandestine years are not a parenthesis in his Parisian life. They are the beginning of the integration of his Spanish and French selves, geographically and radically separate up until then, because of political circumstances. This was not a "political" period devoid of literary growth. On the contrary, his authorly identity was wrought from within his political role, as he crafted—with great independence—his own constantly evolving job description. There is an intermittent use of code in his reports, ostensibly to dodge censors, but he otherwise speaks quite frankly about the situation in Spain and uses people's real names. The fear of his reports falling into the wrong hands seems more pronounced during his first year in Spain, in 1952, when Jorge describes the party as "the business" (el negocio), and the comrades as "shareholders" (accionistas). He disguises communist activities in capitalist terminology, and seems to relish the creativity involved in dissembling: "All is well here. The weather is good, and business is booming. We will hold the shareholders meeting in mid–March. The project with the students is getting results."[218]

Over the course of several years, over a decade, Jorge had worked his way to the top of the PCE. He used his charm, self-discipline, imagination, and patience, and in his free time he wrote earnest, ideologically correct literary works. He had been proving his mettle as the PCE's writer-in-residence since 1946 when he wrote the play *Soledad*, about a group of anti-Franco students. This play and other works were important practice for his later literary career, and they gave him credibility and stature within the party. Most comrades did not have the education, talent, or will to be writers.

Soledad, his odes to Pasionaria and Stalin, and his 1953 play *"¡Libertad para los 34 de Barcelona!"* are all examples of his creative propaganda. The soundtrack for ¡*Libertad!* could not have been more traditional; the Communist anthem "The International."[219]

In the late 1940s he wrote a poem "Canto a Dolores" ("A Hymn to Dolores"), in honor of Dolores Ibárurri.[220] He also wrote poem about Pasionaria's son Ruben, who was killed fighting in Stalingrad, and a Hymn to the Party (*Canto al Partido*). Though some of these verses were never published, Jorge shares them at the beginning of his 1977 memoir *Communism in Spain* (*Autobiografía de Federico Sánchez*) as evidence of his once total and profound Stalinization. *Communism in Spain* is the self-critique of a dissident; it is a conversion tale of a man who lived in the dark as a devoted militant until he saw the light and grew out of the stale ideology of Spain's Communist Party.

He explored his political convictions and critical spirit in a notoriously damning review of Carmen Laforet's 1943 novel *Nada* in the magazine *Cultura y Democracia*.

Cultura y Democracia was a short-lived publication, but it served as a platform for Jorge to impress his superiors with his ample cultural references and his ideological dogmatism. One of his first articles was his review of Carmen Laforet's book. *Nada*, a bestseller in its time, paints a harsh and sordid portrait of postwar Spanish life under

Franco. It is not explicitly political and made it past Franco's censors, and even won the first Nadal literary prize. Jorge's review was written in 1950 and tore into the novel's success and what he saw as the author's counterproductive "nihilism" and "pessimism." *Nada* was not an example of Communist revolutionary ideals, and he calls it "rubbish." He also drops many names, from Faulkner to Mao Tse Tung. He proclaims he is not going to stoop to such nonsense such as asking whether the author is blond or brunette. It seemed to rankle him that a successful novel had been written by a woman who lived in Spain under Franco. This review of *Nada* was a winning audition for PCE cultural leader. It showed a Jorge who was intransigent, confident, worldly, and not afraid to call out what he saw as Franco-supported culture. He was parading his adherence to a true bunker sensibility. That Laforet's novel—which has been translated into many languages and is a respected classic to this day—was already seven years old when Jorge's review came out shows the disconnect between the "interior" and the "exterior." The PCE, consistently, was several steps behind in the cultural war it was waging, and it would have to catch up quickly through the 1950s and '60s if it hoped to connect with Spanish youth.

It should be noted that for decades the PCE only existed officially in exile and in secrecy. Since its leaders Santiago Carrillo and Dolores Ibárruri had both been active during the time of the Spanish Civil War and could not risk setting foot on Spanish soil, they ruled from afar, from Paris and Moscow, respectively. The consequence of this remote leadership was that no matter how many clandestine agents or secret reports they had at their disposal, they were out of touch with life in Spain. This complete lack of direct contact went on for four decades, until after Franco's death. The PCE faced other external and internal challenges, but remote rule was a significant and long-standing handicap. The fact that the bosses were not on the scene themselves probably made it especially enticing for Jorge to be one of the few sent to be on the ground, within Spanish borders. The exclusivity of his role, and the risks involved in getting to and from Spain, made the "secret agent" lifestyle irresistible. It was also the only way to finally, after sixteen years in exile, go home. The trips were temporary and illegal, but he could again bask in the familiarity of his childhood streets and hear his mother tongue spoken everywhere around him. He also had new parental figures, Carrillo and Ibárruri, to fill the void left by his long-deceased mother and absent father. Though he took his ambivalent younger brother Carlos along as a fellow agent during part of his clandestine adventure (1955–1957), Carlos and the PCE were not meant to be. Jorge found he could also replace his siblings with comrades, most of whom he outshone in terms of education, and worldliness. At the same time, this was a return to his childhood dream of becoming a Spanish political leader. The PCE was the only apparent route toward the removal of Franco from power.

Jorge's was a peculiar role in the Spanish party from the beginning. His distinguished family origins were a plus, not a minus. Though he often said he had to prove himself more than others to dispel any noxious influence from his haute bourgeois origins, this was easier than one would think. Paradoxical as it may seem, the Spanish Communist Party leaders were snobs, and they loved having a well-born, handsome, young intellectual as their gentleman mascot. They could not revel in trumpeting his "brand" because he worked clandestinely, but he nonetheless brought an erudite outlook to the party's cultural program. The PCE worked to recruit new blood from Spain's up-and-coming university students. Carrillo sensed that the youth of Spain would find Jorge irresistible, and he was right. Nobody, however, knew him as Jorge Semprún. He lived in Spain under a series of aliases, along with false passports and all other necessary papers, that included Federico Sánchez, Juan Larrea, and Jacques Grador, among others. Sometimes he assumed the identity of a French Hispanist, other times he passed as a Spaniard. Federico Sánchez was his first adopted persona:

Federico Sánchez was born, at first without a surname, in 1953, during my first clandestine trip to Spain. The purpose of this first trip, which started in Barcelona, was to make contact with people and organizations. I had letters of intro- duction, and some of them said I was Spanish, and others said I was a French Hispanist. . . . My colleague who spe- cialized in border controls said that every week I should send a phony letter back (to Paris) just to say hello. To them it would mean that I was still alive and that I had not been arrested. I had to choose a name with which to sign these letters, and I chose Federico, I don't know why. And I chose Sánchez because it is a totally banal and commonplace sur- name.[221]

Though he says that he does not know why he chose "Federico," we could hazard a guess that it was in honor of Federico García Lorca. Spain's most famous poet was also a powerful political symbol: he had been murdered by Franco supporters in the first weeks of the Spanish Civil War. As a nom de guerre, Federico was synonymous with free- dom, poetry, and antifascism. By the time Jorge became Federico Sánchez, he and his future wife Colette Leloup (the former Mrs. Martinet) were a serious couple, and her apartment was Jorge's home. The couple lived there with Colette's daughter Dominique. His life as a clandestine agent had to be hidden from the people around him in Paris as well, and he had to cover up his trips with lies and omis- sions. The latter, combined with his personal magnetism, all added to his enigmatic presence in Parisian society. Costa-Gavras remembers seeing Jorge during a weekend at the country house of Yves Montand and Simone Signoret, and asking Signoret who this mysterious fellow was. She answered protectively and evasively, fueling the curiosity around her guest. A few select and trusted people were eventually let in on the secret: there was a Spanish revolutionary and secret agent in their midst. But it was all kept very hush-hush.

The man in charge of producing the fake identification cards for PCE members was Domingo Malagón, an artist by training. He was a genius counterfeiter, and nobody was ever detained on suspicion of false papers. From his Parisian base, he made many passports, French and Spanish, for Jorge, with whom he also worked on a committee devoted to Spain's internal politics. Malagón recalled the relationship between Semprún and Carrillo:

> Santiago Carrillo, Julián Grimau, Semprún—they were all part of this committee. Semprún reported on how his work in Madrid was going, with students, intellectuals, and so forth. He was an extremely precise man, down to the last detail, and he was very sharp. Seeing him working alongside Carrillo, I never thought they could fall out as they did. To the contrary, they seemed to complement each other perfectly. Semprún was highly motivated, and Carrillo completely convinced of the merits of his right-hand man. As I understand it, Carrillo's first notions of what would later be called "Euro communism," as well as his 1956 strategy of "national reconciliation," were both taken from Semprún.[222]

Jorge's work was primarily focused on Spain's intellectual world, a milieu in which he could blend in. As Malagón explains:

> The intellectual, student, and artistic milieus enjoyed a social prestige that protected them a bit more from possible persecution. . . . As our contacts in that world grew, we addressed the need for them to have direct political support. In the 1950s, Semprún was the ideal person for the task. He was an intellectual, a loyal and brave militant, and he didn't look like a traditional clandestine militant Communist agent. Furthermore—and we were all aware of this at the time—if he was ever arrested, his record from the period of the Civil War would be clear, and his last name and family

background would make him easier to defend in national
and international campaigns.[223]

His *informes* to the PCE leaders naturally reflected his Communist
values, but there is more to them than meets the eye. The reports,
which seem objective, are actually a blend of genres: autobiography,
epistles, and diary entries. They simultaneously convey a personal,
private tone and self-consciousness that they are official documents
that will be read and analyzed. In all of them he is giving a portrait of
Spain but also a self-portrait that recounts his progress, and a passion
for his work. It could be argued that these letters to his bosses are the
real seeds of his autobiographical genre, the "auto-fiction" that Jorge
Semprún was to make his own. They are lively, candid, political, and
one day should be edited and published.

Clandestine work gave Jorge a new lease on life. He was, perhaps, one of the most optimistic men in Madrid. He was home again,
while most of the Spaniards he met only dreamed of getting out.
His return was far from a proper homecoming, but it was his first
postexile experience. Though he was contentedly living with Colette
Leloup in Paris, his other nuclear family for nearly a decade were the
PCE leaders Carrillo and Ibarruri, and the party members he worked
and lived with in Madrid, including the entrepreneur and film producer Domingo González Lucas (Dominguín), the film producer
Ricardo Muñoz Suay, and the young intellectual student Jorge himself recruited, Javier Pradera.

Ironically, his Communist work would bring him into alignment
again with the monarchist members of his conservative Maura family. Jorge's mother's brother, Gabriel Maura Gamazo, Duke of Maura,
was eager to have Franco brought down so that the monarchy could
be restored. His other uncle, Miguel Maura, had returned from exile
in France to live in Barcelona, where he remained a firm believer in
the lost Spanish republic. These disparate family members, Jorge and
his two uncles, had conflicting political orientations—Communist,

monarchist, and Republican, respectively—but they were overridden by a common goal: to bring an end to Franco's rule. They were not alone. As Jorge observed in his travels around Spain, this desire was widespread, though understandably latent due to the regime's repressive apparatus. Franco's power had been built on executions, torture, and censorship.

Nearly a hundred years earlier, in 1842, the French writer George Sand had described Mallorca as being stuck in a primitive time warp. Jorge's description of Franco's Spain echoes the French writer, and suggests that the entire country had been beaten back to a quasi-medieval time.

On his first trip back to Spain, he took the train from the French border at Port Bou, the town made famous because of philosopher Walter Benjamin's suicide in 1940. As soon as the train left the French station and crossed into Spain, Semprún wrote, it seemed as if the clock had been turned back half a century. He describes the country-side as completely primitive, and full of idle, dirty children clothed in rags, wandering the railroad tracks and the highways. Barcelona was dirty, abandoned, and decaying except for the main squares and central avenues. Valencia fared a bit better because of its surrounding agricultural bounty, and Madrid was the "darling of the regime" even though building sites were prehistoric, with workers carrying bricks around in sacks hung around their necks by ropes. Everywhere there were uniformed guards: the infamous *guardias civiles* with their capes and shiny black tricorn hats, armed police, soldiers, and armed highway patrolmen.[224]

In counterpoint to the new, homegrown repression and dire poverty, the city was also littered with physical signs of the 1953 economic and military "Madrid Pact" between Spain and the United States. Franco's success in wooing President Dwight Eisenhower was a thorn in the side of the PCE. How could anti-Francoist forces garner international support to bring down the regime when it was being bolstered by a superpower like the United States?

In exchange for a billion dollars that would enter the country throughout the 1950s,[225] the American military was allowed to build bases in three strategic locations in Spain: Rota, Morón de la Frontera, and Torrejón de Ardoz near Madrid. Following the military bases, a huge American commercial industry was also about to move to Spanish soil: motion pictures. The empresario (and nephew of Trotsky) Samuel Bronston built huge studios outside Madrid, and imported executives and talent from the blacklisted ranks of Hollywood. One of those imports, the screenwriter Bernard Gordon, was amazed by the incongruity of being an American, persecuted at home, yet welcomed in a right-wing Spanish dictatorship. While the average Spaniard was impoverished and oppressed, Gordon says that the upper-class madrileños were living a decadent dolce vita. Their soirées were held at exclusive and debauched locales like the Marqués de Riscal, where there was no shortage of cocktails, glamorous women, and partner swapping. This was not what a progressive Jewish American had been expecting from a repressive Catholic regime. Franco Spain was full of paradoxes. Gordon remembered the impressive extent of North American influence in Madrid, and how the city became a cultural and financial colony:

> Eisenhower had made a deal with Franco to establish major air force and naval bases on Spanish territory. . . . The thousands of servicemen who worked there needed living space, schools for their children, restaurants, and recreation. . . . Bronston was not the only American producer who had discovered the advantages of filmmaking in Spain. . . . It was frequently cheaper for Americans to come over to Spain with the cast and much of their crew than to work in their own backyard at home. In addition, American films completely dominated the screens in Madrid. Down on the Gran Vía, which was the Broadway of the city, all the film palaces featured American films. The only concession to the Spanish

was that the films could not be exhibited in English with Spanish subtitles. . . . Along with the filmmaking (and the dollars it brought in) and the film exhibiting (and the dollars it took out), the Americanization of old culture had really begun. Coca-Cola and Marlboro billboards dominated the landscape. American music was even more ubiquitous.[226]

The Bronston entourage included Ava Gardner, who made her first movie in Spain, *Pandora and the Flying Dutchman*, in 1951 and lived in Madrid from 1955 to 1968. Needless to say, for these wealthy movie stars and other members of the film industry, Spain was a very different country than for Spaniards. For the foreigners it was sunny, cheap, and provided a convenient gray area in terms of taxes—all the benefits of Switzerland with flamenco and beaches instead of cuckoo clocks and Alps.

Inevitably Semprún compared the present-day city to the Madrid of his childhood. He noticed evidence of North American imperialism everywhere, and the urban landscape had been dolled up to appeal to its new backers. He paid special attention to his childhood haunts, and found that Franco's government had lavished attention on the Prado Museum and the Retiro Park, and that the main avenues, such as de Calle de Alcalá, were lined with banks—also stationed with pairs of armed guards—and American-style cafeterias with alien American names such as Nebraska, California, and Alaska. One of them, California 47, would be one of the last holdout meeting places for Spanish fascists until it was bombed in a terrorist attack in 1979. How incongruous these new, spotless, air-conditioned, bland sandwich shops must have been amid the smoky Spanish bars, where patrons traditionally crushed their cigarette butts with their heel on floors covered in toothpicks, prawn shells, napkins, and other debris. Semprún was horrified by the blind lottery vendors seen on every corner, whose salesman's pitches ("¡Para hoy! ¡Para hoy!") became part of the regular drone of Spanish street life. The cultural life of Madrid had been reduced to buying lottery tickets. What he didn't see was much pro-Franco spirit and he wondered how the regime managed to forge ahead without "Francoists."[227]

He was also dismayed that the Prado had opened a "coffee" shop that served American coffee as opposed to European *café*.

While thousands of Spaniards lived in shantytowns, two entire middle-class neighborhoods with swimming pools and parking areas had been built to welcome the Americans toward the north of the city. These were sarcastically dubbed "North Korea" and "South Korea" by indignant locals. Not only were Americans enjoying a much higher standard of living in Madrid, they were driving the prices up and the standards down for the locals.[228]

The Spanish-American pact was a betrayal to Spanish democracy, and many people were outraged that it was being marketed as a wonderful breakthrough:

> There is a youngish doctor, until now apolitical, who has recently expressed aggressive "anti-Yanqui" sentiments to our contact (in whose house, by the way, I am staying). He has also begun to show concern and an interest in our activities, and in the USSR. Criticism of "Yanqui" movies has become a means, within these middle class and even in bourgeois circles, of opposing North American policy.[229]

He added that the patronizing tone of the United States toward the Spanish people would not be tolerated:

> We must not forget, in any case, that the volume of American propaganda being spread by the embassy is vast, even if the content is completely stupid. They address themselves to Spaniards as if Spain was a backwards country with a mental age of ten years old.[230]

Furthermore, the Spanish people seemed to be indifferent to the invasion, and didn't even seem to care when the first North American battleship, *Northwestern Victory*, docked at Cartagena with great fanfare and air shows of US planes. Spaniards had lived through a brutal war on their own soil. These interlopers, by comparison, were pure Hollywood.[231]

Despite his "anti-yanqui" impressions, he would always cherish his encounter with Ernest Hemingway. Domingo Dominguín brought them together at the Madrid restaurant El Callejón, in 1954. Alas, for security, Jorge had to use a "cover' and Domingo introduced him using one of his multiple aliases: Agustín Larrea, sociologist. Hemingway was drinking, and was vocal in his contempt for sociology. At the same time, through the drunken haze, he very rightly suspected that Jorge/Agustín was not who he said he was. Hemingway feared he might be a journalist in disguise. Jorge would have given anything to come clean, but he couldn't, and Hemingway died in 1961—long before Jorge could be himself in Spain.[232] A frustrating encounter perhaps, but he had met Ernest Hemingway, one of his literary idols.

Jorge noted that the book fair (Feria del Libro) on the Calle Recoletos had a handful of customers. Books were expensive, and a luxury that few could afford. This dovetailed perfectly with the. Regime's patriotic dumbing down of the Spanish masses. Reading was censored and discouraged, and soccer and bullfighting were being promoted as the new opiates of the masses. Interest in these two sports had efficiently eclipsed potential conversations about political unrest.[233]

Yet despite the disheartening elements he saw, Jorge was full of hope. Despite Franco's apparent vise-like hold on his own country and international opinion, Jorge and the leaders of his party were convinced that the regime was a failure and that it could not last. Most of Jorge's optimism was pinned on university students. He knew how to approach them: after all, he had been a student himself when he had been recruited to join the French Resistance.

The young Spaniards were educated, they represented the future, and they had not lived through the Spanish Civil War. They did not have the firsthand fear their parents had lived through. Ironically, the infiltration of Franco-sanctioned American culture would make them aware that there were other options beyond Spanish borders. The deal with Eisenhower was a double-edged sword for Franco: the influx of dollars made him more popular with some, but they also revealed chinks in his dictatorial armor: his repressive tactics of the past had been protected by enforced isolation isolation that he was now glad to loosen, renting or selling to the highest bidder.

The PCE was not the only group trying to woo the students and gain power within the university. There were multiple factions vying for new recruits: monarchist supporters (directed by Rafael Calvo Serer); Catholic groups such as Opus Dei and Acción Católica; and the right-wing antimonarchist Falange leaders including Dionisio Ridruejo and Pedro Laín Entralgo. The Falange, once inextricably linked with Franco's mission, had lost power in the postwar years, but they officially ran the student union or SEU (Sindicato Español Universitario).[234] Jorge noted that there were hardly any Falange banners or flags flying during the July 18 annual celebration of the outbreak of the civil war. If the Catholic church and Opus Dei set out to corrupt, capture, and intimidate (*"corrupción, captación e intimidación"*), Jorge would try a different tack: seduce, capture, and educate.

Many of the factions looking for new members shared the conservative politics and Catholic values of Franco's regime, but they had been disenfranchised by his monolithic approach to government. Dissident representatives from these splinter groups were infiltrating the universities, and the PCE had to compete for students' attention.

Jorge made inroads with students, publishers, film producers and directors, and bullfighters. As he spent more time in his mother country, he reported back on the restlessness he sensed within Spain:

"Francoism is no longer capable of governing Spain. It needs to be replaced. This is, more or less clearly, expressed in all the conversations I hear about politics, and made clear by all the activities of various social forces in play. The question is: What should it be replaced by?"[235]

At the same time that each group waged its propaganda war, it suddenly seemed possible that these disparate factions might eventually coalesce to form an anti-Francoist front. The point was to get rid of Franco. Nobody had thought through what the next steps might be.

Just as Jorge was getting the hang of his new role in Madrid, and gathering momentum in his first few months of work at the university, the summer interrupted his activities.[236] The campuses emptied for the long vacation period (July–September), and between the heat and the Mediterranean cultural norms, even professional revolutionaries were forced to slow down and take a break. The PCE leadership had paid vacations every other year in Crimea and other Soviet spots. Jorge was still a few years away from enjoying these privileges, but in the meantime he spent the summers, and other periods, in France. In Paris he would meet secretly with Carrillo and other party leaders, and resume his "normal" life with Colette and his stepdaughter, Dominique.

Jorge quickly became the leader of the PCE's cultural insurgence aimed at Franco Spain's universities, publishing, and film worlds. His letters to his superiors in Paris through the mid-1950s show that he was optimistic yet worried about how to publicize the cause and educate his recruits. There was a scarcity of materials and books, and he complained that the party publications were not arriving on time. But despite short supplies, his commitment to the cause did not waver:

> Semprún became a booster, and a publicist in the truest sense of the word. He was a bridge between the party

leaders and the cultural world, first in exile (in Paris), and later inside Spain. There are two phases to his work: the first one started in January 1950, with the launch in Paris of the magazine *Cultura y Democracia*, and lasted until 1953. In the summer of that year, Semprún traveled clandestinely to Spain for the first time, thus starting the second phase, which would end ten years later in 1964 with the crisis in party leadership and his expulsion.[237]

In the 1950s, the university system in Spain was "rigid and static, and had not recovered from the devastating Franco purges of the faculty."[238] The Republican thinkers had been weeded out during and after the war, and what remained were professors who had collaborated in the purge of free thinkers. Closed-mindedness and strict Catholicism reigned. PCE events were designed to mobilize the students, to make them aware that they had both rights and voices. The regime was complacent and unprepared for student protests.

To understand why some of the events were subversive, it is important to keep in mind the cultural tensions in Spain in the early 1950s. Attending the funeral of a great, elderly writer, such as Pio Baroja, could be a charged statement against the regime. Circulating a non-Catholic philosophical text or a poem could be cause for suspicion. In the literary world, the latest scandal was an issue of the magazine *INDICE*, dedicated to Pio Baroja. The issue passed the Franco censors, but it was pulled at the last minute because of pressures exerted by the church.

The first official PCE event planned was a student homage upon the death of the Philosopher José Ortega y Gasset, and the second was a series of conversations about poetry. Gregorio Morán highlights the key role of Semprún in these illegal cultural activities:

In the summer of 1953, using the alias Federico Sánchez, Jorge Semprún arrived clandestinely in Spain from the safety of his Parisian exile. He managed to set up an infrastructure that was especially important for the Spanish film world (Muñoz Suay and Bardem), but also among university students thanks to the young Enrique Múgica. . . . The work he did with respect to the Spanish university essentially consisted of organizing cultural activities that provided an ideal forum to attract students and allowing them to express nonconformist opinions.[239]

Students risked prison for participating in any unofficial event, and many were arrested and served long sentences. These detentions impressed and galvanized other students, and planted the first seeds of dissent in Spain's postwar youth. In its approach the clandestine PCE was like a small-scale Spanish Communist version of the CIA-sponsored Congress for Cultural Freedom. Jorge Semprún, as Federico Sánchez, was key in organizing and influencing a network of Spanish students, artists, intellectuals, and editors who, in turn, slowly infiltrated Franco's repressive dictatorship where "ideas" were dictated and controlled by the Church.

As his work attracted new members, Jorge reported that everything was coming up roses as far as the PCE was concerned. The conservative SEU was losing its grip on the students, Spaniards on the street were turning against the arrival of the United States bases and money, and students were ready, willing, and able to lead the revolution. Was Jorge looking to give himself a positive performance report or was he truly optimistic? Was he just telling Carrillo what he wanted to hear? A few times he concludes his upbeat assessments by saying, "As you can imagine this is just a sample of a thousand things I will tell you more about, when we have a chance."[240]

He made a compelling case for his mission and for hope. On the economic and intellectual fronts, he thought, Spain was about to burst. He seemed sure that the enduring financial crisis, despite the American injections of cash, was pushing the average Spanish citizen to the limit. On February 24, 1954, he shared some general impressions and claimed that the economic frustrations were pushing people into radical political positions:

> Since the last time I reported, the situation here has become characterized by a sharpening radicalization. The contrast between the haves and have-nots has become more extreme with an ever-diminishing middle class. One sees more and more poorly clad people in the street . . . cuts in electrical supply . . . restrictions placed on industry and commerce; the agricultural crisis . . . the catastrophe that is the fishing industry . . . these are the most common themes in the surprising conversations I have had. . . . This great economic discontent is being translated, along with other factors I will mention later, into a radicalization of political attitudes.[241]

And he was extremely positive about the inroads the party was making in Spanish intellectual life:

> Above all, the new generations—thanks to the warmth and influence, however indirect, of our ideology—are really changing. Our political position is taking hold, and there is an enormous interest in the USSR. It is indeed heartening to see the progress we've made in the last few months. . . . Apart from a few cases of subjugation when faced with the regime's tactics—put into place out of fear of being overwhelmed by the intellectual movement—the general feeling here, on the contrary, is one that favors democratic positions. These are being reinforced by an older, liberal university generation and by groups of bourgeois intellectuals like those following Ortega y Gasset, and the odd progressive Catholic movement . . . along with other groups with more complicated ideological stances. . . . But above all one sees

it in the younger students coming along fired up if only indirectly by our ideology, our political position, and by an enormous interest in the Soviet Union. Seeing the progress made during these past months is very encouraging.[242]

The party seemed to have most of its hopes pinned on the students, and so far Jorge's efforts to educate his pupils were paying off. He was a first-rate professor, a talent he would maintain throughout his lifetime. His recruits had become natural revolutionaries, without even being aware of it. After a demonstration in which some students were beaten and arrested by the police, he wrote:

> What the students care about is that their classmates have been beaten. What they have started to demand is a change of regime; they have started to wage a fundamentally political battle, and they are—spontaneously—taking up the positions of our party. . . . The students disassociate themselves from the demonstration organized by the SEU. The Gibraltar issue does not interest them. What does interest them is that their classmates have been beaten. . . . What is implicit in what the students have been demanding is a change of regime; they've begun an essentially political battle spontaneously espousing the same positions our party does. . . . The great mass of students, without even realizing it, are developing initiatives on their own that could only called revolutionary.[243]

One of the most interesting people Jorge came into contact with was Dionisio Ridruejo. Ridruejo had been an engaged Falangist and *Franquista* until the end of World War II. In fact, he had been one of the coauthors of the Falangist anthem *"Cara al Sol."* During the Spanish Civil War, Franco made him Minister of Propaganda; however, his strong character and loyalty to the Falange above all led to his dismissal. By the mid-1950s he was an active anti-Francoist, and Jorge made contact with him. Ridruejo was an important figure in the dissident movement, and thought the PCE had a good shot at shaking up the regime. He had an insider's perspective, and insights that were useful to the PCE, as Jorge reported:

> The central thesis of Ridruejo is that in this day and age it is easier to fight against communism with the sort of regime seen in France than it is with the Franco regime. He said that the regime in France can withstand a strike lasting many weeks without having to make radical changes but that in Spain now, a strike lasting three days would bring it all down.[244]

According to Ridruejo, there were 10–15,000 Communists in Spain in 1954, all of them identified by the police.[245]

Jorge also noted his frustrations at trying to make contact with the publisher of a magazine identified only as "C," which may very well have been the literary and cultural journal *Clavileño*.[246] He confided that he was afraid, but he still seemed too boyish to earn people's trust. He signed his report affectionately "a big hug to all,"[247] and concluded another with the words of dutiful son who had been scolded for not writing longer letters: "As you can see, I have taken to heart your reproach about not writing enough." In another memo he simply expressed his sheer joy at being in Spain again.

He also gave updates about cultural developments in Spain, including new films such as Luis García Berlanga's *Novio a la vista*, and a screening he was organizing of *Battleship Potemkin*. He shared a joke that he overheard a retrograde monarchist tell: "A gentleman goes to a newsstand to buy the evening paper, and has the following exchange with the news agent: "May I please have a copy of *España*?" "Sold out." "What about *Pueblo*?" "All out." "And *Informaciones*?" "Go to the American embassy."[248]

In March 1954 he writes about his uncle, Miguel Maura, and refers to him as "Jorge and Gonzalo's uncle," thus slightly encrypting the fact that he himself is Jorge. He confirms that his uncle is back in Spain, that he has been able to reinstate his credentials as a lawyer, and is trying to garner anti-Francoist support from the student population:

> From the society pages: they have allowed Miguel Maura to register again with the College of Lawyers . . . Jorge . . . is assiduously developing relations within the university. It is clear that the students are interested as well especially in light of recent events.[249]

This note seems to suggest that Jorge was in touch with Miguel Maura and other members of his family in Spain. He mentions spending a few days with a female cousin, and his brother Alvaro must have known Jorge was in Madrid. This means that he was not always undercover.

In early 1954 Jorge was convinced that he and the PCE were on the right track and that their labors would soon bear fruit. He had been encouraged by meeting a law student at the Universidad Central (Complutense) who was "from a very good family" and spoke openly about the political engagement on campus.

> 9-2-54 . . . The importance of what is happening is spreading among many who have been participating without being conscious of what they were doing. For example, I had the opportunity to speak with a law student who comes from a "good family" and he described to me the battles going on within the Central University as if it were the most natural thing in the world, unaware of their enormous importance. What confidence this inspires! What most impresses me is being able to feel with my own hands the flow of vitality in these youths, easily oriented in the right direction as soon as you begin to work at it.[250]

In summary, in early 1954 Jorge knew that it would take time to change the situation in Spain, but he had hope that the day would come. He was deeply optimistic.

In 1956 Jorge spoke at the sessions of the PCE in Prague, and his optimism remained firm. These meetings were held after the XX Congress of the Communist Party of the Soviet Union, and the speeches reflected an awareness of the "new era" the Congress had inaugurated:

> We have entered a new period in the history of humanity, a new era of the Communist and workers movement throughout the entire world. . . . The (Spanish) student movements of February didn't come from a void. They are the fruit of approximately a year and a half of activity led by a coalition of opposition forces. . . . The idea of a National Congress of Students had taken off and is becoming an extraordinarily deep mobilizing force.[251]

A group of engaged students had written a manifesto, made public on February 1, in which they asked for the right to hold a National Congress of Students. The manifesto was written by a committee of students, including Jorge's recruit Javier Pradera.

The manifesto called on all students to participate in demonstrations and strikes to coincide with the meeting of the Executive Committee of UNESCO in Madrid on the 12th and 13th of April.

> We do this on this date—says the text—we the children of the victors and of the vanquished, because it is a date fundamental to a regime incapable of integrating us into any authentic tradition, to propose any sort of common future, to reconcile the differences between us and with Spain itself.[252]

This manifesto led to serious disturbances, which in turn led to the Falange being permanently marginalized because of its use of violence. On February 9, there had been a student meeting and the armed Falangists started a fight. In the ensuing violence, a young *falangista* from a very modest background was seriously wounded. Falange seized on this "providential blood" to denounce a supposed "Communist conspiracy" organized by the Soviet Embassy in Paris. In doing so, they evoked the memory of the horrors of the Spanish Civil War in the hopes of discouraging any kind of anti-Francoist activity. But their plan backfired, and they only fanned the fires of the anti-Regime students who raced through the streets yelling "Franco must die! Falange must leave! Down with the SEU!"

By the end of February 1956 the University in Madrid was firmly and quite unanimously opposed to the regime. This was a decisive step toward Spain's future.

> Quite suddenly, during those days in February, a unanimous feeling crystallized throughout Madrid society: the realization that it (Falange) was abnormal, contrary to the interest of public order. In the consciousness of large numbers of people, the Falange was discredited as being antithetic to the national good. And this will have enormous political consequences.[253]

Thanks to his effective role coordinating the clandestine resistance in Madrid, Jorge was made a member of the Executive Committee of the PCE in the summer of 1956, and through 1960 he continued to work, patiently and optimistically, to bring an end to Francoism. In these later years, the PCE's work became much more public. They wanted the foreign press to pay attention to Spain, and to collaborate in denouncing—to an international audience—the brutal repression Spaniards had lived under since 1939. They wanted networks of people to back them, in Italy, Belgium, and France. Foreign support, and pressure, was key to bringing amnesty and reconciliation to Spain. The PCE leaders had realized that they needed a vast coalition, from within and outside of Spain, to translate their goals into action.[254]

As the clandestine years passed, Jorge came to feel at home again in Spain. Some of the best descriptions of him in those years come from his friends and collaborators. Everyone seemed to remember his great talent for clandestine activities, and his seductiveness. Josep María Castellet recalled an episode in February, 1962, in Barcelona, when Jorge, aka "Federico Sánchez," appeared, as if by magic, in the elevator of his apartment building:

> I was driving quickly toward my house. There wasn't much traffic. Back then, the building facades in Barcelona were all still dirty from the civil war, and the streets were quite empty. . . . I parked on the corner of Provenca with Roger de Flor. . . . From the corner to Roger de Flor 215 there are about thirty meters. Visibility was clear. I automatically looked toward the entrance of my building, where I often ran into neighbors. Nobody was there. When I got to the gate, I looked toward the back of the lobby and walked in. I picked up my mail from the mailbox, went to the elevator, and opened the door. There was a man inside. It was impossible. It took me a few seconds to recognize him, in part because of the shock, because in the time I walked through the lobby and opened the elevator door nobody could have gotten past me. "José María," he said. . . . And suddenly I recognized the face and the voice: it was Federico Sánchez, Member of the Executive Committee of the Communist Party of Spain, which at the time was, obviously, a clandestine operation. I had met him a couple of years before. . . . He had certainly made an appearance . . . I asked him how he had gotten into the elevator, and he answered, laughing, that he was a professional of the clandestine world, and that he couldn't give his secrets away.[255]

One of the "safe houses" was that of Domingo González Lucas. Domingo came from a great family of bullfighters (his brother was the world-renowned Luis Miguel Dominguín), and he was a member of the PCE. In his highly entertaining memoir,[256] his son, Domingo Jr., recalls what it was like to have "a secret agent" as a frequent houseguest in his boyhood room, and how Jorge crossed the French/Spanish border whenever he pleased:

> As for Semprún, despite what anyone says, he got around in Madrid without any problems and was quite at home in my house especially. Next to my bedroom was a small storage room. I had the wall knocked down and an armoire built with an escape panel. It was a hiding place he could get into in case the police ever came looking for him because when he was in Madrid he often slept in my bedroom. He came to Madrid whenever he wanted to, by train or by a regular flight on Iberia. I don't recall him ever having to use the hiding place.[257]

Domingo also points out that his father, who was largely financing most of the PCE clandestine activities, never trusted or liked Carrillo:

> My father always said that Carrillo did not inspire confidence and that he was not the ideal person to lead the party because he was anchored in the communism of an earlier time, that he was a Stalinist and not equipped to understand the actual needs Spain had. He wanted to be like God in the Spanish Communist Party, to be everything, and he was not crazy about my father or Semprún, or Múgica or Pradera for that matter. In the end, all of them, intellectuals and various union leaders, left the party because of their bad relations with Carrillo.[258]

Semprún stayed in many people's houses during his clandestine
period. For a while, his brother Carlos worked with him, and his
recollections of the secret agent lifestyle are colorful and very different from Jorge's. The brothers were still close in the early fifties—
hence Jorge's interest in bringing Carlos along for the ride—but there
is no doubt that Carlos's memories are colored by their subsequent
falling-out. Nonetheless, they provide an amusing and lively contrast to Jorge's serious portrayal of the clandestine life. Carlos paints
his return to Madrid to work secretly for the PCE as boring, ano-
dyne, and pointless. He clearly would not have signed up for the job
if he had other options. He and their other younger brother, Paco,
had been practically abandoned in the chaos and poverty of the war
and postwar. During the 1940s and '50s, their adolescence and early
twenties, they lived without direction, ambition, or security of any
kind. He was predisposed to sign up for an adventure:

> Essentially we lived off a miniscule family pension while
> searching for and rarely finding opportunities to teach
> Spanish or do translations. When it was announced that the
> pension was about to run out, Paco and I had many anxious
> conversations about our future. He often arrived at the con-
> clusion that we should kill ourselves. The idea of actually
> going to work was not even considered! We didn't have any
> marketable skills anyway or diplomas, not even a basic high
> school diploma. My first two "jobs" that paid me anything
> were a translation of a thesis by a Latin-American student
> about varicose veins, and writing the prologue for a catalog
> of paintings by the Venezuelan artist Alejandro Otero.[259]

Carlos had always wanted to be like Jorge, and he became a clandestine PCE agent out of his fraternal admiration combined with his
penniless state. But he was never a true believer, as Jorge appears to
have been, and he was of inferior rank to his boss-brother, "Federico

Sánchez." Moreover, he seemed flummoxed by the lack of direct action in the party's activities. The slow, indirect, discreet tactics the PCE had adopted were frustrating to the slightly younger wannabe revolutionary. In Carlos's memories, the clandestine work in Madrid was disappointing:

> My first assignment, my first mission as a "professional rev-olutionary," took place at a café on the Calle San Bernardo where Federico Sánchez brought me to meet with Enrique Mújica, the first student who had asked to be admitted into the Spanish Communist Party. Seated next to him was a poet called Eugenio de Nora, who I took an instant dislik-ing to. This instantaneous antipathy was not only because he had written some dull poems dedicated to the *Pasionaria* using the pseudonym "Carlos del Pueblo," but also because of the way he spoke and dressed, and his ridiculous little hat.[260]

Carlos, deeply unimpressed by this "revolutionary meeting," is given his first official mission by Jorge: attend poet Eugenio de Nora's talk on social poetry at the University, and "take the temperature" of the masses in the audience. Nothing happened at the lecture: no police, no uproars. Carlos continued in this role of "human thermometer" at student cultural events and football games, and became, briefly, the Secretary of the Committee of Student Communists in Madrid. He remembers long hours of boredom during his "professional agent" period in Spain, and the details about his downtime and his sardonic tone are what make his perspective a memorable counterpoint to Jorge's accounts. Carlos gives a better sociological portrait of an agent's life than Jorge: his hotel room, at the Inglaterra on the Calle Echegaray, was surprisingly nice; he spent lots of time in his room. He couldn't walk around roaming his childhood haunts because his hard, cheap leather shoes had become torture instruments. He didn't know how to order a black coffee in Spanish ("*solo*," not "*negro*") and was worried that a banal everyday slip such as this might get him arrested. He enjoyed the three square meals at the safe house of Doctor José Antonio Hernández, while Jorge was fed, lodged, and had his naps at the superior home of film producer Ricardo Muñoz Suay, a former comrade of Carrillo's in the Unified Socialist Youth Party (JSU) during the war.

Jorge also had access to the rooftop swimming pool of his host family's apartment building. Carlos was never invited to come along for a swim, but he liked to go hang out with Ricardo Muñoz Suay when Jorge wasn't around. He also noted that though these host families had largish apartments, they couldn't afford to eat meat every day, and that what in France was a most basic car—the Citroen Deux Cheveaux—was a much-anticipated luxury for Doctor Hernández. Whenever Carlos came from Paris he did so with an enormous false-bottomed suitcase stuffed with propaganda materials, including PCE publications. That suitcase, part of the debris of history, is now in the attic of his first wife's home in a small village in rural New Hampshire.[261]

After Carrillo introduced them to each other in Paris, Jorge and Muñoz Suay grew close. The latter recalls their first meeting:

> After a few days of sharing information, Santiago Carrillo introduced me to Jorge Semprún in the dining room of some French house, the sort that would become so familiar to me. Jorge and I arranged to meet some weeks later in Madrid. It was then that we began to work at the rarely easy task of gathering together groups of communist intellectuals. Starting with a nucleus made up of people connected with the film industry, we expanded our efforts finding intellectuals who, preferably, were either tied to the film or literary world.[262]

In the Muñoz Suays, Jorge found another family. He especially liked spending time with Ricardo's wife, Nieves Arrazola. She was a few years older than Jorge, and had spent two years in prison (1946–1948) for anti-Francoist activities. She was also a fantastic cook and a savvy survivor who knew Franco Spain much better than Jorge and Carlos. She promptly told Jorge to get himself some Spanish shoes, and instructed Carlos to cut his Parisian long hair. She feared they would stick out like sore thumbs and put them and everyone they worked with at risk.

> It was not as if I had hundreds of contacts and so sometimes I'd go to the Prado Museum or to Muñoz Suay's house. Hanging out there mostly meant hanging out with Nieves (his wife) because in those days Ricardo worked very hard. Being there was sitting in their library, having a coffee, having paella and long talks with Nieves. I've a weakness for hearing stories and Nieves was a wonderful conversationalist with a brusque style and sectarian points of view. She was an old-school, authentic communist, the real thing. We got along famously. It was a true delight to be there with her in their house. She stopped criticizing me for my shoes when I got some Spanish ones. She was absolutely right that I ran an unnecessary risk wearing French ones, something the Guardia Civil might notice.[263]

Berta, the Muñoz Suay's daughter, agreed with her mother, and remembered that even Jorge's cologne—Guerlain's Vetiver—gave him away as a foreigner. She also recalls that his affectionate party nickname, *Pajarito* ("little bird" in Spanish) was thanks to her inability to pronounce "Federico."

> I can still remember it. I would get home from school and know before I even opened the door if Semprún was there because he wore a particular cologne. Jorge was an actor. The library and the dining room were separated by a pair of

doors with mottled glass panes. Suddenly they would open and there he'd be. He was like a movie star. I had trouble pronouncing the name "Federico" and so I called him *Pajarito* and that is how he got that nickname.[264]

Jorge, and Carlos—in his subordinate, naysayer role—had curious and unique lives going back and forth to Spain illegally. It was a strange routine, but the higher ranking PCE members were too wellknown to travel, and few among the lower ranks were trustworthy or polished enough to mingle with the Franco-era university students without blowing their cover.

Carlos left the PCE in 1957, and it wasn't until 1962 that he was able to openly return to Spain, reconnect with family he had not seen since 1936, and claim his inheritance. Jorge never mentions claiming his. During the trip Carlos saw his father's sister, Mercedes (who Alvaro had boarded with in the early 1950s) and his own sister, Susana. The sibling reunion was a disappointment and sheds light on the damning combination of family tensions and political differences that tore the Semprún Maura generation apart:

> Between my time as a clandestine militant with the PCE that came to an end in early 1957 and my return to clandestine life working with the FLP[265] starting in 1962, I made just one trip to Madrid. I went there to retrieve a small inheritance because in Paris we had nothing and in Madrid at least there was a little something. A certain Señor Domínguez who administered the Semprún estate as well as those of much wealthier families advised me not to sell my shares in the Aguila beer company, in the Madrid Metro and the few others I had. He said it was a terrible moment to sell and that some of them would soon rise in value significantly. Regardless, I sold everything immediately, for a terrible price, horrendous, as if I was ashamed to have money in Franco Spain, but not being

brave and honest enough to renounce the inheritance for that same reason. I think I cleared around 300,000 1962-valued pesetas, which was a huge sum for us but, in real terms it was not all that much and it lasted a very short while.

While I was there I did all I could to avoid running into any former PCE comrades because many had left the party but I wasn't sure who exactly and so I spent my time visiting with family. I saw almost all of them. The most amusing was Mercedes (Mercedes Semprún de Smith—yes, friends, she had married an American with that original last name—but he had died in 1959 and that's all I know about him). She expressed her monarchist anti-Franco sentiments with such fervor at various cafés we frequented that sometimes I feared for my life. Mercedes had some sort of relationship with the Prado Museum, either professional or as a benefactor, and she organized tours and conferences there.

But the strangest case was that of our older sister Susana. Informed of my presence in Madrid by Señor Domínguez who told her which hotel I was in, she called to invite me to meet her at a cafeteria right next to where she lived. I could hardly recognize her. . . . She apologized for not inviting me up to her apartment, claiming some excuse or other about some guests she had staying with her, but the truth was that her husband, a man with the amazingly long last name of Aguirregomezcorta, refused to see anyone even remotely affiliated with the Left. We had a very dull conversation that left a bitter taste in my mouth.[266]

In retrospect, it is hard to imagine that during his nine clandestine years, 1953–1962, Jorge really believed his initial vision that the Franco regime was on its last legs and that revolution was imminent. Was there a true link between elite Spanish university students and the working class? Did anybody ever think for a moment that such a link could be capable of galvanizing a people's movement that would send Franco and his army running for the hills? Carrillo's forecast, from a distance, was based on his constant analysis of the Spanish press, and Jorge's reports. His conclusions were always clear: the regime was "extremely" weak, and en route to self-destruction.[267] He always pointed to its weaknesses, and avoided mentioning its self-evident strength: its total power in Spain.

And what about the weaknesses of the PCE? Nearly twenty years had passed since Franco's victory. What kind of real revolutionary progress were they making? By the time Jorge had spent seven years as a clandestine agent, he started to question the party's approach. There had been major international events along the way, particularly in the mid 1950s, that had weakened the PCE's potential grip in Spain. The regime's welcome of an influx of North American dollars and culture—Hollywood, grilled cheese sandwiches, tourism, and so forth—had given Franco a positive spin internationally. On the other hand, Nikita Khrushchev's 1955 attack on Stalin's cult of personality and uses of brutal repression had shaken the party to its core. To make matters worse, Spain was also voted into the United Nations in 1955, with the approval of the Soviet Union. How could the Soviet Union, the active supporters of the Spanish republic during the Civil War, and the current PCE backers, vote Franco's Spain into the UN? The PCE leaders and comrades felt deeply betrayed. The Hungarian Revolution of 1956 would also be divisive and cause many comrades and fellow travelers worldwide to distance themselves from their respective parties. In Hungary the revolts were led by students, who were brutally crushed by Soviet forces. In 1960, Jorge traveled to Moscow and was disappointed by his meeting with Mikhail Souslov, the chief ideologue of the Communist Party of the Soviet Union. During their conversation, Jorge realized that Spain was of no interest to Moscow, except insofar as the PCE could be manipulated to bolster Soviet politics and self-image.[268] Given these developments, how could Communism still be held up as an appealing alternative to Francoism?

Jorge didn't give up. He was deeply entrenched in the PCE family by end of the 1950s. In 1958 he had his first party holiday in the USSR, and took Colette and Dominique to spend the summer on the Black Sea in Sochi. They spent days on the beach, and shared meals, with Carrillo and his family. La Pasionaria was nearby. It was not easy to distance himself from the party when even his time off was spent on a "busman's holiday." His was truly a full-time job, and one that required total commitment: to ideology, risk-taking, travel, and lifestyle. In 1960 Jorge and his family would again vacation with the party in Crimea, and along with the usual suspects, this time they were joined by the legendary Colonel Enrique Líster. His military record covered the Spanish Civil War, the Cuban Revolution, and the Yugoslav People's Army. These were vacations in the elite Soviet Civil Servant style. The photographs of Carrillo and Semprún's families together are wonderful propaganda for the PCE: the adults and children pose after a healthy day at the beach, freshly bathed, everyone's hair carefully combed into place, wearing sensible summer clothes.

Semprún had become particularly close to one of his recruits, Javier Pradera. Pradera was eleven years younger, but he was extremely bright and also had an unlikely background for a Communist. He came from a conservative family in San Sebastian and both his grandfather and father were killed by anarchists at the beginning of the Spanish Civil War. Pradera had joined the air force under Franco, but he quickly became an important ally to the PCE. He and Jorge had an excellent political and intellectual relationship, though not without its tensions, and they both saw that the only way to coalesce forces against Franco was to appeal to people's desire to see a national reconciliation take place. They had appealed to students and other young Spaniards by addressing them all in the famous manifesto of February 1956 as "the children of the victors and the vanquished" (*hijos de los vencedores y vencidos*). This was the first time since the end of the Spanish Civil War that it had crossed anyone's mind to publicly suggest that the chasm dividing the Spain's new generations—along the lines of their parents' political fate after 1939—might not be insurmountable. This politics of reconciliation would not take immediate effect, but it foretold the way Spanish democracy would eventually unfold after Franco's death.

Semprún and Pradera's new approach ruffled feathers in the PCE leadership, for it questioned fundamental Communist principles and approaches. Surely, Carrillo and Pasionaria could see that the best they could hope for was to build a coalition and play a part in bringing the regime down. The Communist Party would never have more than a small role in a democratic Spain, and to guarantee that role its members had to experiment with new approaches. But the PCE was not open to auto-critiques.

One of the most significant blows to the PCE had been the complete failure of the Peaceful National Strike, (*Huelga Nacional Pacífica* or HNP). The strike had been pitched as a massive success even before it was supposed to take place, on June 18, 1959. It turned out to be a complete failure with no turnout, and Carrillo continued to hype it up as a victory. Javier Pradera wrote to Carrillo to offer him a first-hand report and correct his delusional, optimistic view. Carrillo did not take well to being told off by a subordinate. This started a series of tense arguments. Jorge, as Pradera's mentor, became involved and, though he tried, he had trouble "repressing" his friend's views because he actually agreed with them. Despite Jorge's optimistic reports, his mission was losing steam. In Paris, Jorge's intellectual party ally was Fernando Claudín. Claudín, eight years older than Jorge, was also a member of the PCE Executive Committee. He too was distancing himself from Carrillo's blind support of Soviet policies, and he was frustrated by Carrillo's ignorance of the new socioeconomic realities in Spain. Carrillo had worked closely with Claudín for so long that he had come to call him his "other self," but, as Paul Preston says, in his biography of Carrillo: "The Stalinist rigidity with which Carrillo reacted to criticisms of his misinterpretation of Spanish reality would convert a potentially creative debate into a debilitating internal crisis."

Much has been written on the internal divisions that led Jorge, and his fellow comrades Fernando Claudín and Javier Pradera, to be expelled from the PCE in 1965. It was a slow, tense, and painful process. First, Jorge was removed from his position as "Federico Sánchez." In 1962 he made his last clandestine trip to Spain. He would wait sixteen years, until 1978, to publish his version of his breakup with Carrillo. He was replaced by Julián Grimau, who already had some experience working in Spain, in Barcelona and Andalusia. Grimau was, tragically, the wrong man at the wrong time, to replace Jorge. The increase in student activism and the failed general strike (HNP) had sharpened the claws of Franco's authorities, and by the late 1950s and early 1960s they were eager to arrest insurgent leaders and make examples of them.

Grimau was a marked man. He had participated actively in the Spanish Civil War as a member of the Republican Police Force,[269] and fled to Mexico and later France during his exile. Compared to Jorge, who the police never identified as Federico Sánchez, Grimau was a "grown-up," a veteran enemy, and useful prey.

Grimau was arrested on November 7, 1962. He was beaten and tortured, and thrown out of the prison window, ostensibly to make his death seem like a suicide and to cover up evidence of torture. To make things more gruesome, he did not die from the fall out the window, and survived to be returned to prison and await his execution for months. For the first time in twenty-two years—since the 1939 end of the Spanish Civil War—the world paid attention to Spain. There was an international outcry to protest Grimau's torture, and his phony trial and the ensuing death sentence. Letters arrived from around the world, and two of the most vocal defenders of Grimau were Simone Signoret and Yves Montand, who had joined Jean-Paul Sartre in making sure the French people finally knew what was going on south of their border. It was at this time that Jorge first became close to Yves Montand, beginning a friendship that would change his life.[270]

Grimau's arrest made Jorge, and those around him, aware of the full extent of the dangers he had been facing for nearly a decade. Inevitably, he thought: why Grimau and not me?

Grimau's ludicrous 1963 trial included charges against his crimes during the Civil War, and no witnesses were allowed for the defense.[271] He was executed on April 20, 1963, at Carabanchel prison in Madrid.

During Jorge's last official period in Madrid in 1961, before Grimau's arrest, he had shared a home on Concepción de Bahamonde Street, near the Ventas bullring, with his comrade Manuel Azaustre and his wife María. Manuel had also been a Republican refugee in France, and had been hired by a work detail under the supervision of the French army.[272] After the 1940 armistice he was captured, along with many French prisoners of war, and deported to Mauthausen. He had survived.

After dinner, when Jorge and Manuel would have their brandy and cigars, Manuel liked to talk about his experiences in the camp, a subject Jorge himself had repressed and compartmentalized for nearly two decades.

> Manuel A. was a survivor of that camp, a ghost like me. Over various evenings he described to me what his imprisonment had been like in Mauthausen. I didn't recognize anything. I could not identify with him. He told his story in a confusing, disordered manner, he got lost in the details. It lacked any sort of overarching vision. Everything he said came from a single perspective. It was testimony in its most brute form.[273]

Jorge tried to help Manuel along as he recounted his jumbled memories, but he was frustrated at his digressions, much like Don Quixote's exasperated edits of Sancho's clumsily meandering tales. Because Manuel could not know Jorge's true identity—he thought he was Federico Sanchez—or that he had been in Buchenwald, Jorge was forced to listen and could only make discreet comments and questions. After a week of such evenings, Jorge woke up in the middle of the night, sat down at his portable Olivetti typewriter, and wrote his own story, starting with the image of all the people crammed into the train to Buchenwald. At first he had no intention of publishing it. How could he, as a clandestine agent? But the manuscript, written in a matter of days between appointments at his comrade's apartment, would become his passport back to the nonclandestine world. When it came out in 1963 under the title *Le Grand Voyage*, Jorge Semprún was reborn.

Carrillo, in his patronizing, paternalistic sketch of Semprún, claims that Jorge had always been a writer—a bourgeois intellectual—and that, from the start, it was a matter of time before he followed his true path:

> In contrast to aspects that characterize his image today, back then Jorge was a simpler soul and even modest. He never spoke about his experiences in the French Resistance or his suffering at Buchenwald; events to which he apparently gave little importance even though they formed the backbone, along with his clandestine activities in Spain afterward, of what would become his literary works. In those days he opted for just living his life, renouncing memories and writing, even though hidden beneath all that was his true vocation, literature.[274]

But Jorge, in his 1978 autobiographical account of his expulsion from the PCE, had the last word. It was a cheap shot on Carrillo's part to retroactively cast doubt on the integrity of Jorge's work, and his decade-long sacrifices on behalf of the PCE and the charismatic leadership he had given the party's operations in Spain. Jorge had been loyal and resourceful, and had put his life on the line for the PCE.

One of the greatest homages to Jorge's work in Spain was published after his death by Fernándo Sáncho Dragó:

When I first met him in the summer of 1954 next to a refreshment stand in the Retiro Park in Madrid, he was called Federico Sánchez. For a long time afterward, despite the intense years of anti-Francoist activity that united us and that sometime split us apart, I never knew he was Jorge Semprún. On that first day, thanks to his counsel and blessing, I joined the Spanish Communist Party.

I did not need much convincing. I was already committed. But if it had been necessary he would have been the man to do it because his seductive power was second to none. The truth is he seduced all of us: Enrique Mújica, Julián Marcos, Javier Pradera, Julio Diamante, Emilio Sanz Hurtado, Alberto Saoner, Ramon Tamames, Jaime Maestro, Manolo Moya, Ángel González, Pepe Esteban and Javier Muguerza.

I don't think any of them still alive would disagree with me when I say that without the activity of Federico Sánchez, who later and mysteriously was also referred to as Agustín, the massive anti-Franco demonstration that took place in February 1956 and the student protests against the regimen would not have happened. His influence in the agonizingly slow process of the regime's deterioration was fundamental and his talent for conspiring worthy of a spy movie.[275]

His work in Spain had come at a great personal expense. Colette had worried about his safety for many years. His son Jaime lived in Paris with his mother, Loleh, and her husband Claude Roy. When Jorge embarked on his clandestine double life, Jaime was five years old. By the time Jorge returned and settled in Paris again, in 1962, Jaime was fifteen, and it would prove impossible to recover those lost years between father and son. Jorge had promised to take his son on one of his party summer holidays to the Soviet Union, and Jaime was thrilled to accompany him, but in the end he was left behind in France. His father brought him a Russian watch as a souvenir, but it was already too late to make amends.[276]

VI

A Star Is Born

I don't think that a political struggle can be compared to
a literary struggle. Literature is less satisfying. Nothing
can replace political action. Nothing can replace the
experience of seeing one's vision transform reality. That is
truly the purest joy of creation for me.
—Jorge Semprún, 1969[277]

The 1960s brought enormous changes to Jorge Semprún's life. During this decade he became a world-famous, prize-winning writer and public intellectual. Fame put the definitive nail in the coffin of Federico Sánchez and all his other clandestine identities, and thrust Jorge Semprún into the spotlight. The man who had been hidden in the dark crevices of the Spanish Communist Party suddenly became an international star. The highlights of these years are better known. Those familiar with him may have read his books from this period, and people of a certain age around the globe will remember articles, images, and interviews from the media.

His transition from secret agent to famous author was not a clean cut. There were overlapping years of tensions and intrigue on the part of his PCE superiors before he was officially expelled. There are multiple zigzags during the 1963–1965 period before Jorge's full emancipation from the party. He had to play a bit of hide-and-seek with the non-PCE world before he could come out of the political closet.

It was after Julián Grimau's 1962 arrest in Madrid that Carrillo decided that Jorge should be removed permanently from any clandestine work in Spain. Carrillo claimed Jorge/Federico Sánchez had been in the field for too many years, and that for everyone's security it was safer to replace him. Jorge did not agree. On the contrary, he thought that it was a high risk to bring someone else in, and that more precautions should have been taken to protect his substitute; but the decision was approved by the PCE Executive Committee and he acquiesced.[278]

Just before Grimau, Jorge was first replaced by José Sandoval, a comrade who had spent all of his exile years in the Eastern bloc. Their initial encounter in Madrid was in front of the Prado Museum.[279] Sandoval had been a Communist since his youth, and was committed to the party. But he was ten years older than Jorge and a native of Asturias (vs. Madrid), and had the veneer of a Soviet apparatchik. Sandoval lasted a year and a half, until his arrest in 1964. He was tortured and sentenced to fifteen years, of which he served ten.[280] The shorter sentence was thanks to the partial amnesty law that came into effect after Franco's death in 1975. His arrest was part of a generalized crackdown on PCE allies and infiltrators at the University of Madrid.

From the time Sandoval filled in for Jorge in Madrid, the latter's responsibilities were severely reduced to being a member of the Executive Committee and working with the Communist intellectuals in exile, such as the writer, and also PCE Executive Committee member Jesús Izcaray.[281] Izcaray may have been a writer, but he was a party writer and an ideologue, not a cultivated thinker like Jorge.

Carrillo suggested that Jorge take advantage of the end of his clandestine duties to straighten out his legal residency in France, and in 1963 Jorge sorted out his papers and started living under his own name. To help speed the process along and preclude any complications, he used his connection with the influential Catholic resistance hero Reverend Alexandre Glasberg (*l'Abbé* Glasberg).[282] Glasberg was an old Semprún family friend who had helped Jean-Marie Soutou escape imprisonment by SS Captain Klaus Barbie.[283] Despite Jorge's years of work in the Communist Party, conservative family ties and Catholic power still played a part in his life.

With his legal status in order, he married Colette in Villeneuve-Loubet, a village on the Côte d'Azur between Nice and Cannes. The wedding banquet was held at a restaurant called *La Toque blanche*, between La Colle and Saint-Paul.[284] It had taken Jorge and Colette many years to marry—until his clandestine work was over and he could legally apply for a marriage license. This moment was Jorge's

debut as an official husband and father. He would eventually adopt Dominique, and Claude Roy (Loleh Bellon's husband) did the same for Jaime. It was a complex intergenerational stepparent game of musical chairs. It cannot have been easy to wait for Jorge while he was Federico Sánchez, but Colette was a sturdy *parisienne* with *bretonne* roots, and she was much more resistant than her delicate features might suggest. She was, in fact, the ideal companion for Jorge. Though Jorge would continue to travel frequently over the years, he and Colette stayed together until her death in 2007.

Her first husband, Dominique's father Jacques, had also been a prominent Communist and the head of the famous "722" Saint-Germain-des-Prés cell. And her father Marcel Leloup was a war hero who had volunteered during World War I and fought valiantly before having his arm blown off by a German machine gun. He was part of Léon Blum's cabinet, became General Director of France's Forestry and Water commission after the liberation, and moved on to be the International Director of Food and Agriculture Association at the United Nations. In short: his new father-in-law was a man Jorge could openly and enthusiastically admire, and the feeling was mutual. Leloup single-handedly organized Jorge and Colette's beautiful wedding. Colette was, perhaps understandably, never enamored of Spain, and from 1963 onward Paris was Jorge's home base, while Spain receded into the background of their daily life.

Semprún's personal, intellectual, and professional lives all started to undergo a "transition to democracy." He was starting to shake off the oppressive ideologies—fascism and communism—that had shaped his fate for nearly thirty years. He had declined his 1962 paid party vacation in the Eastern bloc, and opted instead to spend the summer holidays in Capri, at the home of Mario Alicata, the Director of *L'Unita*.[285] Alicata was a Communist, but he was Italian, and a man of letters. The major Italian Communist leaders, including Giancarlo Pajetta and Rossana Rossanda, were modern politicians connected to contemporary events. They weren't stuck in a post-1945

no-man's-land like Carrillo. In Italy, Jorge and Colette spent time with Spanish writer Juan Goytisolo and his future wife, the French writer and editor Monique Lange. These new friends would be a great help to him, and their friend Florence Malraux, the film editor who was the daughter of André Malraux and the wife of film director Alain Resnais, would be crucial to his future.

Goytisolo, an expat from Spain who also had settled in Paris, was a new kind of friend for Jorge. He was a serious author, and a maverick in every way. Though he opposed the Franco regime and had sympathy for the PCE, he was an idiosyncratic fellow traveler. His priority was freedom, and he eschewed ideologies because, to him, they all required the sacrifice of some liberty or other. Jorge admired Goytisolo, and may have been a bit envious of his independence. Goytisolo, in turn, was impressed by Jorge, and may have been a bit daunted, as time progressed, by his burgeoning superstardom. In other words, they were worthy friends. Jorge described their first meeting in 1961 at a café terrace on the Castellana:

> There began to crystallize between us that strange nebula of feelings that eventually constitutes a friendship . . . full of shared surprised, passions, silences, and tears.[286]

Goytisolo recalled:

> Though nobody had told me about Semprún/Federico Sánchez's double identity, it didn't take me long to put things together and figure it out. Monique was also fascinated by him, and his Janus-like double face. In contrast to the other Spanish exiles, who were leaden and clumsy, and whose eternal nostalgic discourse about Spain was like an old, unbearable broken record, Jorge was cultivated, seductive, poised, and brilliant. He was right at home in the French intellectual scene.[287]

Goytisolo and Monique lived on the rue Poissionière, and their home became a salon for Jorge and Colette, and for Fernando Claudín—also still a member of the PCE Executive Committee—and his wife Carmen. Jorge and Claudín's intellectual and personal concerns had outgrown the narrow PCE confines, and they were glad to have a milieu where ideas could be exchanged freely. It was also at this time that Jorge's friendship with Yves Montand and Simone Signoret began to develop. The seeds were planted for a productive and affectionate relationship with Montand, whom he would come to call his "real" brother. He was not as enthusiastic about his relationship with his own six siblings, and Montand had a difficult relationship with his brother, Julien, so both men celebrated finding a new fraternal ally.

While still a member of the PCE Executive Committee, Jorge was establishing important personal and professional connections in the literary and cinematic milieus of Paris. If we think of his situation in matrimonial terms, it is as if he was still legally married to Carrillo, but had moved out and into his own apartment for a trial separation. Divorce was not far off.

Thanks to the encouragement of Monique Lange, Jorge had started to circulate his manuscript of *The Long Voyage*. The editor who decided to publish it was, curiously enough, Claude Roy.[288] Roy worked at the legendary publishing house Gallimard, and Jorge knew him because he was now married to Jorge's first wife, Loleh Bellon. Roy was also Jaime's new father, to all intents and purposes. The circles of the Parisian intelligentsia in the early 1960s were quite small indeed.

The Long Voyage was originally published in France in May 1963, and in his review in *Libération*[289] Roy himself hailed Semprún as "the revolutionary Proust." Jorge later gratefully remembered, "It was Claude Roy who discovered *Le grand voyage*. It was thanks to him that it was published, and that I exist as a writer."[290]

The publication was Jorge's baptism as the engaged European literary man of the moment. This first novel was awarded the 1963 international Prix Formentor.

The Formentor was a major prize at the time and the jury knew its decision would launch the writer's career. The Spanish editor Carlos Barral recalled the competition, and the tension among the jury members, in the following way:

> There were wars, skirmishes, and not all of them were above board. In May '63, in Corfu . . . the principal candidates to the Premio Formentor were Mario Vargas Llosa's *La ciudad y los perros* . . . and the French-language novel *Le grand voyage* by Jorge Semprún. . . . It worked against Vargas Llosa that the previous year's winner had been a Spanish-language book, Juan García Hortelano's *Tormenta de verano* . . . and like it or not, these international awards take the rotation of languages and countries quite seriously; it's a kind of secret law. In Vargas's favor, on the other hand, was the fact that Semprún was a Spanish writer, although his novel was written in French, and that Vargas's book was much more ambitious. The opinion of the seven editors on the jury was split down the middle. The Spaniard, the Scandinavian, and the English members were for Vargas; the Italian, North American, and French members were for Semprún. It was quite obvious that the Parisian contingent, led by Monique Lange, were all rooting for Semprún.[291]

Juan Goytisolo also remembers the enthusiasm Monique had for Jorge's book: "We went to Capri one summer, Monique Lange and I and Jorge was there (I already knew he had been Federico Sanchez), and we got to know each other then and saw a lot of each other. It was at some point then that Jorge mentioned his manuscript of *The Long Voyage* and he showed it to Monique. She was very impressed with it and it was she who proposed it for the international novel prize that was celebrated, in Corfu that year I believe, and Jorge won the prize with that novel.[292]

The award and the enthusiastic press reception secured Jorge exceptional publishing deals: *Le grand voyage* was simultaneously translated and published in fourteen languages. The English language version, *The Long Voyage,* was published by Grove Press and translated by the American editor, publisher, and translator Richard Seaver.

The great secret of Federico Sánchez's identity was not so easy to conceal now that Jorge was a public figure. The writer and Federico Sánchez recruitee Fernando Sánchez Drago was shocked to see a photograph of his former political guru in an Italian newspaper. The caption said his name was Jorge Semprún, and that he was a novelist:

> It was in the early 1960s, '63, I think, when Federico Sánchez ceased to exist and Jorge Semprún showed up. It was a tremendous shock to me. I was having breakfast at the bar of a café in Padua. I opened *L'Unitá*, and saw on the first page that Carlos Barral, Gallimard, Einaudi, and other prestigious editors had given . . . the Formentor prize to one Jorge Semprún. I looked down, saw the photo that went along with the headline, and I dropped my cup of coffee on the floor . . . when I saw that it was Federico Sánchez, or Agustín, my party liaison, and my boss, who had won the prize with a novel titled *The Long Voyage.*[293]

Jorge was pulling away from the PCE leadership. He had read Alexander Solzhenitsyn's *A Day in the Life of Ivan Denisovich* and discovered the systematic brutality of the gulags. The impact of this book led him to profoundly question and overhaul his political thought. He had intense conversations about these matters with Fernando Claudín, and Javier Pradera. His disappointment with the Soviet Union was only amplified by his frustration at Carrillo and La Pasionaria's retrograde and fanatic loyalty to Moscow. With the failure of the 1959 General Strike in Spain (Huelga Nacional Pacífica), they should have finally realized that they were out of touch with Spanish reality. As Jorge saw things, based on his years of experience in Madrid, the transition to post-Francoism could only happen under a bourgeois hegemony, not a popular uprising. The best Spaniards could hope for, which was not bad—though it required endless patience—was to become a European democracy like Italy, or France.[294] This vision went against the rigid Stalinist ideals of the party. To the PCE leaders, Semprún and Claudín were "right-wingers," "defeatists," "anti-Stalinists," and "social democrats."[295]

By the end of 1964, Jorge and Claudín were having intense arguments with the rest of the PCE leadership, and the situation became even more hostile at the Executive Committee meeting, held at an old castle in Prague in April, 1964. Semprún and Claudín were provisionally suspended from their positions on the committee.

In December 1964, Claudín submitted the famous "Divergencias" report to the PCE, in which they outlined their issues with the party line, and by January 1965 they were expelled. Carrillo concluded that "It was better to be wrong with the party, inside the party, than to be right from the outside, or to go against it,"[296] and La Pasionaria dismissed Claudín and Semprún as "bird-brained intellectuals."[297]

Claudín's daughter Carmen (named after her mother) has a powerful childhood memory of what it was like when her father was expelled from the Communist Party. It was comforting to her that Jorge and her father continued to be friends after those ties were broken:

> My father and Jorge were arguing with the party all during 1964 and then there was the famous meeting of the political bureau that took place in a castle in Prague, the one he writes about in a number of his novels. I didn't know anything about any of this of course back then but both of them knew with certainty that they were going to be expelled. It was not a surprise to them in the least but they wanted to air their views, to be heard. The details of their expulsion

are contained in a document that was called "the little blue book" that must still be around somewhere, that includes their analysis of the situation as they saw it.

I had no idea what was happening within the party. I didn't know who my father was within the party. To me they were all the same; Jorge, all of them. The key year for me was 1964, the year when I first got to visit Spain. I discovered Spain in the summer, and then that Christmas too, and during that time I'd no idea my father had been expelled from the party. I think he and my mother were waiting for some sort of adequate moment to tell us. But then I found out about it in the most banal way that I will tell you now. The way I discovered that my father had been expelled is very illustrative.

There was another party member who was called Pepe who came to our house pretty much every day, a house where the only people who visited were trusted party stalwarts. And given how young I was Pepe seemed like a much older man to me. On top of that his hair was gray and the word "Pepe" was one French children used for "grandfather." And so here was this man who came to our house so often and who was so close to my father and who always took the time to chat with us children, giving us candy and kisses always before shutting himself into a room with my father for one of their serious talks and then being equally kind to us before leaving. He was like my adopted grandfather. And for me he was the same as Semprún, as Carrillo, they were all alike to me.

That Christmas in France I went with my mother to the market next to where we lived, in that neighborhood that was the home, the emblematic *banlieue* for the French Communist Party where they celebrated the *l'Humanité* and all of that. So there we were shopping for a few special

things for the Christmas meal when all of a sudden I saw
Pepe and before my mother had time to react I ran up to
him and put my arms around his neck. I adored him. He
was my Pepe. I was thirteen or fourteen years old and he
was a large man and I was hanging from his neck, my feet
off the ground, when I realized he was not reacting. He just
stood there like a statue. He didn't hug me or try to ease me
down or say anything. I turned my head around to look at
my mother and she, with tears running down her face, said
to me, "Carmen, come, come back." Pepe did not dare risk
giving that thirteen-year-old a kiss on the cheek. He didn't
dare.

Because of this incident my father sat me down and
explained things. I remember it very well, the two of us
there together, and by the way, speaking of Jorge, when my
father explained that it had been the two of them who had
gone through the disagreeable experience together I thought
to myself, "Good," because Jorge was my very favorite of all
of them. It is hard to describe but in a way he and his family
were our family as well back then and they lived in an apartment that fascinated me, it was nothing at all like the drab
typical flats assigned to party members, like the one you see
in *La Guerre est finie*, each one with its little framed print of
Picasso's dove. My parents had a very different aesthetic but
the apartments were always the same. Jorge's apartment in
Saint-Germain-des-Prés was amazing. I remember thinking, the fact that my father and Jorge would continue to be
friends was something important for me.[298]

For both men the expulsion had been a brutal experience. They were
both long-standing professional revolutionaries, and without his job
Claudín had no papers, money, home, or income. He was slandered by
the party and was subsequently pressured, and intimidated, to accept

a "generous offer" to resettle permanently in obscurity in the Soviet Union.[299]

The new economic reality of the Claudín family made their life impossible and they depended on the help given to them by Jorge and Colette to keep going for a time:

> When they expelled my father his steady salary, his party stipend and all of the logistical support the party provided evaporated. All of the Spanish Communists we lived close to, and their children, treated us like pariahs. My sister was ten years old at that time and my parents lived in constant fear we would be kicked out of our apartment. My father finally went to speak with the party member in charge of the neighborhood asking him to at least give us a month's notice before an eviction so that we might have time to find another solution. He didn't say yes or no. But I think Carrillo ordered them to leave us alone. Everything else disappeared. There was no money to live on at all.
>
> For a while we lived thanks to help from my father's family and friends like Jorge who helped us greatly and took us on vacations. It was especially hard for my mother. She is ninety years old now and has still not recovered really. Thanks to the three Communist friends of ours who did continue to speak to us my mother finally got a job teaching in a private school. She couldn't work in a public school because she was not a French citizen. She taught math, Russian, and Spanish. Suddenly we were living thanks to my mother's salary. My father, who had always been out and about and involved with the revolution, now stayed at home all day long while my mother who had always been at home became the wage earner, getting back late at night. Ours was a wartime economy and in truth we survived thanks to the kindness of people like Jorge and Colette.[300]

Jorge's situation was less drastic because he resided legally in France had a beautiful home with Colette, and a promising literary career. Nonetheless, getting kicked out of the PCE infuriated and hurt him deeply. Twelve years after the fact he published his 1977 *Communism in Spain* that recounts his clandestine years and his expulsion. It is a great literary example of revenge being served cold, or at least *semi-froid*. The lively narrative is fueled by a staccato of intense anger that leaps off nearly every page.

The year 1966 was a milestone year in Jorge's life. His friend Florence Malraux had given her husband, filmmaker Alain Resnais, a copy of *The Long Voyage*.[301] Resnais, who had made the movies *Night and Fog*, a short about the Nazi camps, *Hiroshima, mon amour* and *Last Year at Marienbad*, was fascinated by Jorge. In addition to a shared artistic and historical interest in the camps, they were both drawn to experimental narratives and memory. Resnais asked Jorge to write a screenplay about his clandestine work in Spain, and the product was *La Guerre est finie*. Yves Montand was cast as Diego, Jorge's fictional alter ego, and the film won several prizes.

Suddenly the forty-four year old Jorge Semprún, the ex-Communist, was a prize-winning novelist and screenwriter. *La Guerre est finie* was nominated for the Academy Award for best original screenplay in 1968, and his next screenplay, for the 1970 film *Z*, cowritten with and directed by Constantin Costa-Gavras, was nominated for best screenplay "based on material from another medium." Jorge did not take home an Oscar, but the nominations were huge international honors, and *Z* did win Oscars in two other categories: Best Foreign Picture and Film Editing. It was the first film in Hollywood history to be nominated for both Best Picture and Best Foreign Picture.

In 1966, Jorge's father, José María Semprún Gurrea, died in Rome. He was seventy-five years old, and had lived in exile for thirty years, since 1936 when the Spanish Civil War broke out. Jorge had not spent much time with him in the last two decades of his life. José María and his wife Annette had found a cozy refuge in Rome. José María was

given a religious funeral with maximum Catholic pomp and circum-
stance. Carlos recalls that all the siblings were at their father's deathbed except for Jorge: "Jorge wasn't there. He was at a film festival,
Karlovy-Vary, I think."[302]

Strained father-son relationships seemed to run in the family.
Jorge's son, Jaime, turned twenty-one in 1968. Though Jorge had dedicated the 1963 *The Long Voyage* to him ("*A Jaime, parce-qu'il a 16 ans*"),
their relationship was in decline and they would soon sever all ties.
Jorge would not mention Jaime again in public, nor would he dedicate
any more books to him. According to those close to Jaime, it was his
decision never to speak to his father again, but he died before Jorge so it
is impossible to know directly from either party what really happened,
and their relatives have remained quiet about the estrangement.

Jaime was an exceptionally handsome fellow, and like his father,
he was involved in the film world. He was a close friend of Philippe
Garrel, a well-known French actor and film director. Jaime had a role
in one of Garrel's films *Le lit de la Vierge*, which was filmed on location in Morocco, and he made two films of his own: the suggestively
titled short *Le meurtre du père*, and a feature-length film, *La Sainte
famille*, both from 1968. He was also a radical thinker, a disciple of
Guy Debord, and a Marxist theorist who had a major role in galvanizing the May 1968 revolts in Paris, and he was highly influenced by
the *International situationniste* movement. At the time, there was a brief
article in *Le Nouvel Observateur* about Jaime called *Le repas le plus long*:

> Jaime Semprún, the son of Loleh Bellon and Jorge Semprún,
> is a handsome 20-year-old who hasn't done much (as he
> himself says) since passing his baccalaureate, aside from
> making a color film short for television. *The Father's Murder*
> tells the day in the life of a young man who wants to kill his
> father at all costs. In the end, he doesn't go through with it.
> Jaime Semprún says that the film is entirely autobiograph-
> ical. Despite all this, he seems to be a family man, since he

asked Maurice Garrel and his son Philippe to okay, respectively, the roles of the father and of the son. It seems that Jaime Semprún's keen sense of family is still going strong: his first feature-length film has been christened "The Holy Family." . . . The story is quite surprising as it all takes place during a meal (a family meal, of course), which lasts from 1870 to the present. . . . As "history" accelerates, according to Jaime Semprún, the structure of the family disintegrates. . . . Someone yells "To Cuba" . . . others sign petitions for the liberation of Greek and Russian writers, and we hear bits of conversation, such as, "Not only is he in prison, but he is also a truly great poet."[303]

Jaime questioned all the values dear to the pre- and postwar generations: the family, the Catholic church, and "great" literature. His irreverent, farcical take on religion, the institution of the family meal, and his subversive spirit are evocative of the experimental vision of filmmaker Luis Buñuel.

Jaime remained close to his uncle Carlos Semprún, and they even wrote a book together, *Revolution et Contre-revolution en Catalogne*. Jorge had grown distant from Carlos ever since the latter abandoned the Spanish Communist Party in 1956. As time went by, the rupture with Carlos would also become complete, and permanent.

Jorge's breakup with Jaime constitutes a rather dark chapter in his life. Jaime was much like his father in many ways: handsome, charismatic, intelligent, and politically engaged. He was also the child of a broken home, and had the experience of being a stepchild: Claude Roy was his stepfather, and Colette Leloup his stepmother. However, there were also many differences. Jorge had been born in Madrid into a large, conservative, Catholic, bourgeois family. During his adolescence he had experienced the Spanish Civil War, exile, World War II, and Buchenwald. He had been a militant Communist for many years. Jaime was an only child, a born-and-bred Parisian, his mother was a well-known actress, his stepfather, Roy, a poet and editor for Gallimard. His coming of age was spent riding the wave of Paris in May 1968, and he was perfectly suited to the antibourgeois, creative fervor of that time. With his long hair, beautiful smile, and artistic and radical friends, he was very far from his father's ideology and culture. And he was not a rebel without a cause: he translated, edited, and published a good deal of George Orwell's work in France, wrote several political essays about Portugal and Spain, and in 1991 founded the publishing house Les Editions de l'Encyclopédie des Nuisances. He felt connected to his half-Spanish roots, felt implicated in the country's political evolution, and thought about buying a house in La Fresneda, a beautiful village in the region of Aragón.[304] But he considered the Spanish transition to democracy a sell-out, and a triumph of bourgeois capitalism. As a firm disbeliever in any political system, he distrusted his father's past as a Communist leader, and believed the expression "Stalinist for a day, Stalinist forever" ("*Stalinien un jour, Stalinien toujours*").

One of Jorge Semprún's screenplays, for the 1978 *Les routes du sud* (directed by Joseph Losey), addresses the Jorge-Jaime relationship. It was a kind of sequel of *La Guerre est finie*, with an older protagonist—Jean Larrea (Yves Montand), a play on the name Juan Larrea, one of Jorge's clandestine aliases. Jean has a son in the film, Laurent, who is the same age as Jaime Semprún, and in one of the climactic scenes the father and son have a violent argument. The son asks his father why he is stuck in the past, and says he should have organized Franco's assassination instead of wasting "twenty years" on ineffectual clandestine work. The father tries to explain his perspective, and why Communism was so important to him. He says that the blood spilled by Spanish republicans tainted his dreams for forty years, and that the son knows nothing about Spain. This sentiment is a leitmotif in Jorge's work. Jorge, via Diego in *La Guerre est finie*, says the same thing to some well-meaning Parisian acquaintances: the French don't understand Spain, they think it's a country of folkloric clichés. Jaime, unlike his father, was French, so there was the age gap and a huge cultural divide.

In *Routes du sud* there is no hope for the father-son pair. Laurent tells his father that he's tired of hearing the same old story and memories from the past. He says that the only dreams that count are those of the future. Jean says that nobody can understand the future without knowing about the past, and he tells his son to go to hell as he gets into his car and slams the door. This film is the only artistic reflection of Jorge's falling-out with Jaime. Jorge could not accept that a few years after being hailed as the "revolutionary Proust" he would be seen as a stodgy old-hat Stalinist—by his own son! The cultural upheavals of the mid- to late-1960s had distanced the new generation from the old, and Paris was the Western eye of the storm. Jorge had gone from appearing to have it all—political credibility, a beautiful flat, famous friends—to being almost swept aside by the radical youth culture. He was a former Resistance fighter, Nazi camp survivor, retired clandestine anti-Franco agent. These achievements carried no currency with Jaime's generation. It is easy to imagine the tensions between Jorge's new celebrity status, his home with Colette and her lovely daughter Dominique, and the estranged son, Jaime. Jorge was a writer, an engaged intellectual, but he and Colette had a decidedly bourgeois lifestyle since he had split from the PCE. In fact, Jorge was now a true bourgeois for the first time since 1936. He had only had a second brief glimpse of luxury and comfort when he had been under Edouard-Auguste Frick's tutelage in the late 1930s, but that had ended brutally and was followed by the Resistance, Buchenwald, and his life as a Communist. He was not about to sacrifice his newfound stability and life of ease for the whims of his long-haired, unkempt, fiery son.

From Jaime's point of view, his father was a fraud.[305] What kind of revolutionary wears a Cartier watch? It was a classic generational culture clash cast in the specific light of the *soixante-huitards* and their violent rejection of existing values and ideologies. The overarching tensions between Jaime and Jorge mirror those that Jorge had with his own father. José María Semprún had been horrified and scared—for his own safety—when Jorge joined the Resistance. He had also abandoned his active paternal role and chosen to invest his time almost exclusively in his new wife, Annette. Jorge had been disappointed in his ineffectual, old-fashioned father, and this dynamic was reproduced—with its own particularities—in his relationship with his own son.

As Jorge's family relationships crumbled, Yves Montand became the most important male figure in Semprún's life. He played the protagonists Jorge created on the big screen—in addition to *Les routes du sud,* and *La Guerre est finie,* there was also *Z,* and *L'aveu* (1970, also Costa-Gavras). *L'aveu* was based on Artur London's autobiographical book, by the same name, about the Prague trials; instead of Carrillo and Claudín, Yves Montand and Costa-Gavras became the new axis in Jorge's life. The three of them were Mediterranean, French by adoption, passionately creative, and politically engaged. They made a world-renowned filmmaking team for a few years in Jorge's life, 1968–1970. During this period they all spent weekends at Montand's luxurious country home in Autheuil, and it was in this glamorous, relaxed, and friendly atmosphere that Costa-Gavras asked Jorge to work on adapting the novel *Z,* by Vassilis Vassilikos, into a script. The film told the story of Grigoris Lambrakis, a Greek Member of Parliament who was an antifascist and pacifist, who was murdered by members of the extreme right in 1963. Jorge enthusiastically accepted, as he was already familiar with Lambrakis's story, and he identified with the Greek struggle against military dictatorships.[306]

Costa-Gavras remembers how important his friendship with Semprún was and his collaboration with Semprún and Yves Montand, starting with the award-winning film *Z:*

> We were "The Mediterraneans!" Simone Signoret would say, "Jorge is Spanish, Montand the Italian and Costa the Greek," and so we covered almost the entire Mediterranean region. I said to Jorge one day that I'd like to make the film

Z and I asked him if he knew anything about the story of Grigoris Lambrakis and he said he knew it very well. Nobody in Paris at that time knew about Lambrakis. It was a profoundly political tale concerned with great changes taking place in Greece, connected with the Greek Civil War, and Jorge knew about it because he saw so many parallels with what had happened in Spain. I told him I wanted to make a film about it and that I'd like him to collaborate with me. He said, "Whenever you want—why not right now?" He was very popular during this time and sought after and so we could only find time to work now and then in Paris. I told him that the best way to write the script would be to stay somewhere in the country, but I had no friends with country houses except for Yves Montand, and he and Simone Signoret spent a lot of time there, so it would have been difficult to isolate ourselves. Jorge finally found us a place, owned by a friend of his, a doctor I think, about sixty kilometers from Paris. We holed up there and worked every single day for five weeks. We only stopped to eat. Sometimes we would cook for ourselves at the house and sometimes we went to a small local restaurant. Sometimes I played pinball and I got good at it. Our wives came to see us a few times but we were working so well we didn't even want them to be there. And that's how we wrote the script for *Z*, five weeks of intense work. We argued a lot but Jorge came to see what he had already learned from working on *La Guerre est finie*, that you often do not need dialogue when an image will tell you all you need to know. It was very serious work. The final draft was two hundred pages long, which scared a number of people.[307]

After *Z*, Costa-Gavras also collaborated with Jorge, on his film *The Confession*:

I had read Arthur London's book and I asked Jorge to write the script. I asked him, "Do you think all of this is true?" And he said, "Absolutely!" Jorge had gotten to know Josef Frank—one of the accused in the story who was executed—in the Buchenwald concentration camp. He said they had charged Frank with working for the CIA but that he knew it would have been impossible. I told him I wanted Montand to play the lead role. Montand was interested in the story for personal reasons. Though he never joined the Communist Party, he was linked to it and his brother had an important post within the party.

Jorge and I began to work on the script together and since we had already done *Z* together the experience was much easier. He was very familiar with the story. The idea was to write a story trying to explain an impulse to accuse oneself of something for the good of the party. Jorge felt close to the theme because they had tried to talk him into doing something similar once and he had refused. He preferred to leave the party in the same way he left the government of Felipe González years later in what was an act of great moral integrity. After *The Confession* we often spoke of working together again.

In 1975 we finally did *Special Section* together. Then came the period in which he was named the minister of culture in Spain. I wanted to make *Missing* with him in 1982. We really should have done that but by then he was spending most of his time involved with Felipe González. His relationship with González was intense and it left him no time for anything else. I even said to him, "Listen, we could try and film *Missing* in Barcelona," and he went and spoke to Felipe González about it. We almost did it. I was convinced I could shoot parts of Barcelona and Cataluña for Chile. But he was very involved with Felipe by then and sensed how far González and the Spanish Socialist Party would go. Later I came to understand how important Spain was to him. It was always Spain. Shortly before he died we came back to the idea of working on a new project together, to make a film based on Malraux's *L'espoir*, but soon after that he was hospitalized.[308]

Montand was Semprún's longest-lasting French friend, however, and the most important male influence on Jorge for nearly thirty years, between 1963 and Montand's death in 1991. Jorge first met Yves Montand in 1963 thanks to Colette's daughter, Dominique, who attended the École Alsacienne in Paris with Simone Signoret's daughter, Catherine Allegret.

The first encounter between Montand and Jorge was a *coup de foudre*, as Montand recalls:

> It was almost love at first sight between us. We met at the Colombe d'Or. He was sitting at our table, with Simone and his wife, Colette, and he was in my chair against the wall. I came in and thought, "Who is this guy who's taken my seat?" I gave him a dirty look. Simone introduced us. For half an hour I was curt with him, and then we found out we had an amazing amount in common. It was a love story. He was a man I loved the way you love a woman. I truly love him—without the slightest ambiguity—and he loved me back, even though in background he was more reserved than me and showed his feelings less.[309]

Jorge even wrote a 1983 book about his friend, *Montand, la vie continue*.[310] It is more love letter than biography, and as much about Jorge as it is about Montand. The book's raison d'etre was Montand's phenomenally successful 1981 world tour. He performed to packed stadiums in Brazil, and the Metropolitan Opera in New York. Jorge accompanied him, and he uses the book to report on tour highlights, pay homage to Montand's meteoric career, and reminisce about their friendship. He also takes the opportunity to reminisce about some of his own highlights that are completely unrelated to Montand. These include the day that Francois Mitterrand invited Jorge to lunch at the Elysée. This type of digression is classic Jorge Semprún: as an aside, he will launch into an anecdote that includes a reference to a well-known person, and that at the same time reminds us of his militant past, in Buchenwald or Spain. It's a kind of bonsai autobiography within the longer narrative, which is about another subject altogether. In the case of the Elysée anecdote in the Montand book, the invitation is mentioned in a nonchalant tone, but this was clearly a momentous occasion for Jorge since he spends a paragraph describing how punctually he arrived at the engagement. His punctuality was not—he points out—because of eagerness, but due to the discipline ingrained from his clandestine years. These dual threads of glamour and political engagement ran through the rest of Jorge's life, and much of his work.

Montand and Jorge had a good deal in common—including the difficult relationships with their real, biological brothers—and they also complemented each other in a yin-and-yang kind of way. Jorge was extremely well-educated and had been born into splendor, whereas Montand had started life as a talented go-getter with no schooling. Jorge could be shy and distant in social situations, and Montand could charm anyone just by saying "bonjour" in his famously seductive voice. But Montand yearned for credibility and substance; he had a voracious appetite for learning about politics and ideas. In Jorge, he found his ideal professor.[311]

From the early 1960s onward Jorge was an unstoppable whirlwind of creativity. His multiple roles as screenwriter, novelist, memoirist, and public intellectual reached their highest pitch in the 1960s and 1970s. It was also no small feat that Jorge had achieved this great success in a language that was not his mother tongue. Though he had been forced to learn French quickly, and fluently, at the age of thirteen, it is surprising that he could become a respected writer in what was, in fact, his third language. His mastery of French was phenomenal. Very few people before him had been able to become established authors in a language acquired after childhood. There are exceptions, such as Joseph Conrad, who mastered English in his twenties, and Irishman Samuel Beckett who wrote in French, or Vladimir Nabokov, who wrote in English, but it is a rare talent. In addition to writing in a foreign language, Jorge Semprún faced—like many exiled Spanish authors—the added obstacle of censorship in his native country. It wasn't until the late 1970s, after Franco's death, that his books were translated and published in Spain.

In reading Jorge Semprún's work, and listening to his interviews, it is clear that he had a gift for French. His command of the language was greatly enriched by his lifelong, voracious reading of French literature: Queneau, Guilloux, Valéry, and Stendhal are among the many authors he cited as his favorites.[312]

He directed one film of his own, the 1972 documentary called *Les deux memoires*, which was put together during the long eve of Franco's death. It is a fascinating portrait of Spaniards from across the political spectrum and their views on the Spanish Civil War. The film is not commercially available,[313] which is a shame because it has an all-star Spanish cast of thinkers and leaders including Juan Goytisolo, Fernando Claudín, his daughter Carmen Claudín, Dionisio Ridruejo, and Santiago Carrillo. The film is divided into five parts, each focusing on pivotal episodes concerning the Republic and the Spanish Civil War. In typical Semprúnian fashion the sequences are not chronological. It starts in February 1939, with the Republican exodus across the border into France, then shifts to July 1936 in a segment titled "War and Revolution in Spain." The next section is a flashback to the "Bourgeois republic" and the origins of the civil war. The penultimate subject is Soviet aid to the Spanish Republic, and the film concludes by exploring the end of the war in March 1939. Most of the interviewees were Republican supporters, yet their views are by no means homogeneous. Semprún chose the title to suggest that "there are always two memories of events, even among those who fought on the Republican side."[314]

Much of the filming took place in the Chateau de Roche, the home of the American anti-Francoist, historian, and book collector Herbert Southworth. The movie was, in fact, supposed to be a collaboration between Southworth and Jorge. However, as one of the interviewees, historian Gabriel Jackson, recalls, Jorge soon took control. He conducted the interviews and directed the camera. Jackson's recollections give a sense of the tense atmosphere on the shoot, and Southworth's frustration:

> What I remember clearly were the circumstances of the shoot. Herbert Southworth had telegraphed me at UCSD to get on the first plane available, that Semprún and his wife were coming to the Southworth home (at that time a disheveled chateau in central France) and that he and Semprún were making a film, which he defined as a collaboration between the two, and it was clear that for Herbert it represented an opportunity also to have his own work become better known. Since the chancellor's office at UCSD had never heard of either Semprún or Southworth, it took a lot of persuasion on my part to get permission to go to France (not even to Paris or to a major French institution!) for a week during the spring quarter.
>
> The plane landed in mid-morning after a near-sleepless night crossing the continent and the Atlantic. The village taxi driver didn't know where Southworth lived, dropped me in the center of town, and as I was inquiring of a storekeeper whether he knew Southworth, the old boy himself appeared in the same street. At the chateau I was introduced to Semprún, then sent up to sleep for a few hours in a spare bedroom in one of the towers of the castle. Mid afternoon

we had a sumptuous lunch, including a beautiful red fish that
was said to be the pride of the river valley. Then the filming
session, of which I recall very mixed personal emotions
because on the one hand I was very favorably impressed by
the whole project, and by Semprún's personality, but on
the other I realized that Herbert was feeling "left out" by
Semprún's total control and his rather dismissive attitude at
moments toward Herbert.

Semprún had left the PCE, but not his leadership status. *Les deux memoires* was a project that involved many of Jorge's friends and family:
Colette, Dominique, and filmmaker Chris Marker edited the film,
and Jorge's youngest brother Paco composed the music. It is worth
seeing, and it proves that, at least in the early 1970s, Jorge Semprún
and Santiago Carrillo, were still on speaking terms, despite everything. That would change.

   It has been impossible to see or find a copy of *Les deux memoires* until very recently. Shortly after Jorge's death it was restored and
shown in Paris, Barcelona, and Madrid. Carmen Claudín went to see
it again, many years after she had first seen it screened, and was taken
by surprise:

   I hadn't seen it since it premiered. My father appears in it,
   Carrillo, Jorge. It was so much more interesting for me
   seeing it for a second time. More than *"dos memorias"* it's
   really just one, a *memoria* of the defeated. Something I've
   reflected on seeing it now is how difficult it was then to
   speak with those who had won the Spanish Civil War, at
   least with those who were actually part of the system. There
   is a fascist priest who appears and then Dionisio Ridruejo
   who has a lot to say and who is fascinating but by then he
   was no longer part of the system either. Up until this film
   was made no one on the losing side was interviewed in any

sort of organized fashion. In this documentary all kinds of people who lost are interviewed, not only communists but anarchists, Trotskyites, Republicans who were not of the left, all of the anti-Francoists, their opinions and memories. It is totally unique. It was shown commercially in France but the last thing you might call it is a commercial film. It is a film that in France is really just for an erudite audience or for a Spanish audience. Though it was shown in Spain originally it made little impression because there were so many other more pressing things going on like consolidating democracy and the consensus that was brewing about historical memory, the decision to not look too deeply into things. And this film of Jorge's goes into all of that so it was not received the way it should have been. It wasn't ignored deliberately or anything like that, it just didn't work. His film is dry and one has to be quite connected to our history to want to go and see it, although I must say the young people in the audience with me this second time around were very impressed by it.[315]

Jorge wanted to be able to travel to Spain whenever he wished but when he applied for a Spanish passport for the first time in 1967 he was refused. He asked the dashing bullfighter Luis Miguel Dominguín to intercede on his behalf. Dominguín was an important friend to Jorge and to other communists and ex-communists although he himself had nothing to do with politics. Juan Goytisolo tells an amusing story about a dinner Dominguín attended in Russia:

It was a curious journey. While we were staying at the Astoria Hotel in Leningrad—which is what it was called back then—I was there having lunch with Jean Paul Sartre and Simone de Beauvoir when Luis Miguel Dominguín strode in. I introduced him to Sartre and Simone and we

had a very good time. Later that evening there was an official dinner and Dominguín was there along with a woman
who translated his Spanish into Russian. One of the officials asked him, "How does the poor nation of Spanish people live under the tyranny of Franco?" And he answered,
"They live fabulously well." "How do you mean 'fabulously
well?'" "I mean it," he said. "They live very well indeed."
"How can you say such a thing?" they asked him. "Look," he
said, "who runs things here in Russia?" "The Communist
Party," the official replied. "If I lived here in Russia I would
be with the Communist Party," he said. "But given the fact
that Franco runs Spain, well, I'm with Franco." "That is
so cynical," the party official said. "Absolutely cynical,"
Dominguín agreed. But he was pulling their leg. He was a
very charming fellow.[316]

When Semprún first applied for his Spanish passport in 1967, his
request was denied, based on a sophomoric Spanish internal police
report about him. In it, he was described as a dangerous anti-
Francoist, and a wanted man, who had often traveled to Spain under
the pseudonym Federico Sánchez. Ironically, part of the information
in the police document was drawn from his own screenplay for *La
Guerre est finie*. In other words, life was imitating autobiographical
fiction. The police openly used the film as a source: "According to
references to the plot of this film, it is about an exile who is forced
to return to Spain, but not to visit his ailing mother, or anything like
that. He returns to become the leader of a group of guerilla fighters
who are under threat by the "Fascist police."[317]

How could Jorge have been expected to return to Spain with the
virtuous motive of "visiting his ailing mother" when she had died in
1930? The of police report used hypothetical and fictional nonsense
to damn Jorge's character. And in 1967, he was no longer a political
threat.

When Jorge finally got his Spanish passport, quite likely thanks
to the the repeated pressure of his friend the bullfighter, Luis Miguel
Dominguín, he was a bit disappointed. Recovering his legal Spanish
status, with Franco still in power, seemed like a sign of failure. He
was no longer Federico Sánchez, Franco Spain's public enemy number
one. His revolutionary mission had expired before the dictatorship. It
was all a bit too anticlimactic:

> So that was that. I was just another tourist, another traveler,
> a Spaniard who lived abroad, coming home to breathe the
> air of my homeland. . . . The truth was, I was of little conse-
> quence, and doubtful importance. I was just a French writer
> of Spanish origin. The whole thing made me want to cry.[318]

But there was not much time to mourn the past, because Jorge was
rapidly adapting to his new full-time role as a writer and celebrity. In
1969, he wrote *The Second Death of Ramón Mercader* (*La deuxième Mort de
Ramón Mercader*). Ramón Mercader was the Spanish Stalinist agent who
murdered Trotsky with an ice pick. Mercader had infiltrated Trotsky's
home, and gained his trust, before picking an opportune moment to
attack. Jorge's novel was loosely inspired on the figure of Mercader,
and is the story of a clandestine KGB agent who is being pursued by
Stalinists and by the CIA, and who is found dead in his hotel room
in Amsterdam. The novel has not, perhaps, aged as well as *The Long
Voyage*, but it is still worth reading for fans of complex espionage novels, or to learn more about Semprún. Mercader was clearly a kind of
doppelgänger for Semprún/Federico Sánchez, and the story is, perhaps,
a creatively hypothetical exploration of how Jorge's story might have
ended differently. It could also be seen as an exorcism of his fears, and
his staking a further claim to the safety of the public sphere outside the
party. It was a literary way of saying to his real or imagined enemies
"I'm out, and don't think I'm ever going to end up dead in some hotel
room because I've already thought of that and written a novel about it."

Claude Roy, who had been Jorge's first official fan when he approved *The Long Voyage* for publication with Gallimard, was disappointed that this labyrinthine new novel overindulged in the techniques of the "nouveau roman." Jorge adamantly denied any association with this literary trend, and responded to Roy's comment, saying:

> He is absolutely wrong about that. I don't know the first thing about the "nouveau roman." If my work suffers from flaws, they are of another nature. I've been accused of excessive showmanship, virtuosity: and that proves that I am naturally inclined toward excess. I need to make an effort to pare things down. Left to my own devices, I am baroque and sophisticated. . . . I don't delete enough.[319]

The novel won Jorge his second major literary prize, the Prix Femina 1969. This was a huge achievement, and helped secure Jorge's place in the company of great authors. The 1968 Femina had been awarded to Marguerite Yourcenar.

This prize also guaranteed a new media blitz. Though some of the coverage makes it clear that the press still did not know quite what to make of him. Was he a writer or a political activist? A Communist or an ex-Communist? In an extensive roundtable interview for the French magazine *L'Express*, Jorge was grilled by the writers Michèle Cotta, Jean-Louis Ferrier, and Francoise Giroud.

The pointed questions included: "What is a revolutionary like you doing on the literary prize circuit? How does that make sense?" Jorge tackled all the questions calmly, and answered eloquently, except for one. When asked if he had wanted to go back to Spain after the Liberation of France he said that he did, but knew that it was pointless because it was clear that there was no hope of changing anything. There was, he said, an agreement between the Allies and the USSR to leave Spain under Franco. The major powers had enough problems to resolve without bringing up the Spanish question. The interviewer responds by saying: "But you did return to Spain between 1952–1962, under a false name, to recruit students and intellectuals for the clandestine Communist Party; and you were a high-ranking leader in the party, and an active anti-Francoist, like your character played by Yves Montand in *La Guerre est finie. Oui ou non?*" To which Jorge answered obliquely: "Let's just say that I'm not some intellectual who suddenly found out, when he died, that Stalin was a bad guy. But I refuse to answer your question."[320]

Were the journalists pressing him inappropriately, given the fact that Spain was still under the same military dictatorship he had worked to overthrow? He had written a screenplay about this facet of his life, so they must have thought the subject was fair game. In any case, Jorge had little patience for these "Western" intellectuals who thought it was still breaking news that Stalin was "a baddie."

It was also during 1969 that *Z* came out, and Jorge traveled to New York City for the premiere. He also spent part of the year in Prague with Costa-Gavras in preparation for shooting *L'Aveu*, which would come out in 1970.

His next film project was another collaboration with Alain Resnais, *Stavisky*, starring Jean-Paul Belmondo. The story was based on the true story of Alexandre Stavisky, an impresario, con man, and bon vivant. No expense was spared, but the luxurious-looking sets and costumes did not guarantee international success. The story was complicated by a disconnected subplot in which Trotsky shows up on the Côte d'Azur. The film was well received in France when it came out in 1974, but Stavisky's real-life son took issue with the portrayal of his parents' relationship and interfered with the movie's distribution.

In 1973 Francisco Franco resigned as prime minister, and chose his alter ego, Admiral Luis Carrero-Blanco, as his successor. Just a few months into office, the sixty-nine-year-old Carrero-Blanco was assassinated by a car bomb planted by the Basque separatist movement Euskadi Ta Askatasuna (ETA). The assassination, right in the heart of Madrid's posh "*barrio de Salamanca*," came as a shock to a country that was already on edge, not knowing what political direction Spain would take once Franco died. The regime had made many arrangements to ensure its enduring power. One had been the new role of Carrero-Blanco as prime minister, and the other was to make Juan Carlos de Borbón, son of Spain's rightful heir Juan de Borbón, his heir-apparent. He was named "Prince of Spain" in 1969. Franco shrewdly skipped a generation in the royal lineage because he feared that Don Juan was too liberal and would not uphold his legacy and ensure the regime's continuity. On the other hand, his tall, handsome thirty-year-old son, soon to be Don Juan Carlos I, had been personally chosen and molded by Franco, and he was confident that he had invested in a loyal ally to perpetuate his values.

Carrero Blanco was replaced by the minister of the interior (*Jefe de Gobernación*) Carlos Arias Navarro, who was, in turn, promoted to prime minister. Another seasoned and staunch Francoist, the sixty-six-year-old Arias Navarro had forged his reputation during the Civil War, where his harsh repression of Republicans had earned him the nickname "the butcher of Málaga" (*el carnicero de Málaga*). The new prime minister may not have seemed like the right candidate to shepherd Spain into democracy, but he did not have much choice. After close to four decades without elections, political parties, or human rights, Spaniards were ready for change. Spain had moved on without examining its recent past. The transition was described by some as "the pact of amnesia."

On October 30, 1975, Franco gave full Head of State powers to Juan Carlos de Borbón, and two days after Franco's death the Prince was proclaimed King Juan Carlos I. The new king selected Adolfo Suárez to be prime minister, and under his leadership the Law for Political Reform was passed. The much touted "transition to democracy" was underway, and on June 15, 1977, Spain held its first democratic elections in forty years. Suárez was reelected. He had been an integral part of the Franco apparatus, but at forty-four years old he was younger than most of the dictator's cronies, and quick to see the opportunity to become a key player in a new Spain. The winning political party he created, Unión de Centro Democrático (UCD), was too conservative for some, and too democratic for others, but his tenure was peaceful and essential to the Spanish political evolution. Juan Carlos I had made a savvy choice. By 1978 a democratic constitution was in place. The king remained head of state and commander-in-chief of the armed forces. Though he had no executive powers, Juan Carlos I faced huge challenges and proved himself to be a true democrat.

On February 23, 1981, there was a military coup d'etat. The fledgling Spanish parliament was stormed by armed soldiers who falsely claimed that the king was backing them. Juan Carlos spent a long night sorting out the situation, and made an emergency television appearance to reassure Spaniards that nothing would threaten their constitutional democracy. This failed coup had hoped to destabilize the transition, but it had the opposite effect. It brought Spaniards together as never before to defend their new political freedom, and the king's response caused his popularity to soar. He went from being an unknown quantity, and Franco appointee to boot, to becoming the people's hero. In 1982, the Socialist (PSOE) Prime Minister Felipe González was elected. Spain had its first Socialist government in nearly half a century.

In 1978 the *New York Times* published an unusual lead story on Spain titled "Ex-Communist Upsets Spanish Party with a Book About its Past." The article described the book, and its destructive impact on the Spanish Communist Party:

> A 342-page memoir bearing the innocuous title *Autobiography of Federico Sánchez* has exploded like a delayed-action bomb in the Spanish Communist Party and has thrown its secretary general, Santiago Carrillo, on the defensive. The book, which appears to be turning into one of Post-Franco Spain's best-sellers, is a former Communist's account in

the form of a novel of his underground years. It was written by Jorge Semprún, a 54-year-old writer who in 1964
was expelled from the party's Executive Committee with
another Communist for advancing some of the arguments
Mr. Carrillo has since embraced and woven into the fabric of
his own Euro communism. While even non-Communists
have criticized Mr. Semprún's one-sided, emotional attacks
on Mr. Carrillo and other Spanish Communists, "Federico
Sánchez" has touched nerves with allegations of Stalinism in
a party that claims to have left Stalin and Lenin far behind. .
. . In leftist intellectual circles in Spain, Mr. Semprún's book
has been received uneasily, in part because its highly personal tone sometimes makes it appear to be an act of revenge
for his expulsion.[321]

In this explosive memoir, Jorge accuses the Spanish Communist Party
of orchestrating Trotsky's assassination, and Carrillo of collaborating
in the murder of Julián Grimau. Even Javier Pradera, to whom the
book is dedicated, "found its 'partial truths'" unsettling.

Communism in Spain is one of Jorge's most compelling works,
and it caused a stir in the Communist world in Spain and beyond.
Semprún had been angry for years, and now that the PCE was legal
he could speak his mind on the record, and people would listen. It
was his first book in Spanish, about Spain, by a Spaniard, written for
Spaniards. It was released in November 1977, and by February 1978
it had sold close to 150,000 copies. It would reach sales of 300,000,
and would remain Jorge's best selling book in any language, anywhere, until his 1994 Literature or Life. Santiago Carrillo had not only
expelled Semprún from the PCE in 1965, but to add insult to injury
he published a volume that year, Después de Franco, ¿Qué?: La democracia
política y social que preconizamos los comunistas,[322] which shamelessly stole
the very ideas that Jorge and Fernando Claudín had included in their
final report, the same ideas that got them kicked out of the party. And

in a 1974 book called *Mañana España: Conversaciones con Régis Debray y Max Gallo*, Carrillo clearly went on the record, identifying Federico Sánchez as Jorge Semprún, and dismissing his/their importance.

In the conversations, Debray raises the subject of Semprún's *La Guerre est finie*, and suggests that it accurately diagnosed Spain's political reality. Carrillo responds to a question about Semprún by saying that "Federico Sánchez"—calling him by his alias, and "outing" him—was proven wrong. He says that his claim that Spain was a "neo-capitalist" country and that the dictatorship could be brought down peacefully, from within, was misconstrued. He also argues that both Fernando Claudín and "Sánchez" brought about their own expulsion through their rash and hotheaded behavior, and that the PCE leaders had tried to convince them to wait a few years to bring their views to the larger audience of the XX Congress. He repeats his oft-used line that "Sánchez" (Semprún) just wanted an out to indulge his desire to become a writer:

> The case of Federico Sánchez is different. I was sure that the work of the party was stifling him, not because of its political nature, but because it was keeping him from fulfilling his vocation as a writer, a creator. The clandestine work was getting to him, which I understood perfectly, and I said to him, "If you want to write, go ahead, but don't cook up a political scandal." He may have been sincerely convinced that the Communist movement had reached a plateau, and that he needed to distance himself from it to become a writer. He chose his path. I recall saying to Federico Sánchez, during one of these last conversations, "Listen, you may be expelled from the party, but my house is open to you."[323]

In addition to insulting Jorge and his alias, he could very well have put him at risk by exposing his real identity. Even if Jorge was beyond the reach of Spanish law—which may or may not have been the case Franco was still alive when this was published and he could have become the target of extremists from either side of the political spectrum.

In retrospect, Felipe Gónzalez sees Carrillo's behavior as predictable.

> Carrillo saw the report (written by Semprún and Claudín) and he thought that they had broken the rules that he had so rigidly enforced. The first thing he did was kick them out, because they had had a brilliant idea on their own. He expelled them, and then he stole their idea. If you look you'll see that Santiago Carrillo's book *Después de Franco* was lifted from Semprún and Claudín's report, and that Carrillo had changed his views. When people change their approach, they first have to get rid of the people who came up with it, the people who should take credit for it.[324]

By 1977, two years after Franco's death, the PCE had been legalized in Spain, and Carrillo was elected to the Spanish Congress of Deputies. He became an important player in Spain's transition to democracy, and much of his rhetoric was based on the "reconciliation" strategy Jorge had fought for twenty years earlier. Carrillo was basking in the Spanish political limelight with Jorge's ideas. Jorge was a literary star, but politically he was nowhere, in Spain or France. He was fifty-four years old, and felt excluded from the new Spain he had spent years working to bring about.

All the bitterness he felt was poured into *Communism in Spain,* a conversion tale, a political self-critique, and a narrative of revenge. It begins, and ends, with La Pasionaria speaking at her podium during Jorge and Claudín's final PCE meeting in April 1964 in a "kafkian" castle in Bohemia. The book is framed by her gathering her thoughts, speaking, and finally calling them *"cabezas de chorlito"* (birdbrains). In the first pages Jorge remembers meeting La Pasionaria, writing poetry in her honor. He was totally seduced by her when he first met her in Paris in 1947, when he was a complete believer in the PCE. In his narrative, she is presented as a quasi-religious figure, and as a mother. She was maternal, a powerful leader, and Spanish. There is no doubt that the twenty-four-year-old Jorge was taken in, and that meeting La Pasionaria was a momentous occasion in his life. She too had been in prison, and had inspired thousands of soldiers to defend the Spanish Republic when they had little but hope to keep them going. Dolores Ibárruri's magnetism was legendary, hence her nom de guerre La Pasionaria. Even in the last pages of *Communism in Spain,* when she is insulting him, Jorge described her voice as "that splendid voice, that was metallic, rough, and harmonious."[325]

The book painfully details Jorge's complete and enthusiastic conversion, his slow climb up the PCE ladder, and his subsequent, chilling disillusionment and expulsion. The book alternates between first- and second-person narratives, and experiments with parentheses, capitalization, and chronology, but it is still a crackling read.

Upon its publication, Jorge became public enemy number one of the PCE, and of the Communist Party Headquarters in Moscow. His "Top Secret" file at the Russian State Archive of Contemporary History (RGANI) has several reports on him submitted over the years to the International Department of the Central Committee of the CPSU by secret agents. To date, they have never been published or studied, and they offer an intriguing glimpse of Jorge Semprún's evolution as perceived by the Soviets. The reports start as the typical party mini-biographies—personal background and useful skills—but turn into warnings. Jorge would have been pleased to know that his critique of the PCE and his talent as a writer were perceived as dangerous threats.

In earlier times, Moscow had seen Jorge as a real catch: an effective "propagandist" or "publicist." They did not like the way he had turned the tables and was now using his abilities against them. He was considered a traitor, and a major anticommunist threat:

J. Semprún's talent is undeniable. He writes in French, and is currently launching massive anti-Soviet and anticommunist campaigns. The screenplays he has written, which are good from an artistic point of view, such as *La Guerre est finie*, *Z*, and *The Confession*, all slander the Soviet Union and the Communist movement openly (*La Guerre est finie* and *The Confession*) or covertly (*Z*). In the words of Luis Balaguer, Jorge Semprún's behavior illustrates how much the Spanish Communist Party needs to try and increase the Marxist-Leninist influence among the representatives of the intelligentsia within the party ranks.[326]

Communism in Spain had singlehandedly launched an anticommunist "bourgeois" campaign in the Spanish press. At the same time, a former Communist Spanish Civil War general, Enrique Líster, left the PCE to create a splinter party, the "Partido Obrero Español." Between the "publicist Semprún" and the "unknown general," the PCE was reeling from new enemies, who were ex-members. They were challenging Carrillo's new adherence to "Euro-communism" and said that he was, in fact, a "Euro-opportunist." The party faithful were especially concerned because, as they saw it, Semprún was being backed by the "millionaire," "reactionary" editor José Manuel Lara Hernández. Lara, who owned the Planeta publishing house, was a media mogul who had fought on the Franco side during the Spanish Civil War. *Communism in Spain* had won the 1978 Planeta prize, and this generated a great deal of publicity and a prize of four million pesetas for Jorge. To the Soviets this was all part of a right-wing, anticommunist conspiracy. A Soviet report from January 12, 1978 informed:

Our correspondent in Madrid from Taniug [news agency] has informed us about the campaign being unleashed by the bourgeois press against the Spanish Communist Party. The motive of the attacks against Communists, according to our Correspondent, is due to two ex-Communists, one of them is an unknown former Republican General, E. Líster,[327] and the other is the propagandist Jorge Semprún.

Over the past few days the "Spanish Workers' Party" has held a congress in Madrid. It was founded by Líster, and its base is a pro-Soviet splinter group. During Líster's speech, and the ensuing debate, Carrillo and "his party" were accused of "Euro-opportunism," of "reactionary deviations" and of "betraying the cause of the working class and the international proletariat." Líster foresaw the "fall of Carrillo's party" and announced that his own party (in reality a splinter group) remains loyal to the doctrine "born of the October revolution;" that it is a "Marxist-Leninist party," and that it is based on principle of "a dictatorship of the proletariat, and proletariat internationalism." According to our correspondent, the bourgeois press has devoted a great deal of attention to Líster's accusations against Carrillo and the Spanish CP. This is why it is difficult to gauge if these accusations will harm or help Carrillo.

With Jorge Semprún, the situation is different, and might have serious consequences among Spanish Communists. Lara, the famous Spanish editor, millionaire, and reactionary, has promoted Semprún's book *Autobiography of Federico Sánchez*, naming it book of the year, and has bestowed him with Spain's biggest literary award, endowed with a prize of 4 million pesetas. At the present time, the book is a best seller, and the source of a massive campaign against the Spanish Communist Party and its secretary general. In his book, Semprún names names, and in a bitter, controversial—and even insulting tone, he accuses Carrillo, Pasionaria, and other members of the Communist Party in Spain of losing sight of the ideal in their quest for power, and of falling prey to Stalinism, sectarianism, and many other errors and deviations. Semprún writes about of all of this brilliantly, and succinctly, and makes use of documentary evidence and conversations that he had access to as a member of the inner circle of the party leadership. The *Autobiography of Federico Sánchez* which the enemies of Communism in Spain and all over the West are promoting like wildfire, is probably one of the most anticommunist books that has been written in Europe in the past ten years. Thus affirms our correspondent from Taniug.[328]

The report continues, saying that the book is "subjective" and that its only value is political (vs. literary). Semprún is accused of "outing" several party members, of insulting Santiago Carrillo, and taking the credit—shared with Fernando Claudín—for inventing the concept of "eurocomunismo". There is also a summary of the review the book was given in *Cambio 16*, an important, new Spanish political magazine:

It should be noted that the reason the book attracted so much attention and won such an important prize has nothing to do with its literary merit and everything to do with political motives. The *Autobiography of Federico Sanchez* is a subjective historical tale about the Spanish Communist Party, specifically in 1964, when members of its Executive Committee rose in protest against the political line promulgated by its secretary general, Santiago Carrillo. The book is also of great interest for its detailed portraits of many key members of the PCE, including Santiago Carrillo, Dolores Ibarruri, S. Sanchez Montero, Romero Marina, Raimundo G. Lopez and others.

In 1964, the author of the *Autobiography* (sic) *of Federico Sánchez*, Jorge Semprún (who also penned novels such as *The Long Voyage*, *The Second Death of Ramon Mercader* and others) together with Fernando Claudín, were expelled from the Executive Committee of the PCE and then expelled from the Communist Party altogether because of their differences with Santiago Carrillo. In his book Jorge Semprún (that is to say, Federico Sánchez) recognizes that during that time he and Fernando Claudín were insisting that the party adopt a political stance currently known as "Euro-Communism." "To be precise and consistent from an historical point of view," writes the author, "one must recognize that it was us, Federico Sánchez (which is to say, Jorge Semprún) and Fernando Claudín who formulated the term 'Euro-Communism' in 1964 along with its basic positions, and it is very gratifying for us to see how our ideas were later confirmed." According to Jorge Semprún, Carrillo took credit for their ideas afterward claiming that it had been he who had invented the term without any basis in fact and that now he continues to advertise himself as the champion and chief theorist of "Euro-Communism."[329]

According to the magazine *Cambio 16*, the most valuable feature of *Communism in Spain* is how it reveals the political evolution of Santiago Carrillo (who now enthusiastically supports the policies he tried to stamp out in 1964) and his lack of political transparency. *Cambio 16* also points out that the book's protagonist (a book that, for however much it is an autobiography, is above all a political document) is the Spanish Communist Party under the absolute control of its secretary general, Santiago Carrillo. "From the pages of this book," the magazine goes on to say, "there emerges an image of Santiago Carrillo as an opportunistic political leader, sly, artful, calculating, cold, cynical and without principles."

With respect to the unity of the Communist Party in Spain—according to this book it would be more logical to speak instead of the "union between the Executive Committee and Santiago Carrillo rather then there being a sense of cohesion between the secretary general and organizations representing the party faithful."

The magazine also points out another important and active personality that appears in the book: a generation of Spaniards who, on the one hand were crushed by Franco's government and on the other, lied to by the Spanish Communist Party.

The next report is from a week later, January 18, 1978, describing Carrillo's counterattack during a press conference in which he claims that in any other country, Semprún's book would warrant "criminal" charges:

> At a press conference held in Barcelona, Santiago Carrillo, the secretary general of the Spanish Communist Party declared the following: "Some of the affirmations concerning the Communist Party made by Jorge Semprún in his book *Autobiography of Federico Sánchez* would, in any other country except Spain, have been liable for legal action." This was his first formal reaction to the book.
>
> But we are not going to bring any charges because we believe the governmental apparatus in Spain has not changed at all and that it continues to represent the past. We are also very aware of the fact that the judges deciding cases today are the same ones who, over decades, ruled against the Communist Party and its representatives. We see no prospects for being able to impede this wave of calumnies, lies, insinuations and outrageous slander against the Communist Party and we've no guarantee more books like the *Autobiography of Federico Sánchez* won't appear.

Santiago Carrillo declared that the Communist Party would soon make all its archives available to historians and that the party itself would publish a diverse range of documents that would show the truth concerning the complicated and confusing history of Spain.

"I wish to draw your attention," continued Santiago Carrillo, "to the fact that the process of national reconciliation must be based on a principle of not stirring up the past. This is a tacit agreement made by all sides so as not to strangle our emerging democracy.

"We renounce the presentation of any kind of complaint concerning the Franco dictatorship of the past forty years; we put aside criticism of how the Spanish Socialist Party behaved during the Franco era, during the Civil War and before it. With respect to the book by Jorge Semprún and the attention it has garnered, it is the opinion of the secretary general of the PCE that the book is an anticommunist trap, supported by a diverse group of people for diverse reasons.

"It is an attempt to destroy the prestige and authority the Communist Party has had in this country," he continued. "The Communist Party shall not respond to these books. The Communist Party will respond to the anticommunist campaign, demonstrating its right to assert its authority with respect to the preparation and realization of a truly democratic congress in which, I am certain, the communists will confirm and totally support the political line of the party."

The final report submitted to Jorge's file from March 31, 1978, was titled "The Situation of the Communist Party in Spain." It states that the wave of dissidence affecting the Spanish Communist Party had become intense, and that the generalized disgruntlement is all because of *Communism in Spain*:

> Over the last few days a wave of dissidence has been convulsing the Spanish Communist Party: numerous disagreements have sprung up at the regional conferences taking place in preparation for the national congress scheduled for the 19th until the 23rd of April in Madrid. Some communists reproach the Central Committee for intentionally rejecting the term "Marxist-Leninist" and accuse the Madrid directive of discouraging any free and democratic debate on this issue within the party.

The first disagreement arose last Saturday at the conference in Asturias. 113 of the 500 delegates walked out of the reunion after one of them was refused acknowledgment, an individual named Horacio Fernández. In an extensive communiqué published on Wednesday these "dissidents" claimed "black lists" were distributed at the conference of people who were not to be elected to the regional committee.

On Wednesday in Málaga (Andalucia) thirty party members published a document protesting the methods utilized by the Communist Party to set up the local conferences a month ago and criticizing the party's lack of democracy.

More and more protests of this sort are appearing in the Spanish provinces. Many define the method by which the Central Committee arrives at its votes as "authoritarian," and by not allowing the "debate to deepen" concerning the use of the term "Marxist-Leninist" which the committee would like to substitute with the term "revolutionary democratic Marxist party."

Many others are discontent with the excessively euro-communist line the party has been adopting recently by direct order from the secretary general of the PCE, Santiago Carrillo, without consulting the members.

All of this discontent began to spread just a few weeks after the publication of Jorge Semprún's "Autobiography of Federico Sanchez," in which the author, expelled from the PCE during the 1960s, accuses Santiago Carrillo of having consistently used the party for his own particular interests. Carrillo made some declarations on Wednesday in Tenerife (the Canary Islands), in which he attempted to calm down the members of his party. "The PCE is not going to renounce Leninism," he said in his concluding remarks, "only certain aspects of it. We continue to believe that Lenin was the first true revolutionary in history."

Jorge had truly used literature to shape politics. By the 1982 general elections in Spain, the PCE was rife with dissent, and the party had lost many seats. Carrillo was forced to step down as party leader, and in 1986 he was expelled from the PCE.

VII
Return of the Prodigal Son

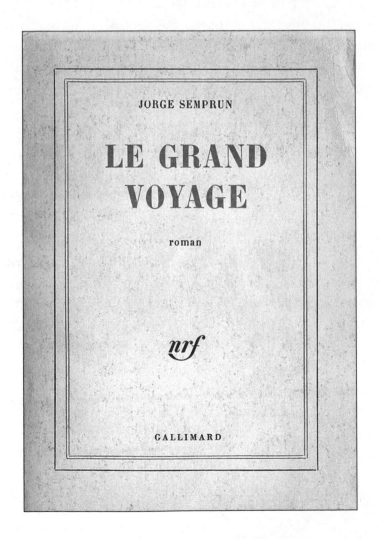

JORGE SEMPRUN

LE GRAND
VOYAGE

roman

nrf

GALLIMARD

By 1983, Jorge had been a writer for twenty years, and he could look back over his as a novelist career with some objectivity and detachment.

> If you want to know the size of my readership, it's easy to figure out. I have a very limited audience. *Le grand voyage* [*The Long Voyage*] has probably sold 30,000 copies between 1963 and today, and about 30,000 more in the Folio edition. *L'evanouissement*, my second book, must have sold about 3,000 copies. *La deuxiéme vie de Ramón Mercader* [*The Second Death of Ramón Mercader*] won the Prix Fémina, which is supposed to boost sales to 100–200,000 copies. I made it to 55,000. *Quel beau dimanche!* [*What a Beautiful Sunday!*], until now, has sold 24,000 copies. So my audience is quite limited, but very loyal.[330]

He was not a best-selling author, but he had fulfilled his childhood dream of writing novels, and he was becoming an enduring media sensation. In France he was a household name; rebaptised as Georges Semprún. The French pronunciation of his first name, and of the "e" and the "u" in his last name make the ensemble incomprehensible to anyone used to the Spanish original. Yet again, Jorge had reinvented himself, this time as a French public intellectual and television star.

One of the key people in this phase of his life was Bernard Pivot. Pivot was a prime-time literary talk show host, and a beloved personality in France. His longest running show, *Apostrophes* (1975–1990) had a faithful audience of 6 million viewers. Pivot used the famous "Proust Questionnaire" to interview his guests. The model was so successful that the American James Lipton copied the questions for his famous program *Inside the Actor's Studio*, rebranding it as the "Bernard Pivot Questionnaire." Pivot was a French cultural phenomenon. Though he had highbrow interests and guests, he managed to make his shows entertaining and accessible to the average viewer. Pivot and Semprún were introduced by their mutual friend Raymond Lévy, and they became close. Pivot understood Jorge. He saw the vast scope of his complicated life. He appreciated everything Jorge had been through, and was able to convey his admiration and respect to millions of French viewers. Pivot recalls their friendship, and their collaboration:

We hit it off immediately. Although we were, I would say, truly opposites. Perhaps that's why I was so fascinated by him. I wouldn't say he was fascinated by me, but he was interested by what I represented. We were just so different. Let me explain. To me, he wasn't just a Spaniard, and he wasn't a Parisian, he was a Spaniard who lived in Paris, who spoke three languages: Spanish, French, and German . . . In my opinion he was a European, a true European. In fact, he was the first European intellectual I had met. Obviously I had encountered writers who were pro-European, but he personified Europe. He personified its history.

He had been a victim of the Spanish Civil War, which was an international war; then he was in the French Resistance, and fought against the Nazis. He was arrested, deported to Buchenwald, and even there he found himself in the midst of a cosmopolitan population. He survived thanks to the languages he spoke: he used his German, his French, and his Spanish. And after World War II, he became a Communist Party militant. Since the party was outlawed in Spain, he traveled all over Europe. He moved around like a cat, sneaking in and out of all the Western countries, and very welcome in the Communist countries. Later, when he abandoned Communism, he became a European writer. In fact, the first literary prize he won, for *The Long Voyage*, was a European prize, the Formentor. . . .

So, in my eyes, he was the authentic European intellectual, par excellence, the European of the second half of the twentieth century. I was fascinated by him, and he saw me as a counterpart. I am very French, a true Frenchman from the middle of France. I don't speak foreign languages, and I have no interest in politics. I love to travel, but I would never go live in a foreign country, unless I was forced to. I think that one of the reasons that my show was such a success was because people, the French audience, identified with me. I was one of them. Jorge and I spoke about this. He often said, "You are obviously very French, and the French people love that." My reflexes and attitudes are indeed French. So I think I was, and I mean this modestly, the exact opposite of Jorge.[331]

Between 1978 and 2003 Jorge Semprún made a total of eighteen appearances on Pivot's shows, *Apostrophes*, *Bouillon de Culture*, and *Double je*. He was invited to talk about his new books and current events, and to share the stage with other writers and personalities, including his pal Yves Montand. Jorge was a prolific and imaginative writer, with a fascinating political, international biography. He was an attractive man, and could speak with authority on fascism, communism, European history, philosophy, and art. These factors gained him entry into the realm of the European cultural elite, but the cumulative effect of twenty-five years on French television played a very important role. Pivot enabled Jorge to become one of the first intellectual media stars, giving him an exposure that he would not have had otherwise. He became a recognizable fixture in French living rooms, and a celebrity.

Even though Jorge was conquering the French general public, he had not forgotten about Spain for a second. Since 1968 he had been able to travel across the border legally, and he did so often. He could have become a French citizen, but he never wanted to give up his Spanish nationality. This stubborn, personal allegiance to his country would soon be rewarded.

In 1975 he met the man who would play the biggest part in the evolution of Spain's democratic future, and a key role in Jorge's own life: Felipe González. González was a young, brilliant politician from Seville. The meeting was another male friendship *coup de foudre* for Jorge. As their relationship blossomed, Jorge's admiration only grew. González, nineteen years younger than Jorge, would take the future of post-Franco Spain in his hands. He had a role that Jorge would have loved for himself, and Jorge was infected with the young leader's enthusiasm and promise. After nearly forty years of waiting around for a dramatic political change in Spain's government, the moment had arrived, and Jorge wanted to be a part of the action:

> I had met Felipe (González) in Madrid, during the dictator's last, long, dying days. I believe it was González who had asked to meet with us, "us" being some intellectuals who were active in the anti-Franco struggle. The young thirty-year-old I met that day caught my attention immediately. It was love at first sight, which can also apply to friendship between men. Back then, he was relatively unknown. We knew that he had been secretary general of the Socialist party for a year, at a meeting held in the outskirts of Paris. . . . I remembered that young fellow, whose hair was too long, who wore corduroy jackets, and who in 1975 launched himself and conquered the brains and hearts of his fellow citizens.[332]

Within the Spanish scene, Felipe González was just the right person to appreciate Jorge Semprún and all that he represented. A clandestine anti-Franco agent from the Socialist camp (his code name had been "Isidoro"), González understood perfectly why Jorge had become a Communist, and why he had to leave the PCE. Though raised in Franco Spain, González had been educated abroad at the Catholic University of Louvaine, where he had exchanged ideas with fellow students from all over the world.

He was well versed in the worlds of exiled Spaniards and the anti-Francoist fight. He might have been one of the best-positioned people in the world to understand Jorge's lifelong political commitment. He was the first person, since Carrillo in the early 1950s, to see Jorge as an asset to Spain. So it was a bold decision to invite Jorge Semprún to be the minister of culture for the new Socialist Party. He was a controversial figure, the author of *Communism in Spain* and a former Communist. He was also perceived with suspicion by Spaniards as being a "Frenchified" (*afrancesado*) by his many decades of living across the border. But González saw a man of the world in Jorge, and a figure who could bring a cosmopolitan veneer to a country that had been internationally tarnished and dulled by decades of a military, Catholic, dictatorship.

González's decision would open new doors for Jorge. For the first time, he wouldn't be a clandestine agent, but hold a real political office. He would return to the Madrid of his childhood, back when the adults in his family were politicians, and not exiles. There would be no more makeshift rooms in other people's homes or *pensiones*. This time he and his wife Colette would be housed in a beautiful old flat located at number 9, Calle Alfonso XI—just steps from where his grandfather, Antonio Maura, had lived. This just happened to be the location of the government-owned flat assigned to him, but the proximity to his family's former home seemed auspicious. Jorge Semprún was finally embarking on a homecoming of sorts, back to his childhood haunts, and even—in his imagination, at least—back to his mother's childhood. It was where his roots were.

> My life cycle seemed to have come full circle. I had left this street on a July morning, in 1936, to head off for my summer holidays. An entire lifetime ago: half a century. It's easily said. One can write about it a single stroke, a few words, but it weighs on one's memory, physically and spiritually. Half a century.[333]

Felipe González's decision to make Jorge an offer had enormous benefits in every way: emotionally, intellectually, and in terms of status. He was, understandably, thrilled to receive the 1988 invitation to be minister of culture in González's government. It was like a dream come true. He was returning to his old haunts, including the Prado Museum, in a chauffeur-driven car with bodyguards. This time, he was in charge of the Prado.

Since 1963, Jorge had been fulfilling one half of his mother's suggested vocations. She had said, "You'll either be a writer, or President of the Republic." In the end he would be both an author and a minister, albeit in a constitutional monarchy. The latter role was clearly something he had patiently hoped for, though never counted on. The position would take him on a completely new series of adventures. For a sixty-five-year-old author, who had not really lived in Spain since 1936 and was not even a member of Gonzalez's Partido Socialista Obrero Español (PSOE), the invitation was irresistible. There were those who said that Jorge lacked the kind of experience necessary to be a minister. In a vibrant, young, new government, he would be the oldest member of the cabinet. Others perceived that González wanted to do a good deed for a veteran anti-Francoist, but in an interview for this biography the former prime minister emphatically denied any charitable intentions on his part:

> From my point of view he had, first of all, an extraordinary symbolic value. Secondly, from an intellectual point of view, it was a luxury to have a minister of culture of his level and stature, and finally, from a human point of view (and nobody seems to understand this), I wasn't doing him a favor: he was doing me a favor. People don't get this, not even in France.[334]

What was it like for Jorge to return to Spain with his own flat, and a ministry to run with a large staff? How would he relate to the other

ministers? He had spent a good deal of time in Spain over the years—
as Federico Sánchez, and later as himself—but for forty years he had
mostly been living in Paris. Paris was his daily life: his errands, his
public transportation routes, his cafés, his commute with his wife to
their country house in Garentreville. In 1988, thanks to González,
many factors were in place for Jorge to feel truly welcome in Madrid,
and indeed, some experiences would even surpass his expectations.
At the same time, there were intense personal and political challenges
that came from being transplanted into a new lifestyle that included
an office job, and a new life in Madrid for Colette.

Madrid is a leitmotif throughout Jorge Semprun's life, and his
madrileño experiences can be divided into three principal periods: his
sheltered formative years, his clandestine visits to the city many years
later as a communist agent, and his official, celebrated, and very public
return as Ministro de Cultura. Combined, these distinctly different
periods span more than eighty years. His relationship to the city fuses
past and present, and seems to physically anchor itself at the Museo del
Prado, where art and memory, past and present seem to become one
in his many autobiographical works.

Federico Sanchez vous salue bien[335] is only his second book written
in Spanish. He in fact wrote a French original, and translated the text
into Spanish himself. In it, Semprún makes the importance of art
explicit by stating that his entire life story could be told in terms of
one painting in particular, Velázquez's *Las Meninas*:

> I could retell my life . . . I could at least try to do it, vis-
> à-vis Velázquez's *Meninas*. . . . Not that there aren't other
> paintings elsewhere in old Europe, paintings that key epi-
> sodes of my life are also attached to, like tattered dreams. . .
> but in this imaginary trek everything begins and ends with
> *La Meninas*. My life is bound to this fascinating painting, I
> never stop coming back to it, and it always crosses my path
> again.[336]

Using *Las Meninas*, we could trace a version of Semprún's biography starting with his weekly Sunday visits to the Prado as a young boy, holding his father's hand. Semprún was initially reluctant to spend his Sundays at the Prado—he would have preferred to be outside playing—but eventually he became attached to his strolls through the museum's empty halls (during this period the museum was often deserted) listening to his father. Jose María Semprún Gurrea used the paintings to explain Spanish history and politics—past and present—to his son.[337] They often stopped before the paintings of Goya, Velázquez, El Greco, and Titian, as well as those of the lesser known Flemish painter Joachim Patinir. The latter's *El paso de la laguna Estigia* would make a profound impression on Semprún and would become a central element in his own work.

Apart from playing a key role in opening the young Semprún's eyes to art, history, and politics, the Museo del Prado introduced him to women and sexuality. His discovery of the female figure in the paintings of the Prado occurred despite his father's best efforts to exclude any dangerous images from their tours—as he recalls in *Adieu, vive clarté* one of his father's main objectives during these visits was to make sure his son's eyes didn't fall on any representations of female nudity. The only painting of a female he was allowed to see was Murillo's portrait of the Virgin. Semprún attributes his enduring aversion to Murillo to this early paternal censorship, and recalls eventually trying to rebel against his father by playfully running off and hiding in the forbidden Rubens gallery. This was disappointing, however, as Rubens's buxom female figures were not to his taste and shed no light on the essential mysteries of the flesh he sought to understand. Confused by his lack of response to Rubens's women, he would finally console himself upon finding a female ideal in the luminous nudity of Cranach's *Eve*.[338]

In stark contrast to this relatively harmonious childhood discovery of life through the paintings of the Prado, under the protection and guidance of his father's affectionate—if puritanical—hand, is the next period of Semprún's visits to the museum. The man who in the 1950s returned to the galleries that the young boy had roamed had a new name and identity as a clandestine Communist Party operative. He had also survived fighting with the French Resistance and living in a Nazi concentration camp, and was working undercover to overthrow the Franco government. This return to Spain was clearly politically motivated, but it was also personal. By 1953 he needed to return to Spain, to try to live in Madrid. His Spanish was rusty after seventeen years of exile and he could no longer express himself with colloquial ease in daily situations. Addressing a taxi driver or a waiter at a café were challenges that exacerbated his feelings of deracination, and put him at risk of being discovered. This linguistic alienation made him feel like a stranger in his own city. He describes his first clandestine voyage back to Madrid in *Literature or Life*, and says that the first thing he did after checking into the hotel was to walk as fast as he could through the city to number 12, Calle Alfonso XI. Facing his childhood home, Semprún was torn by contradictory feelings: a familiarity that somehow made his exiled status more pronounced. This traumatic confrontation with the past was followed by many more trips to Madrid, and eventually he began to weave together the past and the present. He was able to establish parallels between his life as a clandestine operative—the hiding, the waiting—and his childhood games in the Retiro Park.

> It was like a children's game, in a way, like those we used to play in the Retiro Park, long ago—in the lushest, mazelike part of the park, between the Palacio de Cristal and the carriage promenade that goes from the square of the Fallen Angel to the zoo. Inspired by Zane Grey novels or westerns, we use to creep around stealthily, playing tough guys rescuing a prisoner, or robbing a make-believe stagecoach.[339]

The Prado was as central to his clandestine period as it was to his childhood. In *Federico Sánchez vous salue bien*, he describes his return to the museum and the many hours he spent there:

From 1953 (the year of my first clandestine return to Madrid) onward, I often stopped in front of Velázquez's painting and spent hours of contemplative meditation. Several factors combined to make this spot my favorite—childhood memories, without a doubt. . . . In this first period of my return the Prado was an ideal spot to kill time, and relive dead times. And within the Prado, the location and placement of the Meninas was key.[340]

The key line concerning his clandestine return to Madrid is that the Prado is now the perfect place for two main reasons: to kill time, and to revive the long-gone past. Furthermore, it was dangerous for Semprún to return—with his assumed identity—to his hotel or safe house between secret meetings, and the Prado became the perfect anonymous hideout. *Las Meninas* was the ideal spot to stand for hours on end, because it engaged him aesthetically and intellectually. An added bonus was that the painting had a "key position:" *Las Meninas* was displayed alongside a vast mirror. This mirror was placed to the right of the painting and thus allowed the viewer to reproduce the play of points of view that the painting proposes. But Semprún found a more practical and political use for the mirror: he could see—while ostensibly looking at the painting—whether or not he had been followed by a *guardia civil*. Thus in his times as a clandestine operative, *Las Meninas* was *dulcis et utilis*: an engaging work of art, a connection to his past, and a political hideout with a built-in lookout point.

As minister of culture, Semprún again saw *Las Meninas* on a regular basis. Long gone was the man who stood fearfully in front of the painting. As minister, he was not only free to roam the Prado galleries at will, he also had the power to visit the museum when it was closed to the public. In this latest phase, he had the obligation of accompanying official visitors such as the Queen of England to view the paintings he first saw with his father. The Prado Museum became as much a part of his professional, public present as it had been of his private past.

> Official and private tours; memories of childhood and from my underground work in Madrid; ministerial matters related to the art world that might transform the very function and future of this museum: it would have been quite possible to reconstruct these three years of my life in a narrative centered around the Prado.[341]

Semprún saw the Prado as a narrative mirror of his life and of Spanish history. He fantasized about rewriting the museum's history and turning the history of the paintings into the history of Spain. For this, he dreamed up an imaginary gallery that would begin with *Las Meninas*, move on to Goya, and end with Picasso's *Guernica*. The arrangement of these works would trace the figure of the painter—central in *Las Meninas*, to the faint figure overshadowed by royal power in Goya's *Familia de Carlos IV*, and nonexistent in *Guernica*. In this last painting, "Not even the shadow of a painter appears. There is nothing but History, the naked horror of history."[342]

Jorge Semprún tried twice, unsuccessfully, to have the *Guernica* exhibited face-to-face with Goya's "black paintings." The first time was when he was minister of culture, and the second was on the eve of Jacques Chirac's visit to Madrid. Finally, something very close to—and perhaps even better than—his imaginary gallery came into being at both the Prado and the Reina Sofía museums in 2006 with the inauguration of the exhibit *Picasso, Tradición y vanguardia* in which Picasso's works could finally be seen face-to-face with Goya's and Velázquez's. Semprún met Picasso a couple of times between 1946 and 1947, first in Paris, and later at the painter's studio in Cannes. In their conversations, Picasso expressed his desire to see *Guernica* hanging in the Prado, but only after Franco's dictatorship ended. The painter was convinced that *Guernica* would finally be seen properly for the first time in the particular physical context of the Prado, where, he claimed, it would be clear "where I come from, what feeds my own painting."[343]

Picasso died before Franco, and never saw his dream come true, but Jorge followed up on his wish. The exhibit was an occasion to be able to speak about the artist and the Prado, and in a talk entitled *Sueño y verdad de Pablo Picasso* Jorge Semprún described the painting's resonance in words that are evocative of his own literary works: "*Guernica* is and will continue to be for centuries at the center of the debate of what painting and art are. It is a testimony of a concrete event [the bombing of a city by the Condor Legion], but also a universal metaphor for death, and of popular resurrection."[344] Finally, he concluded, Picasso, who was condemned by the left for ignoring the precepts of social realism and by the right for his support of communism, was at the crossroads of all the crises and debates in art and politics of the twentieth century.

For Semprún, seeing Velázquez, Goya, and Picasso together in the same space was the fulfillment of a long-held dream, and one of the most emotional moments of his life. He drew attention to the evident dialogue between the artists, one that is explicit in some cases (Picasso's reinterpretation of *Las Meninas*), and subtle and more complex in others. Though his talk focused on Picasso, he was obviously also talking about himself and his own creative origins.

Along with Picasso and Goya, Joachim Patinir's landscape paintings are central to Semprún's writing. Patinir's work was recently rediscovered thanks to a 2007 exhibit at the Prado. In Semprún's book *La montagne blanche*, Patinir's painting *El paso de la laguna Estigia* has an organizing role in the narrative structure. The novel's first chapter is called "Une carte postale de Joachim Patinir" and the title of the last chapter is "Le passage du Styx." In the opening chapter the postcard of the painting has been sent to Paris by a friend in Madrid called Juan Larrea, who has just visited the Prado. Larrea gives the following report of his tour: "Later, as usual, I confirmed that Patinir-blue is still what it was. What it used to be. A mad, and very definite, blue."[345] Within these brief lines, in French, like the rest of the novel, the Spanish *"solía ser"* stands out as it repeats the idea—already stated in French—of "that which used to be."

The writer of the postcard is a regular of the Prado and the tour he has taken is a habitual one. He reassures his friend that in the museum nothing has changed, and that most importantly the shade of Patinir-blue is still the same fixed and mad blue it always was. This color—the Patinir blue—is the color of the river Styx in the painting *El paso de la laguna Estigia* and the particular shade—often defined by Semprún as *"marine claire"* or a light navy—is a hallmark of the artist's work. The use of blue for the areas of the composition that seem most distant from the viewer is common throughout Patinir's paintings, and the blues are so intense and characteristic that they almost define the painter's identity. The blue skies in the distance are an infinite lofty paradise compared to the darker brown and green tones of the foregrounds, in which the human figure is dwarfed and often in flight. Microscopic analyses have shown that while Patinir indeed used the same materials as other Flemish artists of the time, through his technique he was able to achieve blues of legendary intensity.

Throughout Semprún's long exile, Patinir's blue became the symbol of an irretrievable world: his childhood in Madrid under Patinir-blue skies. Like amber, the shade is rich but transparent, and holds trapped treasures from the past. The color is a touchstone for memory; the paintings seem to be the only unchanged objects in the city from which the past seems to have vanished. In his book *Veinte años* the narrator remembers a quote from Baudelaire: *"La forme d'une ville change plus vite hélas!, que le coeur d'un mortel,"* (A cityscape changes more quickly, alas, than the human heart) and laments that "the truth is that Madrid has changed more quickly than the old heart of the human, more mortal by the minute, narrating this story."[346]

In *La montagne blanche* the main character Juan Larrea has returned to Madrid with a French girlfriend, Nadine. They are staying at the

Ritz Hotel, just blocks from Semprún's childhood home. Larrea is seducing Nadine—as he has other women—with this privileged trip to his childhood haunts. Their hotel room looks out to the Prado Museum, he takes Nadine for walks in the Retiro, they visit the Prado every day. But just as this romantic trip seems to be going well, a sudden glance up at the Madrid sky causes Larrea to disengage completely from the present, from the false and repetitive amorous relationships he pretends to involve himself in:

> The sky above his head was the same blue as before, the blue of childhood. The blue that preceded the proliferation of the industrial suburbs built by the Franco regime, the blue of a courtly, bureaucratic, slightly provincial capital and not the metropolis of urban, cancerous expansion it had become. The blue there had been before the existence of the crown of smog of daily pollution that now eclipsed what had been Europe's bluest sky. But on this day, the blue of Madrid's sky became all blue again . . . a dense blue, but pure, even purified—without the viscosity of some tropical blues. . . . Dense yet light; almost unsustainable in its dense lightness, its infinite blueness. . . . Juan had looked at the blue sky. . . . He was no longer a part of that April day that had started off so well. . . . He felt lost . . . abandoned, forgotten. Forsaken by God's hand. . . . The blue of a childhood sky seemed to unmask life: There was nothing behind the mask. Nothing but the banality of life itself.[347]

At the end of La montagne blanche Juan Larrea drowns himself, drawn in by the blue water of a French river. As he lets the water flood his body, words and images of Patinir's blue and of his childhood fly by his eyes in fragments: the blue of April, the intensely blue skies of Madrid near the Retiro, the indigo of the French river. Colors become words, not spoken, but cried out. Larrea dies bombarded with words for shades of blue that sound like the cries of the knife-grinder—the typical early morning sound of Madrid—that he heard so many years ago.

As these few examples illustrate, the paintings of the Prado Museum were central to Jorge Semprún's life, his writing, his memory, and the Spanish identity he never gave up. In the following words, we see him in the midst of an unfinished dialogue with one of his favorite paintings:

> I come back to contemplating *Las Meninas*. I still have a few fractions of a second—an eternity in a well laid out narrative—to imagine this admirable screen of the dreams of my life. Or the life of my dreams.[348]

Semprún may not have been able to find the past in Madrid, but he saw part of himself in the city of his childhood: "In Spain I have an identity. It is at times muddled, often not what I would like it to be, but it is there, and very much alive."[349]

Jorge had become a hybrid, and no matter where he was geographically, he was psychologically a bit of a nowhere man. When Felipe González decided to ask Jorge to join his government, he arranged for Javier Solana, his outgoing minister of culture, to call Jorge in Paris and find out if he was still a Spanish citizen. Nationality was a job requirement. Solana popped the question "What is your nationality?" as soon as Jorge answered the phone, and Semprún began to ramble about his cultural identity:

> I didn't really understand the question. . . . I thought it was abstract. "I'm basically stateless," I answered. "Bilingual, hence schizophrenic, hence rootless. In fact, my homeland isn't even a language, as it is for most writers. My homeland is words."[350]

Solana listened patiently and finally laughed and said, "The question is much simpler than that: do you have a Spanish passport?[351] Jorge said he did, and accepted the position.

VIII
Minister of Culture

There will be thrilling moments, and days that are
grey and tedious. You will have friends, some of
them real, and other false. You will have all kinds of
enemies—that's inevitable. Nobody will forgive you
anything, so don't expect them to. That's just the way
this society works. It's still rankled by provincialisms,
class resentment, and archaisms. But the day will come,
on your first official trip, when one of the heads of
the Guardia Civil, will stand at attention in front of
"Federico Sánchez." Then you'll realize that this country
has changed, and you'll know what your presence in this
government means.[352]
— Felipe González

When Jorge was minister of culture, not a day went by
that he wasn't attacked by the friendly fire newspapers for
being "frenchified," a "frog," or "froggy."[353]
—Eduardo Arroyo

Javier Solana very clearly remembers the afternoon he called Jorge
Semprún to offer him the ministerial post:

I had great affection for Jorge; Felipe González did as well.
They were good friends. I was certain the offer would
please Jorge, first that we had thought of him and wished
for him to return to Spain to render a service to his country,
and second to have the opportunity to take charge of and
take responsibility for the country's cultural heritage. I felt it
would be hard for him to turn it down. It was in the afternoon and I was going to the opera—in my official capacity
but also because I was eager to attend the performance—
and I remember how I took advantage of the intermission

to use the director of the opera house's office so that I could call Jorge.

Semprún was taken by surprise because the first question I asked him without mentioning anything else was, which passport did he have, a French or Spanish one. Then we chatted for a bit and I said, "Why don't you come to Madrid tomorrow? I can organize the trip for you if you'd like." And so he came the next day and had a meeting with the president of the government, who made him the offer formally. I had insinuated on the phone what the meeting might be about, the idea of substituting me and such, and once the offer was made by Felipe we were all very pleased and in sync with each other. I changed ministries and became minister of education and he became the minister of culture. After we had both finished the swearing-in ceremony in the presence of the king we went to the Café Gijon. We ordered coffee and a croissant and discussed the best way for me to hand him the reins, the transfer of powers, the most important things he needed to know. Then we walked to the Ministry of Culture that was close by and finished signing the necessary papers.[354]

In countries like Spain with significant state-subsidized cultural enterprises, "minister of culture" or "culture minister" is a post within the government cabinet. The Minister tends to be responsible for the preservation and dissemination—both at home and abroad—of a "national culture." This might include many aspects of a country's heritage: museums, music and film festivals, art fairs, book fairs, schools and universities, and countless other intellectual, artistic, and educational circles. The minister of culture may not have the same substantial ring as, say, minister of defense, but in the right hands it can propel a country into international stardom. André Malraux, Jorge's erstwhile idol, had been the French minister of culture with Charles de Gaulle from 1958–1969. He became a celebrity, thanks to great coups such as sending the *Mona Lisa* to the United States. After a visit to John F. Kennedy's White House, Jackie Kennedy claimed that Malraux was the "most fascinating man I've ever talked to."[355] Starting in 1981, the French Minister of Culture Jack Lang had turned the position into the country's most glamorous political appointment. Lang became a household name all over Europe and internationally, and his political career was launched. He would go on to become a member of the European Parliament.

The 1980s were an exciting time for Spain and for Europe. Spain had been an outlier for centuries, but in 1986 it was finally made a member of what was then called the European Community (since 1993 incorporated as the European Union). Becoming minister of culture in Spain was no longer just a Spanish position, it was also *European*. Jorge Semprún may have very well thought that he would follow in Lang's footsteps, or at least hold his ministerial position for a few terms and leave a glorious legacy behind.

Why did they think Jorge Semprún could be the best possible minister of culture? According to Felipe González:

> First off, throughout the many years we had known each other it was clear we had many things in common; we shared certain fundamental beliefs. I remember him sign-ing books at a book fair in some French city whose name I can't recall; I remember many conversations we had over the years in Paris and here in Madrid once he was able to come and go as he pleased. We had many good friends in common, like Javier Pradera, Fernando Claudín, and Juan Benet, a whole tribe of people. We had a relationship that was fluid and easy. One of the things I most appreciate and treasure in life is intelligent conversation. To be with people capable of adding value to rich conversation is something I did as much as I could, as much as my agenda could permit

back then. As one gets older it becomes more and more difficult to find people of that kind of caliber. Jorge was one of those people and we shared a community of ideas, putting aside ideologies that do not interest me that much, but rather a similar way of analyzing events. Also, to be honest, and this was a fundamental reason for asking him to join my government, I wanted to make some noise, to try and recover the best and most expressive examples of the many brilliant Spaniards who had gone into exile because of Franco. I wanted to give Jorge the freedom to put his own stamp on the Ministry of Culture that enjoyed great transcendence back then. You might remember that in 1982 there was this explosion of energy in the country, an explosion of freedom and cultural expression. And so I thought, Jorge has to come, I have to bring him back to Spain to work with me.[356]

There is no doubt that Jorge had an exceptional background that would enable him to play a compelling role as Spain's minister of culture but there are always adjustments one has to make when taking on a new job. This is how Joaquín Almunia, who was then the minister of public administration, remembers it:

At the cabinet meetings our chairs were always next to each other. I had read his novels and memoirs, the *Autobiography of Federico Sánchez*, and I got to know him personally in the early '80s through mutual friends like Javier Pradera. I remember a number of dinners with him and the enormous interest he always had in Spanish politics. Each time he came to Spain he always asked a lot of questions and liked being up to date with what was going on here. The most contact I had with him, obviously, was in 1988 when we were ministers together.

By order of protocol the ministers of culture and public
Administration always sat next to each other and I think the
event he mentions in his book related to cabinet meetings
had to do with a discussion that took place about butane gas.
It made quite an impression on him.

In cabinet meetings decisions aren't made like they are
when heads of a political party get together. In the latter
the party heads usually engage in an active debate. That
happens now and then during a cabinet meeting, but it's
more like what we now call in the European Commission
a "debate of orientation." I can't remember what we called
it then. I mean if the subject was something like the situation in China each minister would say whatever they
wished, but when it came to approving a project for a law,
or issuing a decree, making a decision about something
concrete which was most often the case, another kind of
debate had already taken place between the ministries
and the president's inner council. These were discussions
aimed at coordinating positions and clearing up any differences of opinion ahead of time. So at the cabinet meetings, even if one of the ministers expressed disagreement
about a particular issue, everyone knew the decision had
already been made—and Jorge did not get that dynamic
at all.[357]

As minister of culture, Jorge had a key role in major developments
in Spain. Perhaps the most significant was a massive project that had
been initiated by his predecessor, Javier Solana: the creation of the
Thyssen-Bornemisza Museum. The basis of this institution was the
gift of a private collection owned by the German Baron Heinrich
Thyssen and his Spanish wife, a former beauty queen who had been
Miss Spain in 1961. The new museum garnered headlines around the
globe for the donors, and even for Jorge:

The government has signed a 10-year agreement with one of world's biggest art collectors to bring paintings by El Greco, Goya and Velazquez home for display. The loan agreement with Baron Hans Heinrich Thyssen-Bornemisza will bring 787 of the works in his priceless collection of classic and modern art to Spain, boosting Spain to the rank of one of the world's leading art centers. The acquisition, which Spanish officials hope will become permanent, also includes works by Holbein, Franz Hals, Tintoretto, Ghirlandaio, Canaletto, Max Beckmann, Van Gogh, Cezanne, Monet, and Degas. The agreement signed Tuesday by the baron and Culture Minister Jorge Semprún caps years of negotiations and represents a success for Spain over such rival bidders as West Germany, Britain, and Switzerland, and the private Getty Foundation in Malibu, Calif. The baron said his desire to have as many people as possible see his collection "was probably the most important motive" in his decision to bring the works temporarily to Spain.

"After ten years, we can see how it works and take a decision," the baron said, referring to the ultimate destination of his collection. He said the final decision would be up to him, his wife and his four children.

That the collection ended up in Spain is due in large part to the influence of the baron's fifth wife Carmen "Tita" Cervera, and to the efforts of the Duke of Badajoz, Luis Gomez-Acebo, the husband of King Juan Carlos's sister, Pilar. The baron's collection of between 1,200 and 1,600 works, rivaled only by that of Queen Elizabeth II as the most impressive private holding of art, has been valued at two billion dollars. That figure is relatively meaningless, however, because of the rapidly escalating prices in the international art market for both old masters and modern paintings.[358]

During his tenure as minister Jorge was also charged with distrib-
uting the legacy of the artist Salvador Dalí. The divvying up of the
works of art, a priceless collection of 190 paintings, stirred a heated
war between Cataluña (Dalí's birthplace) and the capital city, Madrid.
After a year of complex negotiations and controversy, the collection was finally divided—unfairly in the opinion of most *catalanistas*.
Madrid kept some of Dalí's most important works.

Carlos Solchaga, Jorge's colleague and minister of economy and
finance, recalls how well-equipped Jorge was to negotiate cultural
matters:

> From the get-go he was very confident in all the areas he
> was in charge of. Fine arts, museums, the national book
> center (Dirección General del Libro), exhibits. The theater
> world, the film world, performances: he knew these milieus
> like the back of his hand, and he brought a certain style to
> his work. One could say it was the more elegant style of a
> Parisian (vs. Spanish) bureaucrat.[359]

Jorge was so pleased with the way things were going that he planned
to stay in Spain permanently. He saw it as the beginning of a serious
political career:

> I won't write an autobiography about my time as minister.
> Parts of my experience will come out in the media . . . in an
> essay, but not as a novel, nor as a collective portrait. There
> will be no more of that.[360]
>
> When I leave the government, I will stay and live in this
> country, and I will be even more involved in politics than
> I am today.[361]

But all was not well within the PSOE government, and while
Jorge made some loyal new friends, he also butted heads with Vice

President Alfonso Guerra, among others. Jorge's candor during and after his term made him many enemies. He singlehandedly took on Spain's film industry by proposing radical cuts and reforms to the government subsidy program, and accused the president of Spanish television, Pilar Miró, of cronyism. As he was not a professional politician, nor a member of the party he represented, he did not mince his words. What did he have to lose? But his greatest animosity was directed at Alfonso Guerra. Because of the perceived corruption of his brother Juan Guerra, and controversial comments Jorge made about the matter—on the record, in the media—the vice president was forced to leave office. González also asked Jorge to resign after a scandalously candid interview he gave to *El País* newspaper in July, 1990, in which he called Guerra and his followers "opportunists from the Left" (*oportunistas de izquierdas*) and said that the government was in crisis and that nobody was speaking about the politics of it. This was the second, and last, time that he was fired from a post with a Spanish political party for speaking his mind and openly rebelling against his superiors. The interview he gave was truly impolitic:

> **Q:** "How does his relationship with Juan Guerra fit into his case?"
> **A:** "In the worst way possible. It's true the press went to town with it but they didn't make it up, there really was a kind of conspiracy. The story about Guerra came about due to a coincidence of three factors: the brother of the vice president who had an official office and who got rich very quickly. It was made worse by the slow initial, arrogant reaction that attempted to explain things in a very confused manner. Things came out because the press kept on investigating and discovering them."[362]

Carlos Solchaga, the former minister of economy and finance, who was also opposed to Guerra and who always had a great appreciation for Jorge, recalls the obstacles Semprún encountered and created:

> It all worked well for a time until Jorge began to take sides between Alfonso Guerra and myself, most especially with respect to the story about Guerra's brother (Juan Guerra). He sided with me on that one and weighed in against Guerra very clearly. And this threw Felipe off some, changed the way he saw how Jorge fit into his government, fit into his concept of the government and its relation with the Socialist Party. He realized in some way, that while Jorge was a very respected figure, he was not one of us, not someone in lockstep with the Socialist Party, and he wasn't sure how to handle it when the shocks began to reverberate within the party.
>
> This went on for a year, because from the time Felipe realized how difficult it was going to be to prop up Alfonso Guerra, until the moment Guerra stepped down in January 1991 in the middle of the Gulf War, a long year had gone by. Jorge published his article in the summer of 1990, just before Desert Storm and the American invasion of Kuwait. It was a very tough article indignant against Guerra and all that he represented in the Socialist Party. So at that point Felipe surely felt tremendous pressure from leading party figures asking to the effect, "Who is this guy, who doesn't even belong to our party, to be telling us what we should do or not?" The most important point for them, what they kept repeating was: "This guy isn't one of us." It often happens that people who don't have a lot of their own merits will focus everything on belonging. They'll say, "I may not be the smartest one here but I've been around the longest"— that kind of thing.

And then Jorge calls me the day before we were to have a cabinet meeting and asks me to have dinner with him at the Casa Vasca, a restaurant in front of the Zarzuela Theater, close to the "Cortes."[363] And so we sit down and he hands me the letter he received from Felipe González. I read it, and he asked me, "What do you think? What is he getting at?" And I told him, "He's asking you to step down." I think actually by that time Felipe regretted what he'd said. It had happened in a moment of anger, or what have you, and I think he would not have been pleased if Jorge had stepped down just then. The proof is that—I don't know, I suppose Jorge and he had a conversation about this soon after that dinner—they agreed to have him stay on in the government until a new cabinet was to be announced in March of 1991—which is when Jorge left. Colette nursed a permanent grudge against Spain believing it had been tremendously unkind to her husband, especially in terms of what it owed him as an intellectual and as a politician.[364]

Jorge did not stay in Spain, nor did he remain in politics. His poetic return to his family neighborhood and his joining the ministerial ranks once occupied by his grandfather was not to be the grand ending to his complicated life. It was just another frustrated attempt to go home.

Contrary to his previous statements, he did write a tell-all memoir about his experience as minister of culture, his 1993 *Federico Sánchez vous salue bien*. This sequel revenge narrative echoes the 1977 *Communism in Spain*. Here again he is the well-meaning exile returning to the homeland to assume a political role. Yet again he is faced by corrupt leaders who underestimate his wisdom and talent, and yet again he is banished and must return to France with his tail between his legs. There are significant differences, of course. One narrative is about the Communist Party, and one is about the Socialist Party; one is set during the Franco dictatorship, the other after the transition to democracy. But both are angry revenge narratives. In 1977 Jorge still had hopes that he would make a comeback and have a role in Spain's political future. In 1993, the comeback was in the past, he was much older, and the official good-bye rang with finality. Felipe González, his host, was asking him to leave, and he was much younger than Jorge. He could outlive Franco, but not the newer generations of politicians. Though disappointed, Jorge did not blame González. He was much too busy blaming his vice president, Alfonso Guerra. For Jorge, Guerra had become an archenemy, and he relished repeatedly insulting the politician in repeatedly *Federico Sánchez*. If the raison d'etre of this memoir had to be reduced to one, it would be to attack Alfonso Guerra and his brother Juan Guerra on ethical grounds:

> It is true that he had publicly taken a position in the corruption and embezzlement cases in which the presumed guilty party was the brother of the vice president (Alfonso Guerra). Juan Guerra, who was unemployed in 1982 when the Socialists won the elections, later became a factotum for his powerful relative in their home town, Seville. In any case, Juan Guerra was given a government office to work in, and he took advantage of the aura of authority conferred by this office and his last name to make—in just a few years—a considerable fortune.[365]

Combined with his moral opposition to Alfonso Guerra and his brother, he also had a visceral distaste for the vice president. The extensive portrait he offers, that he couldn't stand the thick lenses of Guerra's glasses, his thin face, his reading choices, his "muffled" voice, or his *sevillano* accent. Guerra had been considered the intellectual of the PSOE before Jorge came along, so understandably there was rivalry between them, but for Jorge this tension became a passionate hatred. His criticisms are repeated like machine-gun fire on one page—the adjective "muffled" is used four times in three paragraphs:

Then it was Alfonso Guerra's turn to speak. He spoke in a
weak, muffled voice. . . . His andalusian accent was very
noticeable, and ruined some Castilian words by ignoring
letters and diphthongs, and deformed others. I have come
to the conclusion that Guerra spoke thus to force people to
listen to him intensely. I heard him speak with his muffled
voice, his diction ruined by his andalusian accent.[366]

Jorge may have had to leave Spain, but he had recovered some of his
true identity as an early-twentieth-century *madrileño* ready to look
down on a rival he saw as a provincial parvenu. His portrait of Guerra
is unfair, no doubt, but as Joaquín Almunia recalls, Guerra was not
fair with Jorge, either. Their contempt for one another was a two-
way street, and Guerra never understood why Felipe González had
brought Jorge Semprún on board in the first place.[367]

On the other hand, he had been minister of culture and had played
a political role in democratic Spain. According to Carlos Solchaga,
Jorge also wrote *Federico Sánchez vous salue bien* for other reasons:

You can feel his sense of satisfaction, it's there in the book,
great satisfaction because Spain is finally able to be part
of Europe, then it is a democratic country. And he feels a
necessity to speak about it, to say "Look at what I did in
other times when I lived a clandestine life and then look
at where we are now." Although he tries to say it with a
certain *detáchement* he can't. It is also a book that brings an
end to things, that says, "I want to tell you all that happened
back then because Spain is now a normal country."[368]

Overall, Jorge had exciting, satisfying adventures in Spain between
1953 and 1991. He had been a Communist secret agent and a minister
for the Socialist government. Since becoming minister and moving
back to his childhood neighborhood, he felt reconnected with his

Maura side and with the past. His grandfather had served King Alfonso XIII, and Jorge had now served his grandson. Two grandsons with exiled fathers, Juan Carlos I and Jorge Semprún, had been brought together in Madrid to close some kind of circle that had been violently disrupted by civil war, fascism, and an inconceivably long dictatorship. It was uncanny that the monarchy had been reinstated with Juan Carlos I, and that Jorge Semprún had, for three years, worked with him and his wife, Queen Sofia. The queen was especially involved in the art and music worlds and Jorge had great admiration for her personal and cultural refinement.

In the midst of all his anger at Alfonso Guerra and his followers, he had developed an attachment for many people in Spain, including the royal family. Jorge's former Communist ties did not interfere at all with his new life among the international elite. He enjoyed his work with the king and queen of Spain, and with the other royalty he had the chance to meet in the Prado, including Queen Elizabeth, whom he speaks of glowingly. He says that he and the Baron Heinrich von Thyssen hit it off instantly, and he also writes appreciatively of the baroness, Carmen (Tita) Cervera. On the other hand, he was horrified by the self-centered, ignorant behaviour of Soviet first lady Raisa Gorbacheva.

During the 1939–1975 dictatorship Jorge had lived with a clear priority: fight to bring Franco down. Now Franco was gone, and the Communist Party was legal and Carrillo lived near the Retiro park in Madrid and went home every evening to sit in his armchair and talk on the radio before going to bed. He was on the radio almost every weekday night. People from across the political spectrum hailed Carrillo as a hero of the transition to democracy. He had returned home. But what about Jorge? His own country in the end, Franco or no Franco, always seemed to push him away. His brother Carlos wrote succinctly about Spain's attitude toward its own exiles: "The truth is that post-Franco Spain (and it was already in the 'post' phase even before the dictator's death) has never accepted the concept of exile. Its causes and its consequences have been rejected flat out. Exile is like a handicapped person in a bourgeois family."[369]

Jorge's self-proclaimed desire to spend the rest of his life in Spain and to remain in politics was impossible. Though he was greatly respected for his culture and literary talent, his public outspokenness and cockiness had branded him as a hotheaded troublemaker.

Though there would be many more trips to Spain—to see friends, give lectures, and sign books—he would never live there again. The political power he had so fervently sought for decades remained forever elusive.

As minister he never managed to shake his outsider status. His friend and former colleague Carlos Solchaga says about Spain: "People here don't like outsiders coming to Spain to correct them, or to teach them what to do or say; it makes them suspicious and distrustful."[370]

Jorge's sui generis behavior did not change once he knew he was expelled from the party. He left Spain with his head held high, and even requested a farewell meeting with the king. This was an unheard-of request, according to Felipe González:

> Of all the ministers I've had, the only one who ever asked for an audience with the king to say goodbye was Jorge. And the king said to me, "Don't you think it's a bit odd?" I hadn't had tons of ministers, but over the years I must have had about sixty, and Jorge was the only one who requested a farewell audience with the king. The king, who had a very good sense of the big picture, was intrigued: "So the only minister who wants to say good bye to me officially is the Communist, the concentration camp survivor, the Republican. . . . What does it mean?" And I answered, "Well don't forget that he is a Semprún, but also a Maura. He may have been a Communist, a revolutionary, but he's from a family that knows there are codes of behavior that go beyond ideologies. That's why, and there's nothing else

to it." It was exactly that: Jorge believed he had served democratic Spain, and the constitutional monarchy as a minister. He had to resign his post ahead of time, and it was only natural for him to say goodbye to his head of state.[371]

Javier Solana doesn't believe Jorge's resignation from the Ministry of Culture had any negative impact on Semprún's impressive political arc. When asked if he thought that Jorge had a political vocation, he responded, "Political vocation, absolutely. What I'm not so sure of is if he had a vocation to be a minister of the government, but he showed great political vocation throughout his life. All his life he had an enormous political commitment, understood as dedication to a society in transformation, a desire for change, which is what he always wanted for Spain."[372]

The painter Eduardo Arroyo, a long-standing friend of Jorge's, saw his departure from the PSOE government in a different light. According to Arroyo, Jorge had been used and hung out to dry when he became inconvenient. His recollection of Jorge's last day in Madrid as minister is a pathetic vision of a—temporarily—homeless man and his wife wandering the streets with their belongings after having been abruptly kicked out of their government home and relieved of their official car. Arroyo offered to take them in for a few days, and helped them gather their belongings. The move coincided with the Madrid marathon, and with luggage and no taxis in sight they walked for what seemed like ages through the crowded streets to get to Arroyo's house. If Jorge had come into his post like a swan, he was leaving on all fours, according to Arroyo's version.

No matter when, no matter the circumstances, Spain resisted becoming a permanent home for Jorge. He was doomed to live in a border state, for France was still not entirely welcoming to him, either. Certain people were always eager to point out Jorge's "outsider" status. As Arroyo explains:

The French didn't treat him much better. At the insistence of Jean D'Ormesson and Hélène Carrère d'Encausse, he applied to become a member of the Académie française. That was a mistake, and he should have known better. Several members opposed his candidacy because he had been a Communist, and was Spanish. He, who wrote beautiful, moving pages, in such a precise and rich French. But he wasn't resentful. In any case, it's a useful counterpoint to the Académie Goncourt. They welcomed him as a member, because their only criterion is that the person be a French-language writer.[373]

One of the most insightful tributes to Jorge's time as a minister was written shortly after his death by his cabinet chief, the late Juby Bustamante. She saw him on a daily basis, and they remained close for many years—though as she herself says it was not easy to be "close" to Jorge in the habitual sense. But she sensed his struggles, and the insurmountable obstacles he faced in trying to assimilate to contemporary Spain:

> I never know how to respond when people say to me, categorically, "You knew Jorge Semprún so well." In fact, I think that hardly anyone knew Jorge Semprún very well. His wife Colette is an exception, and a couple of old friends. . . . Everyone else, and I include myself in this group, only saw bits of him, and glimpsed that he was as attractive as he was secretive, as complex as he was contradictory, as warm as he was distant, and as sociable as he was solitary. I can say that I met him when I interviewed him for *Diario 16*, in the late '70s. I can also say that, on many of his frequent trips to Spain, I shared many hours during prolonged gatherings with his legendary friends in Madrid. And, most importantly, that I worked with him for the three years that

he was at the head of the Ministry of Culture of Felipe
González's government. Over many days, and many hours
of every day, I saw him make decisions, reflect, struggle.
He faced bureaucracies that perplexed him, approaches to
politics that were alien to him. He was up against situations
and people who were obtuse, stingy, excessively cunning,
and lacking any real talent.[374]

The dissonance between Jorge and life in Madrid pushed him back
to France once again. But he would always return to Spain when
he could. That said, he never fit in there completely and his literary
works even now have yet to find their place within the Spanish canon.
Jordi Gracia explains this phenomenon:

I'm a professor of literature, and with respect to Semprún
I've had to make the choice of whether to include him or
not in courses I design concerning twentieth-century literature. Though I endeavor to change things around every
year, some of his books have been part of my syllabus for
some time now. Sometimes I assign *The Long Voyage* and for
another course *Literature or Life*. Once or twice I included
Communism in Spain but I soon saw that was a work that
didn't take hold with my students. It's rather like a book
written in code and the students didn't really get it, it
didn't interest them. But they love *The Long Voyage,* and
Literature or Life worked well for them, too. Let's say that
in the ranking of which of his books was the most seductive with students, *The Long Voyage* is the clear winner. He
is difficult to explain to them, and I make a great effort
to reveal Semprún as he was, a Spaniard associated with a
Europe that was cut off from Spain. And this is why he has
not been received with the sympathy he deserves in Spanish
culture, his rhythms and positions are foreign in a manner

of speaking. He functions as a sort of informer with respect to Spanish culture.

It was a shock for me to discover that Semprún did not appear in the *History of Spanish Literature*. Domingo Ródenas and I have just amended this situation and included him as someone who obviously belongs there. We didn't buy the argument that looked to exclude him because he wrote most of his books in French. How could one possibly skip over Semprún? He absolutely belongs to any study of Spanish culture and Spanish literature. If he also pertains to French culture and literature, what difference does it make? He does not fit neatly into any of the prescribed categories of contemporary Spanish writers and this too has been a factor. Another factor is that concentration camp literature has never been valued or paid much attention to in Spain. The famous concentration camp authors have not been valued here. Spain had to wait until the death of Franco for some interest to bloom.

The strangeness of Semprún's odyssey within Spanish culture is directly related to the strangeness of Spanish culture's weird odyssey within postwar Europe. Obviously this is no longer the case, but it was the case for forty years. And I am not only talking about institutional Francoism, because Spain began to change before Franco's demise, something that Semprún had a direct influence on. But to really understand the explanation for the difficulty there has been admitting Semprún's work into the mainstream of Spanish literary culture, it requires an appreciation for the difficulty Spain has had becoming part of Europe.[375]

IX

Paris Encore

On February 24, 1991, Jorge Semprún and Yves Montand made an appearance together on Spanish television.[376] The two guests were on the air as artists cum public intellectuals and experts on international politics. Jorge was still minister of culture, though he had already privately agreed with Felipe González to step down, and Montand had seriously considered a bid for the French presidency in 1988. The two old pals were credible public figures, and both had swung decidedly to the political right. Neither one was at their high point and Jorge looks frankly uncomfortable during some of Montand's more exuberant interventions. Montand died of a heart attack at the age of seventy in November of that year.

Jorge maintained his usual steadfast calm, he was not a ranter, but the combination of his comments and his attitude toward the young female host, Concha García Campoy,[377] were quite hostile. García Campoy, who was about forty years younger than her guests, was polite but firm in her questions, which centered on the first Iraq war.

When one sees the program today, it is easy to wonder: what were these two fellows doing opining publicly about this war to begin with? They were, in this case, both outspokenly prowar, and fully on the side of the president of the United States, George H. W. Bush. Jorge is defensive when García Campoy tries to explore the tension between his current views and his Communist past. The climax of the conversation is when she asks him how a survivor of World War II and former Nazi prisoner can be pro military intervention. He answers that if the United States had intervened when it should have in the late 1930s or early 1940s, he would never have been a prisoner. His debate techniques shine forth in this colloquium, but his political views seem muddled. He had become a supporter of US policies, and given his background, García Campoy's surprise was only natural. There is an unpleasant tension between him and the attractive, and very smart, interviewer. His impatience implies that he had no time for these pesky questions from a female implying he was a turncoat. He soon steered his life away from contemporary international events, and his writing career back to the subject he had the most control over: Buchenwald.

Soon after leaving his ministerial post, Semprún returned to Paris, and his writing returned to Buchenwald. This is a direct parallel to the aftermath of his expulsion from the Communist Party and the publication of *The Long Voyage* in 1963. When faced by political frustration, Jorge turned to literature and memory as figurative safety nets. When excluded by his team in Spain, he again traveled—in his imagination—to Buchenwald. In 1994 he produced a memoir that would become his most successful book ever, *Literature or Life*.[378] The international triumph of this memoir was his best revenge yet. He was seventy-one years old when it came out.

What he managed to do in this latest work about Buchenwald was to spin the subject of Nazi camps into a surprisingly appealing terrain. He employs a seemingly frank and direct first-person narration and a wry tone. The chapters are broken up into manageable, stand-alone portions, and liberally sprinkled with famous names—Louis Armstrong, Pablo Picasso, Thomas Mann. He talks about jazz, cigarettes, poetry, and Smith & Wessons. The memoir was a celebration of life and culture, and an ode to the twentieth century, apparently free of bitterness or resentment. In the category of "Nazi camp memoirs" *Literature or Life* stands out as the supreme nonthreatening book. There are references, of course, to the horrors he has been through and witnessed, but what readers responded to was something else. The tragic death of a Jewish prisoner is checked by the glory of fraternal bonds and the beauty of the Kaddish, the alienation he felt reaching a repatriation center in Ettersburg after the liberation of Buchenwald is converted to joy and desire as the narrator dances with a girl to "The Sunny Side of the Street." There is no reckoning with the Germans, and no criticism of the French and their murky collaboration with the Nazis. Everyone was off the hook. Jorge Semprún had hit the jackpot.

The idea for *Literature or Life* had come to him, he said, when he first heard of author, chemist, and Auschwitz survivor Primo Levi's suicide on April 8, 1987. He did not tackle *Literature or Life* immediately after Levi's death, though, because the idea coincided with the invitation to become minister of culture. It had to wait until he returned to France in 1991, and finished the account of his struggles with the Spanish Socialists, *Federico Sánchez vous salue bien* (1993).

He devotes a chapter of the book to Levi, and within it describes the genesis of the book itself. He says that he took the news of Levi's suicide personally, and was disturbed by the significant parallels between Levi's life and his own:

> Despite the radical difference in the course of our lives, in our experiences, there yet remains one coincidence, and a troubling one. The time span between Levi's first book—a masterful piece of writing; a complete flop in reaching its audience—and his second, *La tregua*, is in fact the same as that separating the failure in 1945 of my attempts to write and *Le grand voyage*. These last two books were written in the same period, published almost simultaneously: Levi's in April 1963, mine in May.[379]

Primo Levi's suicide is, in effect, he said, the inspiration for this book. In Jorge's mind, Levi had chosen "literature and life" by writing *If This Is a Man* (1947) so soon after the end of the war. Jorge found himself unable to revisit the camp in his memory and write in the immediate postwar, and thus chose "life" or political action over literature. He had to wait nearly twenty years, until *The Long Voyage*, to recreate his experience. When Levi killed himself in 1987, it reified Jorge's theory that trauma survivors had to choose between literature—loosely defined as a creation based on deep-sea diving in painful memories—or life—understood as present-day action and denial of the past. Hence the book's title. Jorge appears to be puzzled and disconcerted by Levi's voluntary death. He had thought Levi had somehow been able to escape the claws of the choice, choosing life and literature. Did Levi's suicide prove Jorge right? His evocations and meditations about Levi allow him to pay homage to the late Turinese writer, and at the same time to claim a kinship with Levi and inscribe himself into the canon of Holocaust culture. Rossana Rossanda, who had first told him of Levi's work, had offered to introduce them in Turin. Curiously, Semprún never wanted to meet the survivor and writer he claimed as his Italian doppelgänger. In his explorations of suicide, he also never mentions that his brother Alvaro—who was just a year younger than Jorge—killed himself in 1978 at the age of fifty-three.[380] Alvaro had led a solitary life. He had struggled with depression and schizophrenia and the lack of a secure family life.

Reemerging as a Holocaust witness and survivor, in part thanks to his association with Levi, Jorge had catapulted himself from the role of understudy to star.

Furthermore, he had upped the ante by arguing that "auto-fiction," the memoir-fiction that he had claimed as his particular genre of writing, was the *only way* to give voice to testimony. He argues that straight recollections and testimonial writing were ineffective for conveying the horrors of history. In order to achieve a successful representation, one had to be a witness and an artist. Ideally, one had to be Jorge Semprún. *Literature or Life* explicitly takes on the possibilities of memory and the relationship between memory and art in the context of writing about the Nazi camps:

> There will be survivors. Me, for example. Here I am, the survivor on duty, appearing opportunely before these three Allied officers to tell them of the crematory smoke, the smell of burnt flesh hanging over the Ettersburg, the roll calls out in the falling snow, the murderous work details, the exhaustion of life, the inexhaustibility of hope, the savagery of the human animal, the nobility of man, the fraternity

and devastation in the naked gaze of our comrades. But can
the story be told? Can anyone tell it? All you have to do is
begin. The reality is there, waiting. And the words as well.
Yet I start to doubt the possibility of telling the story. Not
that what we lived through is indescribable. It was unbearable, which is something else entirely (that won't be hard
to understand), something that doesn't concern the form of
a possible account, but its substance. Not its articulation,
but its density. The only ones who will manage to reach
this substance, this transparent density, will be those able to
shape their evidence into an artistic object, a space of creation. Or of re-creation. Only the artifice of a masterly narrative will prove capable of conveying some of the truth of
such testimony. . . . In short, you can always say everything.
The "ineffable" you hear so much about is only an alibi. Or
a sign of laziness.[381]

Many critics and readers would agree with Jorge's case for an artistic testimony, and many would argue that there is no other kind.
Experience is inevitably shaped by our individual perceptions, memory, and imagination, whether we like it or not. On the other hand,
some people saw Jorge's approach as a minefield. He had taken on a
leading role within Holocaust discourse, and he was saying that not
only was it acceptable to invent the past, but that it was in fact necessary. This raised thorny issues vis-à-vis Holocaust deniers who were
always trying to twist the past to suit their own specious arguments.
Fact, truth, and testimony—however slippery those terms might
be—actually had pivotal roles within the history of Germany and the
Jews.[382]

In the French magazine *L'express*, Jorge was asked to take part in a
debate with Alain Finkielkraut, who asked him whether it wouldn't
be better to have rules for fiction about World War II to ward off
Holocaust deniers. Jorge was not at all bothered by Finkielkraut's line

of questioning. He argued that he was free to do as he pleased, as long as he "did not invent things that morally compromised testimony." He went on to give an example:

> The basic rule is: you're not allowed to cheat. One must not build fiction on facts that morally compromise testimony. I don't have the right, for example, to invent the dying Jew who recites the Kaddish in the room for the terminally ill at Buchenwald. I have always respected this rule, and the existence of Holocaust deniers only reinforces the need to follow it.[383]

Yet Semprún's dying Jew reciting the Kaddish in Yiddish gives the scene an air of artifice that seems to directly contradict his "rule." As Yiddish scholar Ruth Wisse points out:

> Semprún inadvertently shows the dangers of falsification in the name of such apparent homage. He goes on to describe a "quite real" Jew who is dying before his eyes in Buchenwald, and to prove his authentic memory, he describes this dying Jew chanting the Kaddish in Yiddish! Even supposing that the man was chanting the prayer for the dead over himself, the Kaddish is Aramaic, not Yiddish.[384]

He also had publicized arguments about the representation of the Holocaust with Claude Lanzmann, the director of the film *Shoah*. But at this point any controversy surrounding *Literature or Life* only fanned the fires of Jorge's rise as a media star and as a moral authority. Timing was also crucial to the relevance of his latest work. Sales in France and abroad hit their stride in 1995 as Europe celebrated the fiftieth anniversary of the end of World War II. Suddenly Jorge Semprún, who had been expelled from the Spanish Communist Party and fired from his post as Spanish minister of culture, was leagues ahead of his Spanish compatriots. Santiago Carrillo and Alfonso Guerra were names that few people outside of Spain had heard of. Meanwhile, Jorge Semprún raked in the honors and prizes across the globe. He was cast as a hero and a moral authority, and he became a voice for a free Europe and one of the most celebrated writers in France, Germany, and Israel. He became a literary-intellectual face of the Holocaust, which was a curious turn for a non-Jewish writer. The book also did well in Spain, where he was able to bask in a newfound glow of media attention. It is always easier to succeed at home when one is an international star.

France and Germany celebrated Jorge as hero, witness, media phenomenon, and long-lost, seventy-one-year-old son. They show-ered him with a steady stream of adoration and admiration he would enjoy for the rest of his life. There are dozens of newspaper and magazine headlines about Jorge from this period. The lead quote for an article in *Le Parisien* from January 18, 1995, is "It's a tough year for camp survivors" (*"C'est un année un peu dure pour les survivants des camps"*).[385] In interviews he is asked almost exclusively about Buchenwald, and about the possibility of forgiveness. By default, he became an expert who was consulted about the German camp. He offered answers about evil, the Nazis, and the future. He became the man of the hour, a star witness to German atrocities, and he topped the bestseller lists.

The honors he received include: the Peace Prize of the German Book Trade in 1994, in 1995 the Prize of the City of Weimar, in 2003 the Goethe Medal, and in 2007 an honorary doctorate from the University of Potsdam.[386] He was also awarded many prizes and honors in France: Le Prix Fémina Vacaresco in 1994, and the Prix Littéraire des Droits de l'Homme 1995. In 1999 he won the Italian Nonio prize, and in 1996 he was elected to the Académie Goncourt.

Jorge returned to Buchenwald twice, in 1992 with his step-grandchildren, and again in 1995. In 1995, the year of the official fiftieth anniversary commemoration of the liberation, he argued for what—to him—was an evenhanded vision of history. He made it very

clear that he did not want to celebrate the liberation of the Nazi camps
by the Red Army, because he did not want to glorify the Soviets and
ignore the existence of their Gulags:

> What are we going to commemorate? We started off com-
> memorating the liberation of Auschwitz by the Red Army
> in January 1945. That's fine, but why shouldn't we remem-
> ber the fact that that army came from a country where there
> were also camps? These commemorations are always one
> sided. If we decide to make a serious project out of memory,
> we would have to commemorate the one-hundred-year
> anniversary of the Gulag.[387]

Semprún's vision shifted the balance of evil by publicly denouncing
Soviet crimes. This brand of objectivity Jorge was aiming for was, no
doubt, soothing to the Germans. In this light they were not the only
country with a history of camps, and, moreover, they were reminded
that they fought a formidable enemy.

    This more forgiving vision of Germany was useful and appreci-
ated, not only as Germany tackled its own past, but more importantly
as the country forged ahead to become the leader of a new Europe.
Present-day Germany had received a powerful public blessing from
Jorge Semprún.

    He loved visiting Germany, and the warmth was reciprocated.
He accepted many invitations to give talks, and he always enjoyed
speaking the language that his *fraulein* governesses had taught him so
many decades ago in Madrid; the language that may have helped save
his life.

    In a 1986 talk titled "Stalinism and Fascism,"[388] Jorge revisited the
liberation scene he witnessed at Buchenwald in April 1945, a moment
he had written about so many times. This version focuses—once
again—on Goethe's oak, and on possibility of hope, exemplified by
rebirth:

I would like to indulge in an evocation, a personal souvenir. At the end of April, 1945, I spent my last afternoon in Ettersburg; and my last hours in Buchenwald before returning to Paris. The repatriation trucks were part of a French Repatriation Mission, though I would not be returning to my homeland. In any case, I took advantage of those last moments in Buchenwald to say my farewell to Goethe's tree. The beech tree, which the Nazis had preserved when they razed the forest to build the first barracks of the camp, was located on an esplanade between the kitchen and the warehouse. A year before, in the summer of 1944 when the American air force had bombed the installations, a phosphorous bomb had hit Goethe's beech. But on that day, my last afternoon, Spring had returned and announced the end of a World War. Some branches of the burned-out tree were turning green again.[389]

It was this ability to portray Buchenwald as a locus of hope and new life that gave Jorge Semprún a particular literary and moral success in the new European scene of the late 1980s, 1990s, and early 2000s. Did Goethe's tree really spring new green branches after being destroyed by the incendiary bomb? Perhaps the easiest answer is one Jorge became fond of saying about his work in general, quoting Boris Vian, "Everything is true because I made it all up."

In 2003 Semprún made a triumphant literary return to Spain with his first novel written in Spanish, *Veinte años y un día*.[390] The central event in this book is the 1936 assassination, in a village in Toledo, of a member of the affluent Avendaño family by local peasants caught in the frenzy of revolution. After Franco's victory, the Avendaños exact their revenge by forcing the peasants to mark the anniversary of their crime with a yearly reenactment of the murder. The novel begins twenty years later, in 1956, and follows the steps of an American scholar named Michael Leidson. Leidson had traveled to Toledo to do some research on the ceremony. Leidson's mother's ancestors were Sephardic Jews from Toledo who carefully preserved the key to the door of their ancestral Toledan home. This key has a symbolic function in opening the doors of the past, and the perpetuation of memory is at the core of this novel's exploration of Spain's untold histories. The plotline darts between the background of the family, the events of the war, and the underground Communist movement in the Spain of the 1950s.

The novel tells the story of the Avendaño family, and of Leidson, but it is also a new recasting of Semprun's own autobiography. Throughout the novel there are real people (Ernest Hemingway, Domingo Dominguín, Semprún's father) mingled with fictional characters. The Narrator (with a capital N) guides us through the intricate combinations of people and time periods. He is also on hand to educate the reader with digressions about major historical events. For Semprún readers, it doesn't take long to figure out who the Narrator is.

The themes that permeate the novel—lost innocence, the horrors of war, but also a vital connection to the past and continuity in a life pervaded by rupture and tragedy—not only unite it to Semprún's oeuvre, but also to the exploration of the past that was prevalent in contemporary Spanish fiction until quite recently. This complex book is an intricate tapestry of many of the themes that dominated his life, and includes pointed criticisms of the strategies of the anti-Francoist Communists in the 1950s, but also of the *franquistas* themselves. The wealthy characters who have reaped the benefits of the dictatorship are portrayed as decadent and perverse. The novel suggests that they will bring themselves down.[391]

Veinte años y un día was awarded the Fundación José Manuel Lara Hernández prize, which came with an award of 150,000 euros. This was a tribute to Jorge's first, and last, novel in Spanish. It was also a belated symbolic homage to an exiled Spaniard who was eighty-one years old and had done a great deal for his country.

But despite the accolades, the frenzied autograph sessions at the book fairs in Madrid and Barcelona, and the regular media appearances, those close to him felt that he never enjoyed the respect he should have in Spain. His close friend Javier Pradera, his best recruit from his Federico Sánchez days, lamented this in the obituary he wrote for Jorge in June, 2011:

> Semprún never achieved the kind of recognition he deserved in Spain, not from the political world, nor from the literary establishment. His painful origins, his transformative goals and his political passion—forged in the international anti-fascist and anti-Francoist fight—made him a stranger on a planet filled with secularized technicians. The extraterritoriality of his citizenhood, back and forth between Spain and France, never allowed him to fit in. Spaniards were only capable of admiring a purely Spanish stereotype, retrograde, and coated with dust.[392]

X

Biriatou-Garantreville

This was a border town, a possible homeland for the
homeless, between the two countries of my affiliation—
Spain, my birth country . . . and France, my country
by choice . . . Here was an ideal place for my perpetual
absence. In fact, if I indulged in this profound desire,
taking into account the inconveniences—at least for those
under the obligation to fulfill my wishes—I would also
request that my body be wrapped in the tricolor flag—red,
gold, and violet, of the Republican flag.[393]
—*Adieu, vive clarté*

María Teresa León, another writer exiled from Franco Spain, often
complained that she was tired of not knowing where to die (*"cansada de no saber donde morirme"*). Losing one's home means not just
figuring out where to live, but also where to die—if one thinks about
such things. Jorge Semprún did. In one of his most moving books,
Adieu, vive clarté (1998), a seventy-five-year-old Jorge asked to be buried in Biriatou. This was the beautiful spot where Edouard Auguste
Frick had taken him—nearly sixty years earlier—to stay at the home
of the Greek shipping magnate with the beautiful wife.

The geographical charm of Biriatou, from Jorge's point of view,
is that it is just minutes from the Spanish border, and one can actually be sitting at a café in France looking over to Spain. So it was in
a border town that Jorge, still a "nowhere man" in his golden years,
thought he would be most at home for eternity. It is also striking that
he asks to be buried wrapped in the red, gold, and violet flag of the
Spanish Republic, a flag that had lost its real significance in 1939. This
is how Jorge Semprún asked to die: in a "countryless" spot, pledging
allegiance to a defunct flag. It was the flag of his mother, and of his
childhood. The world that had irrevocably shattered before he even
had a chance to become an adolescent.

Antonio Maura, safely buried in his family pantheon in the

Cementerio de San Isidro in Madrid, would have been disturbed to know that one of his grandsons had to figure out where to live and die. He had built the pantheon for his descendants, unaware so many of them would embark on a permanent, far-flung diaspora. Each would have to choose his or her own burial spot, in different cities and countries. As his great-grandson Jaime Semprún aimed to show in his 1968 film *La Sainte Famille*, history had sped up, and the family unity had disintegrated.

Colette died in 2007, when Jorge was eighty-four. All his friends say that his health took a sharp downward turn without her. Some recall it was around this time that Jorge seriously considered returning to Madrid to live there, but in the end it was not to be. In the opinion of his friend Claudio Aranzadi, who was minister of industry and energy with Felipe González, Semprún might very well have been disappointed had it worked out:

> We had vigorous discussions often, and one day he said, "Claudio, this is so nice being here. Why don't you try and find me an apartment?" But I always told my wife Inés that I didn't think it was a good idea. Coming from Paris to stay for a week in Madrid seeing friends and such is very different from what it would be like to actually live here. Jorge was not French, even though he settled in France at an early age and even though his dear friend Florence Malraux always claimed that his best and truest friends were all Spaniards. The life he led was absolutely unique. In his childhood he was the nephew of a minister of the Spanish Republic and the grandson of Prime Minister Antonio Maura, the son of a man who went to dinner with Federico García Lorca and that kind of thing. The he disappeared. Then he returned to Spain as a clandestine agent for the Spanish Communist Party. It was a life like no other. Then he lived here as minister of culture and then when back to live in Paris again. I

told my wife that I feared that if he really moved back here
to Madrid, that the day-to-day reality of it would be difficult for him. People going to work every day and adher-
ing to their normal routines. Even so he did fantasize about
moving back, but I don't believe he was truly serious about
it. Keep in mind that he was much more integrated into
French intellectual life than the Spanish version.[394]

The youngest Semprún-Maura son, Paco, died in 1986, and Alvaro
also died when he was fifty-three years old in Switzerland. He had
returned to live with Hélène Reymond, who had helped all the
Semprún children at the beginning of their exile in 1936. She eventually adopted Alvaro, and left him her house in Presinge, where he
died. Susana, the eldest sister who had returned to live in Spain, died
in 2001. Carlos Semprún died in 2009. Jorge's son Jaime Semprún
died at age sixty-three, in 2010, leaving no children of his own. Jorge
had lost contact with him over thirty years earlier, and only learned of
his death when he received, via telegram, a condolence message from
Bertrand Delanoë, the mayor of Paris.

Of all his siblings, Jorge had the best and longest relationships with
his older sister Maribel, and his older brother Gonzalo. The three of
them died in 2011.

Before Jorge's death from cancer on June 7, 2011, he had a complicated operation, and spent a good deal of time in the hospital in
Paris, in terrible pain. One of his consolations in this last period of his
life was speaking in Spanish. Despite his dreams of Biriatou, he was
finally buried in Garantreville, with his wife, Colette. His coffin was
wrapped in the Republican flag, as he had hoped. He is survived by
his stepdaughter Dominique and her children and grandchildren.

On November 26, 2011, his family and friends celebrated a
memorial service in Biriatou. It was most unfortunate that the man
who organized the event, Jorge's dear friend Javier Pradera, died a few
days before it took place and was unable to see the moving outdoor

ceremony, hear the expressions of affection spoken by so many admir-
ers, or appreciate the stone sculpture which weighed close to a ton and
was unveiled by the artist Eduardo Arroyo. Arroyo put a rendering
of Jorge's face upon it and a quote from *Adieu vive clarté*: "*J'aurais désire
que mon corps fût enterré a Biriatou*"—"I would have liked to be buried
at Biriatou."

French and Spanish friends from all the periods of his life were there
that day: his stepgrandchildren, Michel Piccoli and Florence Malraux,
Carmen Claudín and many of those who had been fellow ministers
with him in Spain, among them, Joaquín Almunia, who recalls:

> I often heard Jorge say how he wanted to be buried in
> Biriatou, which is in France but looking at Spain. In the
> spot where we had the ceremony, up high, next to the cem-
> etery, you look down a hill and see a stream, and on the
> other side of it is Navarra.[395]

Remembering Jorge, Almunia also made a point of underlining
Semprún as a true European:

> This was a man who risked his life fighting in the French
> Resistance against the Nazis, who then suffered in a con-
> centration camp, who then risked his life again fighting
> Franco as a clandestine agent for the Communist Party.
> His is a very unique case. And he was profoundly pro-
> European in the best sense, not one of those who feigned
> interest in a European union because of the money they got
> from European funding entities. It was his conviction that
> a united Europe was the space where his aspirations and
> ambitions should be realized. There were not many who
> shared this view. There are still a few, not many, but a few
> from his generation that continue to fight for that ideal.[396]

I started this book with a quote from Jorge Semprún about biographies: "Secrets don't really matter. They only matter if you're writing a real biography, but that should only be done once the subject is dead."

A biographer wants to know everything, but the truth is that subjects always keep many of their secrets. Especially this one. As Javier Solana says of Jorge Semprún: "He was a reserved man, mysterious in a way, who opened up in his own way and rarely. But from my point of view, he always transmitted warmth and humanity. Others may disagree. I always found him to be tender and affectionate in spite of the distance he maintained, the result perhaps of all the unusual things he had to go through during his life. It was as if he kept within him secrets not even he was aware of."[397] Narrating someone's life means putting arbitrary events into some kind of meaningful sequence. Jorge Semprún is an appealing subject because he did just this with his own life for decades: he turned his life into literature. Easier said than done.

As Régis Debray asked himself in 2012: "Do we like Jorge Semprún because of who he was, or because of what he made of who he was?"[398] Despite difficult circumstances, he managed to live many lives, and to achieve some of the success, fame, recognition, and power he had dreamed of as a child. He had talents and gifts to build on, but the greatest one was the ability to invent and reinvent himself, to rise to the top in any given cultural and political context. In this regard, he was a chameleonic genius, who undoubtedly still has secrets up his sleeve. André Malraux said that a man is, for the most part, what he hides. This is true, yet Malraux's biographer Olivier Todd convincingly countered: "No: he is also what he reveals, and what he does."

Bibliography

Archives and Special Collections

Archivo Histórico del Partido Comunista Español, Madrid.

Archivo General de la Administración, Alcalá de Henares.

Archivo Histórico del Ministerio de Asuntos Exteriores, Madrid.

Bibliothèque Litteraire Jacques Doucet, Paris.

Bundesarchiv, Berlin.

Fundación Antonio Maura, Madrid.

Gallimard Archives, Paris.

International Tracing Service, Bad Arolsen.

Library and Archives Reference Desk of the United States Holocaust Memorial Museum, Washington.

Library and Public Archives Unit, International Committee of the Red Cross, Geneva.

Politisches Archiv des Auswärtigen Amtes Paris, Berlin.

Russian Government Archive of Contemporary History (RGANI), Moscow.

Works by Jorge Semprún

Semprún, Jorge. *What a Beautiful Sunday!* New York: Harcourt Brace Jovanovich, 1980. French edition: *Quel Beau dimanche!* Paris: Les cahiers-rouges–Grasset and Fasquelle, 1980.

Semprún, Jorge. *L'écriture ou la vie.* Paris: Gallimard Folio, 1996. English edition: *Literature or Life.* New York: Penguin, 1998.

Spanish edition: Semprún, Jorge. *La escritura o la vida*. Barcelona: Tusquets Fábula, 1997.

Semprún, Jorge. *La Guerre est finie*. New York: Grove Press, 1967; Paris: Gallimard, 1966.

Semprún, Jorge. *Si la vie continue . . . Entretiens avec Jean Lacoutoure*. Paris: Grasset, 2012.

Semprún, Jorge. *The Long Voyage*. New York: The Overlook Press, 2005. French edition: *Le grand voyage*. Paris: Gaillimard, 1972.

Semprún, Jorge. *¡Libertad para los 34 de Barcelona!*, Act VII. Edited by the Federation of Unified Socialist Youth of Spain, 1953. Historical Archive of the Spanish Communist Party, Leaders, Jorge Semprún 26/17.

Semprún, Jorge. "Estalinismo y Fascismo." *Pensar en Europa*. Barcelona: Tusquets, 2006.

Semprún, Jorge. *Adieu vive clarté*. Paris: Gallimard, 1998. Spanish Editon: *Adiós, luz de veranos*. Barcelona: Tusquets Fabula, 1999.

Semprún, Jorge. *Communism in Spain in the Franco Era: The Autobiography of Federico Sánchez*. Brighton, Sussex: Harvester Press Limited, 1980. Spanish edition: *Autobiografía de Fedérico Sanchez*. Barcelona: Biblioteca Premios Planeta. 1977.

Semprún, Jorge. *Exercices de Survie*. Paris: Gallimard, 2012.

Semprún, Jorge. *Federico Sánchez vous salue bien*. Paris: Grasset, 1993. Spanish edition: *Federico Sánchez se despide de ustedes*. Barcelona: Tusquets, 1993.

Semprún, Jorge. Interview by Ceberio, Jesús. "Este gobierno discute poco de política." *El País*, July 29, 1990.

Semprún, Jorge. Interview with Alan Riding, June 12, 2014. Personal archive of Alan Riding. Paris

Semprún, Jorge. *La montagne blanche*. Paris: Gallimard, 1986.

Semprún, Jorge, and Jean-Louis Panné, ed. *Le fer rouge de la memoire*. Paris: Quarto Gallimard, 2012

Semprún, Jorge. *Le langage est ma patrie: Entretiens avec Franck Appréderis*. Paris: Libella, 2013.

Semprún, Jorge. *Le metier d'homme. Husserl, Bloch, Orwell: Morales de Résistance*. Paris: Climats, 2013.

Semprún, Jorge. *Montand, la vida continúa*. Planeta: Barcelona, 1983. French edition: *Montand, la vie continue*. Paris: France Loisirs, 1983.

Semprún, Jorge. *Une tombe au creux des nuages*. Paris: Climats/Flammarion, 2010.

Semprún, Jorge. *The Second Death of Ramón Mercader*. New York: Grove Press, 1973. French edition: *La deuxième Mort de Ramón Mercader*. Paris: Gallimard, 1969.

Semprún, Jorge. *Veinte años y un día*. Barcelona: Tusquets, 2003. French edition: *Vingt ans et un jour*. Paris: Gallimard, 2004.

Selected Film and Television Works

Semprún, Jorge. Television Script and Dialogues. (Director: Franck Apprederis) *Temps du Silence*, broadcast on TV5 Monde, France 2, 2011.

Semprún, Jorge. Screenplay. (Director: Joseph Losey). *Les routes du sud*. Societé Francaise de Production, Trinacra Films, France 3, Profilmes, 1978.

Semprún, Jorge. Cowriter, with Constantin Costa-Gavras. *Section Speciale*. Reggane Films, Les Productions Artistes Associés, Goriz Film, Janus Film, 1975.

Semprún, Jorge. Director and Screenplay. *Les deux memoires*. Aldebarán Films, Fildebroc, Les Films Molière, Uranus Productions France, 1974.

Semprún, Jorge. Screenplay. (Director: Alain Resnais) *Stavisky*. Cerito Films, Les Films Ariane, Simar Films, Euro-International Film, 1974.

Semprún, Jorge. Adaptation and Screenplay (Director : Constantin Costa-Gavras). *L'aveu*. Les Films Corona, Les Films Pomereu, Produzione Internationale Cinematografica, Fono Roma, Selena Cinematografica, 1970.

Jorge Semprún. Screenwriter. (Director: Constantin Costa-Gavras) *Z*. Office Nationale pour le Commerce et l'Industrie Cinématographique, Reggane Films, Valoria Films, 1969.

Jorge Semprún. Screenwriter. (Director: Alain Resnais). *La Guerre est Finie*. Europa Film, Sofracima. 1966.

Jorge Semprún. Dialogues (cowritten with Director, Pierre Schoendorffer). *Objectif: 500 millions*. Laetitia Films, Rome Paris Films, Sociéte Nouvelle de Cinématographie, 1966

Other Works Cited

Abetz, Otto. Correspondence with José Félix Lequerica. Vichy, January 28, 1944. MS. "Länderakte Spanien," 1943–1944, reference-number 2386, and RAV Paris, Strafrecht, "Rechtshilfe in Strafsachen, Interventionen, Auslieferung, Strafvollzug, Gefangenenaustausch allgemein und Namen A-Z," 1942–1944, reference number 2488. Politisches Archiv des Auswärtigen Amtes RAV Paris, Berlin.

Adler, Laure. *Marguerite Duras: A Life*. London: Phoenix, 2001.

Almunia, Joaquín, Personal interview. February 19, 2013.

Antelme, Monique. "Jorge Semprun n'a pas dit la vérité." *Le Monde*, July 8, 1998.

Arroyo, Eduardo. "El hombre que no conoció el rencor." *El País*, June 7, 2011.

Arroyo, Eduardo. Personal interview. July 8, 2012.

Asenjo, Mariano, and Victoria Ramos. *Malagón: Autobiografía de un falsificador*. Madrid: El Viejo Topo, 2008.

"Atrocities in Spain Charged by Bishop." *New York Times*. July 21, 1938.

Augstein, Franziska. *Lealtad y traición: Jorge Semprún y su siglo*. Trans. Rosa Pilar Blanco. Barcelona: Tusquets, 2010.

Barral, Carlos. *Cuando las horas veloces*. Barcelona: Tusquets, 1988.

Boyers, Robert. *Atrocity and Amnesia: The Political Novel Since 1945*. New York and Oxford: Oxford University Press, 1985.

Brodzki, Bella. *Can These Bones Live? Translation, Survival, and Cultural Memory*. Stanford, CA: Stanford University Press, 2007.

Bustamante, Juby. "Extranjero en el mundo." *Diario Público*, June 10, 2011.

Carrillo, Santiago. *Los viejos camaradas*. Barcelona: Planeta, 2011.

Carrillo, Santiago. *Mañana España: Conversaciones con Régis Debray y Max Gallo*. París: Colección Ebro, 1975.

Caso Oviedo, Javier G. "Adiós a un viejo comunista," *La voz de Asturias*. Web. February 25, 2012. http://www.apmadrid.es/images/stories/JoseSandoval.pdf.

Céspedes Gallego, Jaime. "Un eslabón perdido en la historiografía documental." *República de las letras, Revista de la Asiciación Colegial de Escritores de España*. November, 2011, number 124: 40.

Claudín, Carmen. Personal interview. June 25, 2012.

Conde, Francisco. "Spain Signs Agreement for Classic Painting Collection." *Associated Press*. News Archive, December 22, 1988.

Cortanze, Gerard. *Le Madrid de Jorge Semprún*. Paris: Editions du Chêne-Hachette Livre, 1977.

Costa-Gavras, Constantin. Personal interview. March 19, 2013.

Cota, Michèle, Jean-Louis Ferrier, Françoise Giroud. "L'Express va plus loin avec Jorge Semprún." *L'Express*, December 8–14, 1969.

Cruz, Juan "Lo único que he traicionado es a mi mismo." Interview with Jorge Semprún. *El País Semanal*, December 19, 2010.

Débray, Régis. Prologue. *Exercices de Survie* by Jorge Semprún. Paris: Gallimard, 2012.

Dominguín, Domingo. *Dominguín contra Dominguines*. Madrid: España, 2008.

Fernández- Montesinos Gurruchaga, Andrea. "Los primeros pasos del movimiento estudiantil," e-archivo.uc3m.es/bitstream/handle/10016/13919/ primeros_fernandez_CIAN_2009.pdf?sequence=2.

Ferrán, Ofelia, and Gina Herrmann. *A Critical Companion to Jorge Semprún: Buchenwald, Before and After*. Basingstoke and New York: Palgrave Macmillan, September 2014.

Fiscowich, Alfonso (Spanish Consul). Letter to Pedro Urraca (Spanish Police Inspector in Paris). October 30, 1943. MS. Politisches Archiv des Auswärtigen Amtes, Berlin.

Fox Maura, Soledad. "Jorge Semprún: Extraño en todas partes." *Revista de Libros*, January 9, 2011.

Fox Maura, Soledad. Rev. of *Veinte años y un día* by Jorge Semprún. *World Literature Today*. September–December 2004, 78:3–4.

"The Franco Era, 1939–75." *Country Studies*. United States Library of Congress Website. countrystudies.us/spain/51.htm.

Franklin, Ruth. *Lies and Truth in Holocaust Fiction*. New York: Oxford University Press, 2011.

González, Felipe. Personal interview. July 10, 2012.

Gordon, Bernard. *Hollywood Exile: Or How I Learned to Love the Blacklist*. Austin: University of Texas Press, 1999.

Goytisolo, Juan. *En los reinos de taifa*. Madrid: Alianza Editorial, 1986.

Goytisolo, Juan. Personal interview. March 19, 2013.

Gracia, Jordi. "Novelar la memoria o la libertad del escritor." *Jorge Semprún o las espirales de la memoria*. Ed. Xavier Pla. Kassel: Reichenberger, 2010, 87–109.

Graves, Tomás, and Lucia Graves de Farran. Letter to the Editor, *La Vanguardia*, January 20, 1979.

Hackett, David A. *The Buchenwald Report*. Boulder, CO: Westview Press, 1995.

Hamon, Hervé, and Patrick Rotman. *You See. I Haven't Forgotten*. Trans. Jeremy Leggatt. New York: Alfred A. Knopf, 1992.

Hessel, Stéphane. *Danse avec le siècle*. Paris: Seuil, 1997.

Heyde, Veronika. *De l'esprit de la Résistance jusqu'à l'idée de l'Europe*. Bruxelles: Peter Lang, 2010.

Irving, Washington. *Tales of the Alhambra*. London: Henry Colburn and Richard Bentley, 1832.

Judt, Tony. *Past Imperfect: French Intellectuals 1944–1956*, New York: New York University Press, 2011.

Julitte, Pierre. *Block 26*. New York: Doubleday and Company, 1971.

Kertész, Imre. Interview by Luisa Zielinski. "The Art of Fiction." *The Paris Review.* May 28, 2013.

Kogon, Eugen. "Der SS-Staat, Das System der deutschen Konzentrationslager" [The SS state, the system of German concentration camps]. Heyne Verlag: München, 1985.

Kohut, Karl. *Escribir en París.* Frankfurt/Main Verlag: Klaus Dieter Verveurt, 1983.

Levi, Primo. *If This is a Man.* Trans. Charles Woolf. New York: Abacus, 1991.

Lopez Pina, Antonio. *La Generación del 56.* Madrid: Marcial Pons Historia, 2010.

Mainer, Juan Carlos. "Clavileño: Cultura de estado bajo el franquismo," *Bulletin Hispanique,* 2002, volume 104, issue 102–104: 941–963.

Malraux, Florence. Personal interview. June 9, 2012.

Marco, Joaquín. "Veinte años y un día." *El Cultural,* September 4, 2003.

Markham, James M. "Ex-Communist Upsets Spanish Party with a Book About its Past." *New York Times.* February 24, 1978.

Maura, Manuel. *La isla del ayer.* N.d. MS. Collection of Marisol Maura, Madrid.

Maura, Miguel. *Así cayó Alfonso XIII.* Madrid: Marcial Pons, 2007.

Morán, Gregorio. *Miseria y grandeza del Partido Comunista Español: 1939–1985.* Barcelona: Planeta, 1986.

Nicolas, Sylvia. Personal interview. August 3, 2012.

Nieto, Felipe. *La aventura comunista de Jorge Semprún: exilio, clandestinidad y ruptura.* Barcelona: Tusquets, 2014.

Panné, Jean Louis, ed. *Jorge Semprún: Le fer rouge de la mémoire.* Paris: Gallimard, 2012.

Paulding, Gouverneur. "A Time to Hate." *The Reporter.* May 21, 1964.

Pérez Maura, Alfonso. "Valldemossa." January 8, 2014. *Baleares Digital.*

Pivot, Bernard. Personal interview. 21 March, 2013.

Pradera, Javier. "La segunda muerte de Jorge Semprún." *El País*, 8 June 2011.

Preston, Paul. *El Zorro Rojo*. Barcelona: Debate, 2013. English edition: *The Last Stalinist*, London: Williams Collins, 2014.

Riambau, Esteve. *Ricardo Muñoz Suay: Una vida en sombras*. Barcelona: Tusquets, 2007.

Rico, Francisco. *La novela picaresca y el punto de vista*. Barcelona: Seix Barral, 2000.

Riding, Alan. *And the Show Went On*. New York: Vintage, 2011.

Rollin, Léon. "Incertitudes espagnoles." *Politique étrangère* 10.1 (1945): 53–60.

Said, Edward. *Reflections on Exile and Other Essays*. Cambridge: Harvard University Press, 2002.

Samaniego, Fernando. "Jorge Semprún define el Guernica como metáfora universal del dolor y de la lucha." *El País*, July 7, 2006.

Schwartz, Juan. Letters to Jean-Marie Soutou. January 30 and May 22, 1945. Collection of Georges Henri Soutou. Paris.

Scott, Janny. "In Oral History, Jacqueline Kennedy Speaks Candidly After the Assassination." *New York Times*, September 11, 2011.

Seclier, Philippe. *Le Parisien*, January 18, 1995.

Sellier, Andre. *A History of the Dora Camp*. Lanham, MD: Ivan R. Dee Publisher, 2003.

Semprún, Jorge. Letter to Gonzalo Semprún, November 17, 1971. Collection of Danielle de la Gorce.

Semprún, Jorge. Selected Correspondence with Claude Gallimard and Odette Laigle, 1966–1977. Gallimard Archives.

Semprún Gurrea, José María. Letter to Antonio Maura. 5 October 1924. Fundación Antonio Maura, 298/11.

Semprún Gurrea, José María. "A Catholic Looks at Spain." collections.mun.ca/PDFs/radical/ACatholicLooksAtSpain.pdf.

Semprún Maura, Carlos. "Luces y sombras de agosto." *La ilustración liberal*. Número 25.

Semprún Maura, Carlos. *A orillas del Sena, un español*, Madrid: Libertad Digital/Hoja Perenne, 2006.

Semprún Maura, Carlos. *El exilio fue una fiesta*. Barcelona: Planeta, 1998.

Semprún Maura, Gonzalo. ¿La odicea, o la Odisea? N.d. MS. Archive of Santiago Valentín Gamazo.

Semprún, Carlos. "Gros Noyer y la familia" *Libertad Digital*, July 13, 2001.

Semprun-Roy, Sofia. Personal interview. March 20, 2013.

Silió, César. *Vida y empresas de un gran español: Maura*. Madrid: Espasa-Calpe, S.A., 1934.

Smith Semprún, Moraima. Conversation with Jorge Semprún. October, 2002. Recording. Moraima Smith Semprún Papers, courtesy of Roger Kase.

Solana, Javier. Personal interview. June 14, 2012.

Solchaga, Carlos. Personal interview. June 1, 2012.

Soutou, Georges-Henri. Message to the author. 1 April 2014. E-mail.

Soutou, Jean-Marie. *Un diplomate engagé*. Paris: Editions de Fallois, 2011.

Stein Louis. *Beyond Death and Exile: The Spanish Republicans in France 1939–1955*. Cambridge: Harvard University Press, 1980.

Stein, Harry. *Buchenwald Concentration Camp 1937–1945: A Guide to the Permanent Historical Exhibition*. Wallstein Verlag, 2004.

Streiff, Gérard. *Procès stalinien à Saint-Germain-des-Prés*. Paris: Editions Syllepse, 1999.

Wiesel, Elie. *All Rivers Run to the Sea*. New York: Knopf, 1995

Wiesel, Elie. *Night*. Trans. Marion Wiesel. New York: Penguin Books, 2006.

Wingeate Pike, David. *Spaniards in the Holocaust: Mauthausen, the Horror on the Danube*. New York: Routledge, 2000.

Endnotes

1   Semprún, Jorge, "Lo único que he traicionado es a mi mismo," interview by Juan Cruz, *El País Semanal*. December 19, 2010.

2   Goytisolo, Juan, interview by author.

3   Irving, Washington, *Tales of the Alhambra*. London: Henry Colburn and Richard Bentley, 1832, p. 50.

4   Semprún, Jorge, *Adieu, vive clarté*, Paris: Gallimard, 1998, p. 36.

5   Fondo documental de Antonio Maura Montaner del archivo histórico de la Fundación Maura Maura, Leg n° 113/Carpeta n° 24.

6   Sand, George, *A Winter in Majorca*. Classic Collection Carolina: Meudt 2003. Author's translation.

7   Maura, Manuel, *La isla del ayer*. Unpublished manuscript, collection of Marisol Maura.

8   The street that now stands in its place is Calle Gonzálo Jiménez de Quesada. http://antiguoscafesdemadrid.blogspot.com.es/2012 /01/el-cafe-del-desengano-el-toxpiro-de.html

9   Graves, Robert, Interview in *La Vanguardia*, 1979.

10 Silió, César, *Vida y empresas de un gran español: Maura*. Madrid: Espasa-Calpe, S.A., 1934, p. 31

11 Ibid.

12 Ibid., p. 32.

13 Ibid., pp. 34–35.

14 www.ilustracionliberal.com/15/soy-judio-carlos-semprun-maura.html.

15 Maura, Alfonso Pérez, "Valldemossa," *Baleares Digital* balearides-digital.com/?p=11144.

16 hemeroteca.abc.es/nav/Navigate.exe/hemeroteca/madrid/blanco.y.negro/1915/12/26/039.html.

17 ABC, March 2, 1919.

18 ABC, December 11, 1918.

19 Letter from José María Semprún Gurrea to Antonio Maura, October 5, 1924. Antonio Maura Foundation, 298/11.

20 Semprún Maura, Gonzalo, ¿La odicea, o la Odisea?, Unpublished memoir, Archive of Santiago Valentín Gamazo, p. 8.

21 Semprún, Jorge, *Adiós, luz de veranos*. Barcelona: Tusquets Fabula, 1999, p. 74.

22 Spain's last Republican government was overthrown in 1936.

23 Semprún, *Adieu,* p. 20.

24 Semprún Maura, Gonzalo, pp. 8–9.

25 ABC, January 26, 1932.

26 Semprún, Jorge, *Adieu,* p. 76.

27 Semprún, Carlos, "Tío Iñigo y Giner Pantoja," Fragmentos of his manuscript, *Libertad Digital,* July 27, p. 200.

28 Jorge Semprún, *Adiós,* p. 63.

29 www.tabletmag.com/jewish-arts-and-culture/books/75272/partisan.

30 www.diariodecadiz.es/article/ocio/997017/los/semprun/retrato/familia.html.

31 Said, Edward, *Reflections on Exile and Other Essays,* Cambrige: Harvard University Press. 2000.

32 Semprún, Jorge, *Adieu,* p. 158.

33 Stein, Louis, *Beyond Death and Exile*: *The Spanish Republicans in France 1939–1955,* Cambridge: Harvard University Press, 1980, p. 54.

34 Soutou, Jean-Marie, *Un diplomate engagé: 1939–1979*, Paris: Editions de Fallois, 2011, p. 15.

35 "Nationalist" was the designation given to the military rebels by their supporters.

36 Semprún, Jorge, *What a Beautiful Sunday!*, New York: Harcourt Brace Jovanovich, 1980, p. 114.

37 Semprún, Jorge, *Adieu*, p. 244. Nearly thirty years later, in 1964, Paulding published a very positive review of *The Long Voyage*, "A Time to Hate" in *The Reporter*, May 21, 1964.

38 Paulding, Gouverneur, "A Time to Hate," *The Reporter*, May 21, 1964.

39 Semprún, Jorge, *Adiós*.

40 Interview with Leo Barblan.

41 Ibid, p. 93.

42 Semprún, Jorge, *Adiós*, p. 63.

43 Semprún, Jorge, *What a Beautiful Sunday!*, 112.

44 "Atrocities in Spain Charged by Bishop." *New York Times*, July 21, 1938.

45 Semprún, José María, "A Catholic looks at Spain," collections .mun.ca/PDFs/radical/ACatholicLooksAtSpain.pdf, p.12.

46 Susana was taken in as a paying boarder by some non-Republican Semprún relatives who had remained in Madrid, and ended up marrying a shipbuilder and moving to Cádiz. Susana was the only one of Jorge's siblings to ever permanently move back to Spain.

47 commons.wikimedia.org/wiki/File:Grafsteen_Malva_Marina _Reijes.jpg.

48 Semprún, Jorge, *Autobiografía de Federíco Sanchez*. Barcelona: Biblioteca Premios Planeta. 1977, p. 97.

49 Semprún, Jorge, *Adieu*, p. 54.

50 Soutou, Jean-Marie, *Un diplomate engagé*.

51 Semprún, Jorge, *Adiós*, pp. 32–33.

52 Semprún Maura, Carlos, *A orillas del Sena, un español,* Madrid: Libertad Digital/Hoja Perenne, 2006, p. 17.

53 Semprún, Jorge, *Adieu,* pp. 78–79.

54 Ibid., p. 98

55 Ibid., pp. 98–99.

56 Semprún, Jorge, *Adiós*, pp. 98–99.

57 Hazas Antonio Rey, ed. *Lazarillo de Tormes*, Madrid: Castalia, 2011, p. 69.

58 Semprún Maura, Carlos, *A orillas del Sena,* p. 51.

59 Semprún, Jorge, *Adieu*, p. 209.

60 Semprún, Jorge, *Adiós*, p. 153.

61 Ibid., p. 230.

62 Ibid., p. 161.

63 Ibid., p. 93.

64 *Padeia* was the educational approach in ancient Greece, and aimed to create ideal citizens

65 Semprún, Jorge, *Adieu,* p. 97.

66 Panné, Jean Louis ed., *Jorge Semprún: Le fer rouge de la mémoire.* Paris: Gallimard, 2012, p. 34.

67 Semprún, Jorge, *Le langage est ma patrie: Entretiens avec Franck Appréderis.* Paris: Libella, 2013, p. 60.

68 Ibid., p. 61.

69 González, Felipe, interview with the author.

70 Semprún, Jorge, *Adieu,* p. 116.

71 Nieto, Felipe. *La aventura comunista de Jorge Semprún: exilio, clandestinidad y ruptura.* Barcelona: Tusquets, 2014, pp. 31–32.

72 Semprún Maura, Carlos, *A orillas del sena*, p. 49.

73 Ibid., p. 40

74 Ibid., p. 41.

75 Ibid., p. 18.

76 Semprún, Jorge, interview by Alan Riding. Unpublished. Personal archive of Alan Riding.

77 Panné, *Jorge Semprún,* p. 33.

78 Ibid.

79 Ibid., p. 34.

80 Semprún, Jorge, *Exercices de Survie*, Paris: Gallimard, 2012, p. 38.

81 www.auxerretv.com/content/index.php?post/2011/06/08/Gérard
    -Sorel%2C-jardinier-à-Villeneuve.

82 Semprún, Jorge, *Exercices de survie*, p. 56.

83 At times the author refers to himself as Gérard, in the third person.

84 "Paul" was the code name of Henri Frager.

85 Semprún, Jorge, *What a Beautiful Sunday!*, New York: Harcourt
    Brace Jovanovich, 1980, pp. 102–103.

86 Semprún, Jorge, *What a Beautiful Sunday!*, p. 36.

87 www.libertaddigital.com/opinion/carlos-semprun-maura
    /amigos-amores-y-conflictos-de-posguerra-5496/.

88 Nieto, Felipe, Archivo General de la Administración, Madrid,
    Interior 44/10887, exp. 72, p. 33.

89 Rollin, Léon. "Incertitudes espagnoles." *Politique étrangère* 10.1
    (1945): pp. 53–60.

90 Semprún Maura, Carlos. *El exilio fue una fiesta*. Barcelona: Planeta,
    1998, pp. 49–50.

91 Riding, Alan, *And the Show Went On*. New York: Vintage, 2011.

92 Ibid., p. 183.

93 Ibid., p. 229

94 Stein, Louis, *Beyond Death and Exile*, p. 125.

95 Ibid.

96 Letter from Spanish Consul Alfonso Fiscowich to Pedro Urraca,
    (Spanish) Police Inspector in Paris. October 30, 1943.

97 Frances Ferrer was executed in 1909 for leading the uprising in
    Barcelona that would result in the "Tragic Week" (as it became
    known).

98 RAV Paris, "Länderakte Spanien," 1943–1944, reference number
    2386, and RAV Paris, Strafrecht, Rechtshilfe in Strafsachen,
    Interventionen, Auslieferung, Strafvollzug, Gefangenenaustausch
    allgemein und Namen A–Z," 1942–1944, reference number 2488.

99 Lettter from Otto Abetz to Lequerica. Vichy, January 28, 1944,
    RAV, Paris.

100 Ibid.

101 Ibid.

102 Maura, Miguel, *Así cayó Alfonso XIII*, Madrid: Marcial Pons, 2007, p. 558.

103 Ibid.

104 That the person close to Miguel ("*allegado*") was indeed Jorge Semprún was confirmed by Miguel Maura's grandson, Joaquín Romero-Maura, in a telephone interview on 7/11/2014. It is unclear why he is not named in the text.

105 Maura, Miguel, *Así cayó Alfonso XIII*, p. 559.

106 Semprún, Jorge, *Exercices de Survie*, p. 47.

107 Heyde, Veronika, *De l'esprit de la Résistance jusqu'à l'idée de l'Europe*. Bruxelles: Peter Lang, 2010, pp. 197–198.

108 Ibid., p. 198.

109 Ibid., p. 133, note 272.

110 Letter from Juan Schwartz to Jean-Marie Soutou, January 30, 1945. Collection of Georges Henri Soutou.

111 Letter from Juan Schwartz to Jean-Marie Soutou, May 22 1945. Collection of Georges Henri Soutou.

112 Rico, Francisco, *La novela picaresca y el punto de vista*, Barcelona: Seix Barral, 2000, p. 50.

113 Semprún, Jorge, *Le mort qu'il faut*, Preliminary interview, Paris: La bibliothèque Gallimard, p. 12.

114 www.theparisreview.org/interviews/5740/the-art-of-fiction -no-192-Semprún-semprun.

115 www.theparisreview.org/interviews/5740/the-art-of-fiction -no-192-Semprún-semprun.

116 Semprún, Jorge, *Exercises de Survie*.

117 Semprún, Jorge, *The Long Voyage*, New York: The Overlook Press, 2005, p. 47.

118 Ibid., p. 21.

119 Semprún, Jorge, *L'écriture ou la vie* Paris: Gallimard, pp. 381–382. Author's translation.

120 Ibid., p. 319.

121 Ibid., p. 321.

122 Wingeate Pike, David, *Spaniards in the Holocaust*: *Mauthausen, Horror on the Danube*, Routledge: New York, 2000, p. 17.

123 *The Buchenwald Report*, translated by David A. Hackett. Boulder, San Francisco, Oxford: The Westview Press, 1995, p. 29.

124 Semprún, Jorge, *L'écriture ou la vie*, p. 57.

125 Semprún, Jorge, *What a Beautiful Sunday!*, p. 145.

126 Semprún, Jorge, *The Long Voyage*, p. 167.

127 Levi, Primo, *If This is a Man*. Translated by Charles Woolf. New York: Abacus, 1991, p. 193.

128 Wiesel, Elie, *Night*, Translated by Marion Wiesel. New York: Penguin Books, 2006, p. 40.

129 Semprún, Jorge, *What a Beautiful Sunday!*, pp. 145–146.

130 Ibid., 145.

131 Ibid.

132 www.thewhitereview.org/interviews/interview-with-Semprún-semprun/. French original published on nonfiction.fr.

133 www.telegraph.co.uk/news/worldnews/europe/germany /4239663/Petrol-station-used-Nazi-slogan-on-posters.html.

134 *Semprún Semprún: Si la vie continue . . . Entretiens avec Jean Lacoutoure*. Paris: Grasset, 2012, pp. 47–48.

135 Ibid., p. 69.

136 Ibid., p. 71.

137 Sellier, Andre, *A History of the Dora Camp*, Chicago: Ivan R. Dee Publisher, 2003, p. 156.

138 Pierre, Julitte, *Block 26*, New York: Doubleday and Company, 1971, p. 24.

139 Ibid., pp. 48–49.

140 Ibid., p. 49.

141 Soutou, Georges-Henri, interview by the author.

142 Semprún, Jorge, *Le mort qu'il faut*, Paris: Gallimard, 2001, p. 51. Author's translation.

143 Ibid., p. 51.

144 Ibid., p. 155.

145 Ibid., pp. 54–55.

146 Kogon, Eugen, *Der SS-Staat: Das System der deutschen Konzentrationslager* (English title: The SS state, the system of German concentration camps), 15th edition, Munich: Wilhelm Heyne Verlag, translation by Axel Braisz, International Tracing Service, Bad Arolsen. 1985. Eugan Kogon was a prisoner in the concentration camp Buchenwald and deployed to work in the prisoner registration office.

147 "Kapo" is derived from the German Kameradschafts-Polizei.

148 Augstein, Franziska. *Lealtad y traición: Jorge Semprún y su siglo*. Trans. Rosa Pilar Blanco. Barcelona: Tusquets, 2010, p. 179.

149 Semprún, Jorge, *What a Beautiful Sunday!*, pp. 151–152.

150 Wiesel, Elie, *All Rivers Run to the Sea*, New York: Knopf, 1995, p. 93.

151 www.historylearningsite.co.uk/red_cross_and_world_war _two.htm.

152 Email interview of Daniel Palmieri, Historical Research Officer, IRCR, August 27, 2014.

153 Address confirmed in interview with Elsa Grobéty.

154 Semprún, Jorge, *L'écriture ou la vie*, p. 14.

155 Semprún, Jorge, *The Long Voyage*, p. 148, cited in Kertész, *Fiasco* (English, Kindle edition), pp. 46–48.

156 Kertész, *Fiasco*, p. 49.

157 Kertész, interviewed by Luisa Zielinski in *The Paris Review*. www.theparisreview.org/interviews/6235/the-art-of-fiction -no-220-imre-kertesz.

158 Semprún, Jorge, *Le mort qu'il faut*, p. 102.

159 Semprún, Jorge, *The Long Voyage*, p. 75.

160 Ibid., p. 60.

161 Malraux, Florence, interview by the author, June 2011.

162 *The Long Voyage*, p. 70.

163 Gracia, Jordi, interview by the author.

164 Semprún, Jorge, *The Long Voyage,* p. 100.

165 Ibid.

166 Semprún, Jorge, *La Guerre est finie: Scenario by Semprún Semprún.* New York: Grove Press, 1967; Paris: Gallimard, 1966.

167 Semprún, Jorge, *The Long Voyage,* p. 72.

168 Malraux, interview by the author.

169 *The Long Voyage,* p. 182.

170 Semprún, Jorge, *L'écriture ou la vie,* p. 60.

171 Ibid.

172 Semprún, Jorge, *Literature or Life,* New York: Penguin, 1998. p. 35.

173 Semprún clarifies this in *Literature or Life,* pp. 35–37. Also see Ruth Wisse, *The Modern Jewish Canon: A Journal through Language and Culture,* p. 367, note 12.

174 Semprún, Jorge, *The Long Voyage,* 120.

175 en.wikipedia.org/wiki/Buchenwald_concentration_camp.

176 Semprún, Jorge, *L'écriture ou la vie,* p. 17.

177 en.wikipedia.org/wiki/Buchenwald_concentration_camp.

178 Semprún, Jorge, *Literature or Life,* p. 88.

179 Semprún, Jorge, *The Long Voyage,* p. 77.

180 Ibid., p. 110.

181 Ibid., p. 104.

182 Ibid., p. 100.

183 Semprún, Carlos, *El exilio fue una fiesta,* pp. 54–57.

184 Semprún Maura, Carlos, "Luces y sombras de agosto," www .ilustracionliberal.com/25/luces-y-sombras-de-agosto-carlos -semprun-maura.html.

185 Email from Georges-Henri Soutou. April 1, 2013.

186 *In L'écriture ou la vie,* Semprún mentions that his visa expired in January 1946.

187 www.ilustracionliberal.com/25/luces-y-sombras-de-agosto-car-los-semprun-maura.html. Author's translation.

188 Email from Georges-Henri Soutou, April 1, 2014.

189 Judt, Tony, *Past Imperfect: French Intellectuals, 1944–1956.*

190 www.regietheatrale.com/index/index/thematiques/auteurs /bellon/loleh–bellon–1.html.

191 Semprún, Jorge, *Adiós,* p. 210.

192 Gérard Streiff, *Procès stalinien à Saint-Germain-des-Prés.* Paris: Editions Syllepse, 1999, p. 10. Author's translation.

193 Ibid., p. 14.

194 Ibid., p. 91.

195 Ibid., p. 18.

196 Ibid., p. 15.

197 Ibid., p. 120.

198 Adler, Laure, *Marguerite Duras: A Life.* London: Phoenix, 2001, pp. 176–177.

199 Malraux, interview by the author.

200 Streiff, p. 45.

201 Ibid.

202 Semprún, Jorge, Interview by Laure Adler, *Marguerite Duras: A Life*, p. 174.

203 Antelme, Monique, "Jorge Semprun n'a pas dit la vérité," *Le Monde*, July 8, 1998.

204 Semprún Maura, Carlos, *A orillas del sena*, p. 144.

205 Semprún Maura, Carlos, *A orillas del sena*, pp. 143–144.

206 Nieto, p. 168.

207 Jorge Semprún. *Autobiografía de Federico Sánchez.* Barcelona: Planeta, 1977, p. 10.

208 Ibid., p. 16.

209 Ibid., p. 102.

210 Adler, p. 171.

211 Semprún, Jorge, *Autobiografía de Federico Sánchez*, p. 25.

212 Caja 92, Carpeta 64 (1954), February 4, 1954.

213 Goytisolo, interview by the author.

214 For more on Carrillo, see Paul Preston, *El Zorro Rojo*, Barcelona: Debate, 2013; English edition: *The Last Stalinist*, London: Williams Collins, 2014.

215 Santiago Carrillo, *Los viejos camaradas*. Barcelona: Planeta, 2011, p. 174.

216 Ibid., p. 175.

217 Ibid., p. 176.

218 Caja 92, Carpeta 64 (1954), Feburary 22, 1954.

219 Semprún, Jorge, *¡Libertad para los 34 de Barcelona!*, Act VII. Edited by the Federation of Unified Socialist Youth of Spain, 1953. Historical Archive of the Spanish Communist Party, Leaders, Jorge Semprún 26/17.

220 Semprún, Jorge, *Autobiografía de Federico Sánchez*, p. 17.

221 Lopez Pina, Antonio, *La Generación del 56*. Madrid: Marcial Pons Historia, 2010, p. 168.

222 Asenjo, Mariano, and Victoria Ramos, *Malagón: Autobiografía de un falsificador*. Madrid: El Viejo Topo, 2008, p. 223.

223 Ibid., p. 178.

224 Ibid.

225 United States Library of Congress, countrystudies.us/spain /51.htm.

226 Gordon, Bernard, *Hollywood Exile: Or How I Learned to Love the Blacklist*. Austin: University of Texas Press, 1999, p. 115.

227 AHPCE, Jacq 24, Fuerzas Cultura.

228 AHPCE, Jacq 665 (1) Microfilm. 4.

229 Ibid.

230 Ibid.

231 AHPCE Caja 92, Carpeta 64 (1954) 16-2-54.

232 "Del retorno de la memoria," Interview with Jorge Semprún, February 3, 2013, ABC, p. 8. hemeroteca.abc.es/nav/Navigate. exe/hemeroteca/madrid/abc/2003/03/23/008.html.

233 Ibid.

234 AHPCE, Jacq 665 (1) Fuerzas Cultura.

235 Jacques 665 (1) Microfilm, 4.

236 Jacq 665 (1) Fuerzas Cultura.

237 Morán, Gregorio, *Miseria y grandeza del Partido Comunista Español: 1939–1985*, Barcelona, Planeta, 1986. 223.

238 Fernández- Montesinos Gurruchaga, Andrea, "Los primeros pasos del movimiento estudiantil," e-archivo.uc3m.es/bitstream/handle/10016/13919/primeros_fernandez_CIAN_2009.pdf?sequence=2.

239 Ibid.

240 AHPCE. Caja 92, Carpeta 64 (1954).

241 Andrea Fernández–Montesinos Gurruchaga., op. cit.

242 AHPCE, Caja 92, Carpeta 64 (1954).

243 Ibid.

244 Ibid.

245 Ibid.

246 *Clavileño: Revista de la Asociación Internacional de Hispanismo* was published between 1950–1957. See Juan Carlos Mainer, "*Clavileño*: Cultura de estado bajo el franquismo," *Bulletin Hispanique*, 2002, volume 104, issue 102–104, pp. 941–963.

247 AHPCE, Caja 92, Carpeta 64 (1954).

248 Ibid.

249 Ibid.

250 Ibid.

251 AHPCE. Pleno del Comité Central del PCE. 1956. Actas, tomo I. Documentos PCE.

252 Santos, Juliá, *Camarada Javier Pradera*, Barcelona: Galaxia Gutenberg, 2012, p. 233.

253 Ibid.

254 AHPCE, MICROFILM 1960, Reunión del Comité ejecutivo del 23–260.

255 Castellet, Josep María, *Seductores, ilustrados y visionarios*. Barcelona, Anagrama, 2010. pp. 122–123.

256 Dominguín, Domingo, *Dominguín contra Dominguines*. Madrid: Espasa, 2008.

257 Ibid., p. 189

258 Claudín, Carmen, interview by the author.

259 Semprún Maura, Carlos, *El exilio fue una fiesta*, p. 71.

260 Ibid., p. 66.

261 Nicholas, Sylvia, interview by the author.

262 Riambau, Esteve, *Ricardo Muñoz Suay: Una vida en sombras.* Barcelona: Tusquets, 2007. p. 195.

263 Semprún, Jorge, *Montand, la vida continúa.* Planeta: Barcelona, 1983.

264 Riambau, p. 200.

265 The Frente Nacional de Liberación was another anti-Francoist group that operated between 1958–1969. It was unaffiliated with any of the the existing Spanish political opposition groups.

266 Semprún, Carlos, "Gros Noyer y la familia." www.libertad digital.com/opinion/ideas/gros-noyer-y-la-familia-1394.html.

267 Morán, Gregorio, *Miseria y grandeza*, p. 205.

268 Semprún, Jorge and Panné, Jean-Louis, ed. *Le fer rouge de la memoire.* Paris: Quarto Gallimard, 2012, p. 50.

269 Preston, Paul, *The Last Stalinist*, London: Williams Collins, 2014, p. 228

270 Semprún, Jorge. *Le fer rouge*, p. 52.

271 Preston, Paul, p. 228.

272 Semprún, Jorge, *La literatura o la vida,* p. 257.

273 Ibid.

274 Carrillo, Santiago *Los viejos camaradas*, p. 175.

275 Sánchez Drago, Fernando, "¿Jorge o Federico?," *Especiales El Mundo*, www.elmundo.es/especiales/2011/06/cultura/jorge-semprun/firmas_sanchez_drago.html.

276 Grenier, Roger, interview by the author.

277 Cota, Michèle, Jean-Louis Ferrier, and Françoise Giroud, "L'Express va plus loin avec Jorge Semprún," *L'Express*, December 8–14, 1969, p. 153.

278 Semprún, Jorge, *Communism in Spain in the Franco Era: The Autobiography of Federico Sánchez.* Brighton, Sussex: Harvester Press Limited, 1980, p. 186.

279 Caso Oviedo, Javier G., "Adiós a un viejo comunista," *La voz de Asturias,* www.apmadrid.es/images/stories/JoseSandoval.pdf.

280 www.fiesta.pce.es/2012/espacios.htm

281 Semprún, Jorge, *Communism,* p. 188.

282 See chapter 2 on the relationship between Jean-Marie Soutou and Glasberg.

283 Semprún, Jorge, *Montand, la vie continue,* p. 74.

284 Ibid.

285 Goytisolo, Juan, *En los reinos de taifa,* Madrid: Alianza Editorial, 1986, p. 71.

286 Semprún, Jorge, *Communism,* p. 190.

287 Goytisolo, *En los reinos de taifa,* 82.

288 Malraux, interview by the author.

289 Libération, May 7, 1963. Cited in Jean-Louis Panné, *Jorge Semprún: Le fer rouge de la mémoire,* p. 53.

290 "L'Express va plus loin avec Jorge Semprún," *L'Express,* December 8–14, 1969, p. 171.

291 Barral, Carlos, *Cuando las horas veloces,* Barcelona: Tusquets, 1988, p. 45.

292 Goytisolo, Juan, interview by the author.

293 www.elmundo.es/especiales/2011/06/cultura/jorge-semprun/firmas_sanchez_drago.html.

294 Panné, ed. *Jorge Semprún: Le fer rouge,* p. 56.

295 Goytisolo, *En los reinos,* p. 95.

296 Semprún, Jorge, *Autobiografía,* 297.

297 Ibid., pp. 297, 302.

298 Claudín, interview by the author.

299 Goytisolo, *En los reinos,* p. 95.

300 Claudín, interview by the author.

301 Panné, *Jorge Semprún,* p. 57.

302 Semprún Maura, Carlos, *El exilio fue una fiesta,* p. 316.

303 Romi, Yvette, "*Les bruits de la ville,*" *Le nouvel observateur,* March 27, 1968, pp. 38–39.

304 Interview with Sofia de Semprún.

305 Interview with Sofia de Semprún-Roy.

306 Panné, *Jorge Semprún*, p. 59.

307 Costa-Gavras, interview by the author.

308 Ibid.

309 Hamon, Hervé, and Patrick Rotman, *You See, I Haven't Forgotten*. Translated from the French by Jeremy Leggatt. New York: Alfred A. Knopf, 1992, pp. 345–347.

310 Semprún, Jorge, *Montand, la vie continue*. Paris: France Loisirs, 1983.

311 Malraux, interview by the author.

312 Kohut, Karl, *Escribir en París*. Frankfurt/Main: Verlag Klaus Dieter Vervuert, 1983, p. 176.

313 There are copies of the film at the Filmotecas in Madrid and Barcelona, and the Cinematheque in Paris. To date it has never been released on DVD or any other format.

314 Cespedes Gallego, Jaime, "Un eslabón perdido en la historiografía documental," *República de las letras, Revista de la Asiciación Colegial de Escritores de España*, vol. 124, November 2011, p. 40.

315 Claudín, interview by the author.

316 Goytisolo, Juan, interview by the author.

317 Semprún, Jorge, *Autobiografía,* p. 64.

318 Ibid., p. 69.

319 "L'Express va plus loin avec Jorge Semprún," *L'Express*, December 8–14. 1969. 174.

320 Ibid.

321 Ibid.

322 Carillo, Santiago, *Después de Franco, ¿Qué?: La democracia política y social que preconizamos los comunistas*. Paris: Editions Sociales, 1965.

323 Carillo, Santiago, *Mañana España: Conversaciones con Régis Debray y Max Gallo*. París: Colección Ebro, p. 149.

324 González, interview with the author.

325 Semprún, Jorge, *Federico Sánchez se despide de ustedes*. Barcelona: Tusquets, 1993. French edition: *Federico Sánchez vous salue bien*. Paris: Grasset, 1993, p. 302.

326 All documents from the Jorge Semprún folder in RGANI were translated by Esther Gómes-Parra. RGANI (Rossiiskii Gosudarstvennii Arkhiv Noveishii Istorii/The Russian State Archive of Contemporary History). The Jorge Semprún's folder is in Collection: 5; Listing: 109; Documents: 5012, pages 2, 4, 6; 15–19; and 21–34. Copy #65 made on November 12, 2013.

327 Enrique Líster

328 Jorge Semprún papers. RGANI, Moscow. See note 326.

329 Ibid.

330 Kohut, Karl, *Escribir en París,* pp. 179–180.

331 Pivot, Bernard, interview by the author.

332 Semprún, Jorge, *Federico Sánchez se despide de ustedes*, p. 48.

333 Ibid., p. 16.

334 González, interview with the author.

335 This 1993 memoir is a kind of political sequel to *Autobiografía*

336 Semprún, Jorge. *Federico Sánchez vous salue bien*. Paris: Grasset, 1993, p. 145.

337 Cortanze, Gerard. *Le Madrid de Jorge Semprún*. Paris: Editions du Chêne-Hachette Livre, 1977, p. 50.

338 Semprún, Jorge. *Adieu vive clarté*. Paris: Gallimard.

339 Semprún, Jorge. *Autobiografía,* pp. 45–46.

340 Semprún, Jorge. *Federico Sánchez vous salue bien*, p. 147.

341 Ibid.

342 Ibid, p. 165.

343 Samaniego, Fernando, "Jorge Semprún define el Guernica como metáfora universal del dolor y de la lucha." *El País*, July 7, 2006.

344 Ibid.

345 Semprún, Jorge. *La montagne blanche*. Paris: Gallimard, 1986, p. 17.

346 Semprún, Jorge. *Veinte años y un día*. Barcelona: Tusquets, 2003. French edition: *Vingt ans et un jour*. Paris: Gallimard, 2004, p. 238.

347 Ibid., pp. 196–198.

348 Semprún, Jorge. *Federico Sánchez vous salue bien*, p. 147

349 Cortanze, p. 144.

350 Semprún, Jorge, *Federico Sánchez se despide*, p. 19.

351 Ibid.

352 Semprún, Jorge, *Federico Sánchez se despide*, p. 23.

353 Arroyo, Eduardo, "El hombre que no conoció el rencor," *El País*, June 7, 2011.

354 Solana, Javier, interview by the author.

355 Scott, Janny, "In Oral History, Jacqueline Kennedy Speaks Candidly After the Assassination." *New York Times*. September 11, 2011.

356 González, interview by the author.

357 Almunia, Joaquín, interview by the author.

358 Conde, Francisco, "Spain Signs Agreement for Classic Painting Collection" *Associated Press* News Archive, December 22, 1988.

359 Solchaga, Carlos, interview by the author.

360 Ceberio, Jesús, "Este gobierno discute poco de política," Interview with Jorge Semprún *El País*, July 29, 1990.

361 Ibid.

362 Ibid.

363 Spain's equivalent to the House of Commons.

364 Solchaga, interview by the author.

365 Semprún, Jorge, *Federico Sánchez*, p. 59.

366 Ibid., p. 77.

367 After four years of legal battles, Juan Guerra was sentenced for tax fraud in 1995.

368 Solchaga, interview by the author.

369 Semprún Maura, Carlos, *El exilio fue una fiesta,* p. 174.

370 Solchaga, interview by the author.

371 González, interview by the author.

372 Solchaga, interview by the author.

373 Arroyo, "El hombre que no conoció el rencor."

374 Bustamante, Juby, "Extranjero en el mundo," *Diario Público*, June 10, 2011.

375 Gracia, interview by the author.

376 www.rtve.es/alacarta/videos/personajes-en-el-archivo-de-rtve /coloquio-entre-yves-montand-jorge-semprun-1991/1123748/.

377 Concha García Campoy remained a succesful primetime anchor until her premature death from leukemia in 2013.

378 See chapter 3 for analysis of representations of the camp experience.

379 Semprún, Jorge, *Literature or Life*, p. 250.

380 Barblant, Leo, and Elsa Grobéty, interview by the author.

381 Semprún, Jorge, *Literature or Life*, pp. 12–13.

382 The thin line between testimony and fiction is discussed more extensively in chapter 3. For a recent study see Ruth Franklin, *Lies and Truth in Holocaust Fiction*. New York: Oxford University Pres, 2011.

383 Panné, *Jorge Semprun*, p. 75.

384 Wisse, Ruth, *The Modern Jewish Canon: A Journey Through Language and Culture*. Chicago: University of Chicago Press, 2003, p. 367, note 11.

385 Seclier, P., *Le Parisien*, Jnauary 18, 1995.

386 www.buchenwald.de/en/1251/#sthash.o20C8Zg2.dpuf.

387 Panné, *Le Fer Rouge*, p. 76.

388 In the French version of collected essays in which this appears, the title is "L'arbre de Goethe." In Jorge Semprún, *Une tombe au creux des nuages*, Paris: Climats/Flammarion.

389 Semprún, Jorge, "Estalinismo y Fascismo," *Pensar en Europa*, Barcelona: Tusquets, 2006, p. 24.

390 My review of this book can be found in *World Literature Today*, September–December 2004, 78:3–4.

391 Marco, Joaquín, "Veinte años y un día" *El Cultural,* September 4, 2003. m.elcultural.com/revista/letras/Veinte-anos-y-un-dia/7686.

392 Pradera, Javier, "La segunda muerte de Jorge Semprún," *El País,* June 8, 2011. cultura.elpais.com/cultura/2011/06/08/actualidad/1307484006_850215.html.

393 Semprún, Jorge, *Adieu,* pp. 219–220.

394 Aranzadi, Claudio, interview by the author.

395 Almunia, interview by the author.

396 Ibid.

397 Solana, interview by the author.

398 Débray, Régis, Preface to *Exercices de Survie*, Paris: Gallimard, 2012.